GW00480726

FINDING MY WAY

Also by Sylvia Scaffardi

*Fire Under the Carpet: Working
for Civil Liberties in the Thirties*

FINDING MY WAY

SYLVIA SCAFFARDI

Quartet Books
London   New York

First published in Great Britain by Quartet Books Limited 1988
A member of the Namara Group
27/29 Goodge Street
London W1P 1FD

Copyright © Sylvia Scaffardi 1988

British Library Cataloguing in Publication Data

Scaffardi, Sylvia
Finding my way
1. Great Britain. Social Life –
Biographies
I. Title
941.085'8'0924

ISBN 0 7043 2687 6

Typeset by Reprotype Limited, Peterborough, Cambs
Printed and bound in Great Britain by
Camelot Press Plc, Southampton

For Molly,
the catalyst who helped
to make it all come true

Contents

– 1 –
Starting In Brazil

'WHAT is society?' I put it to Miss Hume, who had all the answers. The lesson room was cool behind the veranda. In the blazing garden the green life was held in the pulse of the heat.

Every morning barefoot we took possession. There was no real end to the garden. A raw purple hill of inviting soft clay blocked it at one end, and in the middle it dipped into a cleft. We waded deliciously up through the green water trickling down, maiden-hair fern shivering round our ankles. At the top, long grass...snakes? Broken old trees, easy to climb. A twig snapped off thick with hairy yellow plums, sweet with almond astringency. The wilderness stretched on and up endlessly. Tall trees shed leathery-skinned nuts, good to roast. You looked down into juicy green valleys and the tops of banana trees.

Lydia, always sanguine, had an inspiration: 'Can we have a swimming pool at the top? *Please*, Daddy!'

'We can,' she exulted to me. 'We can – if we dig it ourselves.'

She took the lead with Cassimiro's fork and spade. I followed on, spanking the hard ground. The dazzle of the sun caught and challenged. It cooked and melted me, pricking every small hair in my skin alive. The passionate blue sky spread unrelenting.

Exhausted, we came splashing down, past the chicken-run, where the stream turned and spread to delight the fowls and leave a sticky hazard for bare feet, past the empty stables that housed Cassimiro's secret locked room, the bamboo hedge and the kitchen garden with its plumed orange and purple Indian corn. We made for the tangerine trees, their spiky leaves stiff-set in the heat. Sitting on the swing we tore the skins off the tight aromatic fruit streaked with green, to quench our thirst. Deep beds of cherry-pie and violets exhaled a sophisticated drench, big

1

blue butterflies hovered, spicy white buds on black twigs exuded so pro-
digally that the humming-bird caught in the slip-stream jerked to the
sweet centre. The overgrown entwined hibiscus yielded to us as a ham-
mock in which to lie with a precious book enclosed in pink rosettes turning scarlet before they were shed purple on the ground. We tore round
on bicycles through the front garden, bright with a scentless display of
begonias, hydrangeas, heavy drooping fuchsias and small coconut
palms, past the tall metal gate and spiked grille. Our bullterrier, Jack,
mad with excitement, raring to dart in and worry our bare heels – we
streaked away in mock terror. Clothes sticking, I collapsed on the stone
step to cook my behind in a sweet torment, minute ants tickling. Jack in
the dust, thumping and straining for more.

Miss Hume, of course, knew all about Society. It was our smart Lon-
don-based Aunt Alice who had recommended her as 'just right'. So
Miss Hume had sailed for Brazil to take on the job of governess as a bit
of a lark – and with the prospect of landing a rich husband. She was a
'lad', sporty and dashing, the only girl in a family of boys. She even tried
to flirt with my father. She had made a quick kill with a young junior
diplomat at the British Legation. Mr Handyside kept on calling round
on some excuse or other. 'Meesta Entre-e-sai' (Mr In-and-out) our
black nurse, Caina, cleverly punned on his name.

'Society,' Miss Hume expounded, 'well you've got to be in it, or well
in with people already in it, to get anywhere.'

'Where is it then?'

'Well in London, of course. Especially in the Season. That is if you're
going to be presented and do the Season.' She looked a little doubtful.
'Of course as your mother's Brazilian it might be a little difficult.'

She went on about the Season – balls, the Eton and Harrow match,
Ascot, Henley, the Oxford and Cambridge boat race. I felt that Society
was something to be avoided, a grown-up penalty. It was a little alarming too. All those stiff important people, all dressed up and determined
to go one way. If you weren't in it, and you wouldn't get anywhere, what
were you going to do? And where would you be? In a corner of my mind
I believed that my Brazilian grandmother, Vovó, would give me a very
different answer.

Up to now life had been a delightful kaleidoscope of changing scenes,
the picture never held for long before another was imposed. My earliest
recollection, the sweet-scented cool under the flowering orange tree,
lying safe in the black circle, the white flame of heat licking outside. My
Vovó, with her quick, eager step, brought lively happiness – and deli-

cious, sticky sweets – into our little home in sunny São Paulo. Her confident voice talking to my mother, the cherishing beam she turned on me with the full impact of her strong vital nature, attracted, pulled me like a honey-guide does a bee, establishing a bond that was to hold even against the separation of the Atlantic. Vovô, my grandfather, I see coming towards me across a long shiny floor, a hawk-like glance under his spiky eyebrows. I loved the feel of his silky white whiskers. He set me up in a chair to learn his game of solitaire. His rigid bony fingers dropped the ivory marbles into their wooden sockets, and stiffly jumped and took, till only one was left in the centre. He showed me how to put out the candle with the scissor-like silver snuffers. I was taken to see my precious great-grandmother, Vovó Felicissima, thin and light in the rustle of her clothes, in a high chair. I could kiss her hand and stroke it; it felt like catchy old silk, her rings slipping. She smiled down at me with bright eyes. I was lifted up to be kissed. Mother's third child, a blue baby, died soon after birth. I stood on tiptoe to peep at the big still doll in its dark box, white flower buds round his head and small shut hands. On Vovô's coffee and sugar-cane plantation, in our high-wheeled carriage we drove on and on towards the dangerous lake. The riders ahead dropped their reins to let the horses drink, in spite of crocodiles. In the early morning, in the orchard, I discovered a tiny sapling bearing a single perfect fruit, a golden fluted prism. It was full of sharp juice. On my birthday I was put to bed in daylight, something of a heroine after being pulled out, half-drowned, from the big sluice tank where the coffee beans were washed; I had slipped and toppled over as the water rushed in. In our tree-deep shady house in Rio that was invaded by gentle lizards, my father, in a teasing mood, snatched me up: 'What do you choose, this sweet or Daddy?' I know at once what I am supposed to say, and playing to the gallery, 'The sweet, the sweet!' I cried. I proved him right. But I didn't like the way he laughed as he gave it to me.

Now we were on the Royal Mail plunging through the ocean. I just missed spotting the spouting whale. Ices on deck at eleven, turning into beef-tea nearer England. The shock of the London terminus. It dwarfed and deafened me with its bellow and clangour. A heathen temple with stinking jets of incense exploding to the savage god in the girders above. In my English Granny's garden, at the end of a brick path past the apple tree, there was a little ivy-covered house. Inside, a great wooden seat over a dangerous black hole dropping deep into the cesspit. Her tabby cat caught rabbits. Bee was born there on April the first. Lydia and I waded through buttercups to ask the station-master, Mr Green, if he would unlock the white gate at Little Canfield station to let us gather wild strawberries on the green slopes above the railway line. Lady Warwick – Edward VII's Darling Daisy – sent her pony-trap round to invite 'Granny's little girls' to tea to play with her young relatives, Fortune and Vivian. In the meadow at Easton Lodge we whizzed up and down the switchback landing into piles of hay. A plain English tea in the schoolroom upstairs – bread and butter and jam.

We said goodbye, and were sailing again for Brazil with our jolly young governess, an English rose with a bright hint of cockney in her voice and a wide mouth always ready to laugh. She taught us without tears 'the cat sat on the mat', and how to draw pothooks, and reinforcing Caina's gentle example, that cleanliness is next to godliness. Tidy in the afternoon, in big stiff muslin hats, we sat at a little hotel table high above Rio, looking towards the Corcovado, eating pink-icing cakes, while the carefree monkeys were swinging in the trees below. Enthralled by my newly found power to read I opened the glass-fronted bookcase to breathe in the exciting aroma disengaging from books. I spelled my way through the first chapter of a grown-up novel, *The Heart of a Child*. On the wide empty beach at Copacabana, Lydia and I gathered pink shells, sandals slipping in deep white sand, a safe distance from the cascading Atlantic.

Back in England, in the pageant at Tonbridge, men-at-arms poured out of the castle, torches flaring, peacocks screaming – was this history in the making? The peacocks' cries, again, woke me at night. But in the morning I discovered that it was Edward wailing, just born. Mummy was ill and so was he, till Caina discovered that his smart English nurse was doping him to stop him crying. Mummy told us that her father had been with her, talking to her in the night in such a vivid dream. The next mail from Brazil told us that he had died. We moved to the seaside, to Seaford. Lydia and I went to a local boarding-school, coming home on Sunday after church, and then back to school on Monday. Scratchy woollen combinations gave me eczema. Mummy took me to Buxton to drink the waters. The lift-boy at the hotel taught me how to draw elephants and palm trees, and gave me the low-down on the secret masons who had booked up half the hotel. Lydia was bridesmaid to our English rose who married a rich businessman from Brazil. So now on board ship we had a new, German, governess. She was ugly and grumpy, and soon left us. The mountain railway carried us up higher and higher above hot Rio; we were going live in Petropolis.

There were quite different standards in England and Brazil. In Brazil

I talked French to my music mistress, Portuguese to Romolo and Cassimiro, English among the family and a sort of half-and-half to Caina. But in the cab in London, Aunt Alice stopped me, quizzical through her spotted veil: 'Never say *reely*, dear. That's how *common* little gels talk.' I thought of the lift-boy at Buxton. I suppose he was a common little boy. Nobody that I knew of was common in Brazil. The little princess in Frances Hodgson Burnett's book was treated like a common little girl at the school in London when they thought she had lost her fortune. But when it turned out that she had been rich all the time, then at once she became a little princess again. In Brazil, in contrast, was my early glimpse of the comfort and well-being secured by wealth. This was on a visit to our relatives in their handsome house and garden in São Paulo. Lovely-looking glass floors, and in a long cool room the shining table spread with tempting delicacies. But for our juvenile hosts to sit down to the collation was tedious routine, no appetite. So we too forbore. Their car, the first I had ever sat in, eager now, adventurous, jerked me into a panic when their chaffeur galvanized it into savage life. There was more happiness for me in Vovó's visits to our own little home. Even in the unawareness of infancy I felt the impact of her big-hearted unworldliness, her ardent, robust stand on moral values, the spreading warmth of her trusting optimistic spirit.

In England, at boarding-school on Sunday, I put on my white coat and skirt and daisy hat and was 'holy', kneeling through the litany in the old parish church. Granny took us to church too. I had to surrender my fragrant bunch of sweet peas at the harvest festival. Caina liked church. I found the places for her in the hymn book. Though she couldn't read, she followed and joined in the singing. But in Brazil Sunday was the day when Mummy and Daddy went riding and played tennis at the club, and we had a glorious uninterrupted time amusing ourselves without stopping for lessons or a walk. I only went to church once in Brazil. This was when Vovó came to stay with us in Petropolis and told Mother there was a Presbyterian church in the town. Lydia and I found it with Caina. It wasn't like a church at all. The man said it was all right if people were very poor to give them cups of coffee and chunks of bread, instead of wafers and a sip, because Christ had taught, 'Feed my lambs'. I liked the man and his voice. There was no coffee, but I came away with a lovely text of an orange fox with purple grapes.

Petropolis was 2,000 feet up by vertical cable railway, through the clouds that hung over torrid Rio de Janeiro into the temperate tropics of the mountains above. It was the summer resort of the diplomatic corps from Rio, and the home of businessmen who worked in the city. The marble-fronted imperial palace stood deserted, a reminder of Brazil's recent colonial status in the Portuguese empire. Higher uplands beyond Petropolis caught the clouds. The soft thunder of approaching rain could be heard rushing down, swelling to a susurrating crescendo when it opened overhead, drowning the greedy garden that sucked and gobbled and gave out a grateful aroma.

With the curtain of the rain outside, and the cool earthy tang sweeping in from the veranda, we enjoyed an orgy of reading and painting. The cosy togetherness of *Little Women*. Ellen's breakfast cooking in the New England kitchen in the *Wide Wide World*: brown pork chops covered with stiff white froth of cream sprinkled with flour curdled in hot pork fat. Tom Sawyer spitting and shuffling in the dust, Mrs Molesworth's good little girls in muffs and ribbed woollen stockings, the sensitive heroines of Frances Hodgson Burnett, and Andrew Lang's mouthwatering *Pink, Orange* and *Violet Fairy Story Books*. We would pore over the colour plates, and swill soft brushes in mixes of purple, rose and yellow to embellish the delicate drawings of princesses, dragons and emperors. The American *Queen Zixi of Ix* was different and exciting, the two-tone illustrations in pinkish red and sage green were William Morris-Walter Cranish. A willowy Queen in her magic cloak and convoluted draperies, rubber villain Roly-Rogues – like Michelin-tyre men – original in that time of mostly horses and carriages, and the parodied pomp of full-wigged Chancellor and Keeper of the Privy Purse with caricatured gargoyle faces. (How desperately I missed it, left behind in Brazil.) Best of all, volume after red volume of E. M. Nesbit, in the sandpit, and *The Magic City* and *The Enchanted Castle*.

An ultra-heavy downpour would flood the river that criss-crossed the town under wooden bridges, top it up to spill over its deep-cut bed, cover the high pavements, and run into one vast spread. A few days of hot sun would shrink it back shallow between the high banks. The dust would fly again under the carriage wheels as they rolled their friendly thunder over the arched bridges.

At the weekend the local ladies gathered outside the station to welcome their husbands arriving on the afternoon train from Rio. In starched white, under parasols in open carriages, their freshly bathed tidy children beside them. Very occasionally we were there too. Father would bring us surprises – a pretty woven nest of stems and leaves with pink and blue and red-berry sweets, and once a month the ready-to-be-devoured magazines, *Little Folks* and the American *St Nicholas*. Some-

6

times the surprise turned out to be heavy with a lot of unwrapping. Once it was a kind of magic-lantern, with the picture flickering over and over to make it move. But it showed only a silly dancing mannequin, hardly worth the trouble of all the unwrapping and setting up.

One day the train clanging its bell as it crawled over the last crossing, caught under its slow wheel a friendly inquiring dog. I couldn't avoid seeing the poor red screaming thing that went on crying and crying. The ladies in the carriages behind stood up craning and curious. Lydia was crouching, hands over her ears.

Miss Hume tried to colonize us, to impart snatches and doses of English culture. She sang with infectious enthusiasm the Harrow Old Boys' song: 'Forty years on when afar and asunder...' Then there was the popular 'Tar-ra-ra-*Boom*-de-ay!' and those frightful suffragettes:

Put me on an island where the girls are few
Put me among the most ferocious lions in the zoo
You can put me on a treadmill – and I'll never, never fret
But for pity's sake don't put me near a SUFF – RA – GETTE!

Quotations were all the thing. We had a fat tome. She opened it at random. 'Though the mills of God grind slowly/Yet they grind exceeding small/Though with patience stands He waiting/With exactness grinds He all.' 'My love's like a red, red rose'...'As silent as a painted ship upon a painted ocean'. Sometimes the snatches were tantalizing. I liked the stirring ones best: 'Do noble things, not dream them all day long/And so make life, death and that vast forever/One grand sweet song.' I vibrated to it, swooping on the crest of the swing, or alone on the top of the hill.

Miss Hume had dramatic gifts too. Poetry lessons were followed by Recitations. Right foot a little forward, arms free to gesture. Don't move about. Point, look, raise your eyebrows – surprise! Purse your lips, shake your head, gravely...Smile, pause, drop your voice – last word. Egged on by Miss Hume I enjoyed the grimacing and posturing. I took up my stance, announced the title boldly – and I was off.

A day came when Mother with visitors called me in to have a chance to do my piece with an audience. The grown-up chatter petered out. In the pause between a bite and a smile, they half-turned to me. The veils, the pointed toes, their vague glances cool or indulgent, turned me into a silly little girl to be humoured for a few minutes, and not a brilliant little entertainer. With quailing staccato verve I got through it somehow. My

7

mother smiled and stood me by her protectively. But I was eclipsed. I slipped away.

London and growing up were still a long way off. Perhaps I could just turn into a genius, the best way as it happened in books. Squeezing the juice from bright flowers and shining leaves I would get unusual glowing colours to paint some astounding fresco.

Coming down the garden, I heard Romolo talking to a woman at the back door. She had no business in her state to come into a private garden. He would tell the master. She would get nothing from him, she would only come round again for more. A thin woman in odd clothes, a shawl over her head. But when she turned round – I looked straight into the hole in her face, deep into the nose that wasn't there. She stared at me, and turned away. The grown-up will was against her, as she didn't belong. It was terrible that she was turned away with nothing, with that hole in her face. Caina told me the woman was afraid to go to hospital and to be sent away to a leper colony.

Romolo had a dark smiling Roman Emperor's head crowned with his chef's white hat. His stocky body too young yet to be fat. He and his kitchen were a magnet. When he was slack in the afternoon, he baked in his oven the assorted bits of clay we dug up from the purple hill and moulded into cups, bowls and birds. Most of them ruptured. He heated up sticks of sugar-cane for us, to suck bubbling and juicy. He prepared simple food for our children's meals. The traditional rice and black beans, the rich dark gravy flavoured with pork and a sticky green vegetable like a gherkin, and slivers of banana. Sweet potatoes in their skins, purple grape jellies and preserves made from guavas and peaches. I watched Romolo prepare food for the grown-ups: decorative bunches of parsley whisked in and out of boiling fat, deliciously brittle. I scrunched up the sprigs that splintered off. For birthdays and parties, gnarled chocolate logs with pistachio foliage and almond and marzipan flowers. Sticky egg sweets, white-of-egg swirls, and little pyramids of pink and white coconut. After piercing the hairy hides, he let me have a sip of the delicious milk to be drained off before the shells were crashed open.

There was the occasional health scare. Were we too pale? Getting anaemic? Mother was advised to have us taken to the slaughterhouse to drink fresh blood! Her alternative a raw yolk of egg in clear soup. The disgusting surrealist sun had to be chased round with a spoon till at last it shredded into a slimy yellow sunset.

As I lingered in the kitchen, Romolo talked about Italy. Then he got on to the wars. The soldiers – how they suffered. Yes...I will tell you.

8

You would not believe it...He went on about the sufferings, the tortures, the burying-alive with only the head showing – the sun did the rest. The kicking, the spitting – and more and still more degrading brutalities. Who were the victims? And who were the torturers? The Turks? The Armenians? I never understood.

I don't remember if Romolo's burring masculine voice interspersed Italian with his Portuguese, or if I was making myself stupid, deaf, not to take it in properly. But I heard enough. The rumbling voice went on inexorably. Did he enjoy making a little girl wince and wriggle – too proud to tell him to stop, too silly not to go away? Or was he easing his own mind – even to a child?

One afternoon his young German wife came, carrying their infant son, Hercules. Bosomy and uxurious she took possession of Romolo and his kitchen. No more a Roman emperor, he was an adoring slave, breaking out into soft smiles, looking into her eyes. She was satisfied to have him so. But little Hercules was fretful, fluting away and wriggling in her arms. She undid his wrappings, her solid white hand found his little organ and expertly played with it, until he subsided into sluggish peaceableness.

I was shocked. This splendid pink woman, with her crushing assertion of sex and her mastery of Romolo was one thing, but I felt sorry for Hercules. I felt that he needed protection from that strong manipulating hand.

Did Romolo see, and assent? I don't remember. After that he diminished in my eyes. I didn't haunt the kitchen as much as before. But I still went there as a duty when a bird was to be dispatched. The torture stories...? After these horrors, would Romolo care what happened to a chicken that had to die? Once he used a knife, and the headless bird jigged about spilling blood. But mostly he wrung their necks, and they sagged limp, the fallen head still blinking.

After he had eviscerated and washed it, Romolo showed me the body he had cut open, pointing out in admiration the infinity of eggs stored in the dead larder. They were big and orange at one end and dwindled to minute colourless beads at the other.

Miss Hume got her chance. My father brought home for the weekend the rather simple daughter of the company's big boss. She was captivated by Miss Hume's sophistication and go. And so Miss Hume got a week's leave to stay with her in Rio and never really came back. Only

9

for a short time before she vanished altogether. I heard my father remark grimly that she had 'cooked her goose with Hilda's parents, because she was so fast'.

Her successor, Mademoiselle Gélédent, joined us when we were taking a short holiday in a hotel near the Bay of Rio de Janeiro. The hotel lift went through the top floor to halt on the flat roof. (I would close my eyes and pray it would stop in time, and not topple into the street.) There were ices tasting of melon, peaches, coffee and pineapple. In the morning we bathed on the other side of the white balustrade that circled the bay with its wide mosaic palm-lined avenues. If it was high tide, swarthy moustachioed bathing-men stood planted in the surf like breakwaters, taking it as the waves broke on the narrow strip of beach. We ventured down in limp leggy bathing-dresses, with cork jackets tied round our middles. Two men grabbed each of us by each arm and between them we were ducked through the waves. The biggest hazard as we bobbed about in the retreating swirl was to avoid getting a floating leg thwacked and bruised against an iron tendon in their mahogany calves. But at low tide there were stretches of sand and glorious shallow lagoons of blue with soft running wakes of foam in between; here tireless and safe in our cork jackets we could wallow, swim and float to our hearts' content under the blue sky.

Mademoiselle Gélédent made no concession at all to the tropics. She dressed as though in her native France – a navy costume that fluted unwrinkled into her slender waist, and a batik silk blouse with arabesques of orange or scarlet veined in black. She had disappointed dark eyes with sleepless shadows under them, and a dead olive skin. With a nervous hand she patted a sleek wing of black hair curving from the centre parting, and coquettishly tilted her lean jaw, as though asserting plaintively: 'I am small and elegant, why does no one notice?'

Back in Petropolis she set us a regular timetable of lessons – in French of course; I never heard her speak a word of English. My mother specially asked that we be taught mythology. So we imbibed legends about Zeus, Aphrodite, Isis and Osiris – along with 'Lyon on the Rhone (Export Silk)' in patch-work geography, always confined to the map of France. There was a grey French textbook on the classical origins of history: Babylon, Egypt, the Greek and Roman conquests; (I remember a footnote in which some prurient desiccated pedagogue had carefully recorded obscene details about the treatment of vanquished matrons in a Roman Triumph – to horrify a generation of schoolchildren. Or did the passage scan? Maybe it was a quotation from some Latin poet?)

10

I was longing for the drawing lesson. At last Mademoiselle unrolled a stiff print of a ruin crumbling among twisted trees, fallen masonry and weeds. Drawing books of blotting-paper texture were opened out, and I started with huge enthusiasm. But, square inch by square inch, every wriggle of grass, every crumble and speck of stone had to be rendered exactly. After a particularly smudgy patch of rubbing out, Mademoiselle snatched my pencil to give it a more biting edge. 'Heureusement que vous avez du talent!' ('Just as well you are specially gifted!') she observed acidly.

She moved our schoolroom upstairs to a front room with a little balcony. We knew that this was so that she could get a glimpse of a young Brazilian who banged by in his 'racing' car. With the distant approach we would tactfully get buried in our books, and Mademoiselle absently strayed on to the balcony. He may have slackened his pace, but he never stopped. Mademoiselle grew more pinched and sarcastic.

She made a formal complaint to my mother that I was cheating. She produced feathery writing recording names, dates and places. 'When I ask the question, she keeps looking down before she can answer.'

Mother soothed her: 'She can be annoying. But she tries hard to keep up with her elder sister. Maybe a paragraph or two less for preparation?'

'What's this?' Mother tackled me. 'I can hardly read it. You can write better than that. If you want to remember something, write it down properly so that everybody can see what it is.' She crumpled it up.

Two jolly German girls, Lisa and Trudi, were our new friends. They were coming to tea, or rather our substitute for tea, fruit juice and cakes in the garden. Mademoiselle was adamant: 'Germans – no. I am sorry, but no – impossible!' She declined to meet or shake hands with Lisa or Trudi, and retired to her room.

Soon after this, poor Trudi was slapped hard in the face by her father, in a restaurant in the town. This Prussian way of correcting a little girl in public deeply shocked the Brazilians present. The rumour went round. Mademoiselle shrugged her shoulders: 'But what can you expect? Germans!'

On Sunday morning a new formal Mother appeared, holding up the skirt of her riding habit, smart in her white choker, her hair packed into a double knocker under her bowler, and carrying the little riding crop given to her long ago by her father. My father's shiny mount was already backing impatiently as Cassimiro on one knee cupped his hands and gave Mother a lift into the saddle. Trim and handsome they jogged out through the open gate.

11

A retired French sergeant-major, a ramrod with immaculate white moustachios, stabled their horses, and he taught Lydia and me to ride. Slipping in the polished saddles, silly legs dangling over the huge backs we advanced at a shaky trot, the stern Master ahead with his whip. A mighty crack and he rapped out the order: 'A-A-A-A- D-R-O-I-T-E!' I wobbled. His right? Or mine? But the animal understood and swung sharply, leaving me to fall off the the other side.

After a good ride my parents came home, their horses smoking, to let us get into the saddle and have a little trot round the garden. But that was nothing to the joy of our own rides.

A tall lean Portuguese, much too big for his mount, turned up once a week with a string of scrawny little animals with an ambling gait. No need now to bother about posture, the rise and fall of the trot. We bounced about anyhow, our bottoms protected only by cotton knickers and frocks, bare-legged with sandals in the stirrups.

The riding-man had an intriguing air of villainy. Like the wicked uncle, we never knew whether he was leading us or losing us, or even trying to drown us. Sometimes we would come to a river forded by shallows with big boulders as stepping-stones. The animals would wade in, slip into a hole and flounder. We would get delightfully soaked, clamber off on to a projecting rock, and, as the horse reared up and floundered on, slip on its back again, and steam off in the hot sun.

We tilted up vertical hills to drop down again into luxuriant valleys and discover yellow orchids and green lizards. One darted across the sun-flecked path, and the riding-man caught it in the cruel flick of his whip and immobilized the pretty creature in a prayer for mercy. We slowly climbed stony heights to discover, at the turn of the road, a dazzling waterfall, and we stopped at green clumps by the wayside to gather mouthfuls of huge wild raspberries. When the mood took the riding-man, he would lead the way in a swift canter swinging into a gallop. All the sporting little animals would join in the flight – and we would be in heaven!

Maria, a striking young black girl, half-Portuguese, appeared one day at work in the house – and was gone the next – leaving an indelible mark in my memory. She bounded about the bedroom, tossing the sheets, swinging round the beds in a kind of dance celebrating her youth and arrogance. Underneath her shapeless drab shift you could see the strong Amazon figure, the thrusting breasts.

'Would you like an orange?' she invited me, laughing.

I half-assented, a little doubtful. Leaning over, she offered me through the thin material the bouncing globe of a breast. Unwilling to refuse the challenge I reached out a tentative hand. She seized it, thrust it hard against the tight ball: 'Take it! Don't be afraid!' And sprang away, laughing at making a fool of me.

On my way to the kitchen, Maria was in the ante-room. She was standing on a chair reaching up to a flaring gas jet, from a left-over fixture high in the wall. She was laughing. Caina was remonstrating with her. She came down. In her hand was an infant mouse, its muzzle burnt off. The nest with the rest of the mewing family was under the table.

I snatched it up, ran through the kitchen into the garden, reversed it on to the step. Grabbing a heavy stone I pounded the pitiful orphaned young to a pulp. I slunk off into the hot sun, uncertain whether I was a butcher or a saviour.

My horror at what she had done, did not make me hate the girl herself. I felt her dangerous, in an impersonal way, like a snake or a poisonous berry. Maybe the same kind of savage play prompts some types of immature boys to torture creatures. I saw that too, by the wayside, from an open carriage on the way to a picnic. My father exclaimed in disgust – but did nothing. The carriage rolled on, leaving the creature to die slowly, in the circle of boys, staring and prodding.

Caina – Marcolina Feliciana – was the daughter of a slave, a needle-woman in Vovó's house. I suppose that she was five or six years older than my mother. Her first charge had been Vovó's youngest son, Raphael, thirteen years my mother's junior. She came to us when Lydia was born.

Caina had never been taught to read or write, tell the time, or know the value of money. She ignored these handicaps. Shopping in England, she handed her purse over the counter. She relied on the time-clock in her own head,

Her personal authority and her status were unquestioned. We were her children. She had inflexible moral standards about family behaviour and family loyalty. In my teens, when I chose to stay with a friend from boarding school for the last two weeks of the holiday, and then go straight on to school, without coming home to say goodbye, she gazed at me sorrowfully: 'Nǎo těn coraçǎo' ('You have no heart').

Caina had summed us all up in her own way. My elder sister, Lydia, with her large soft eyes, always tidy, prepared, methodical, who rode her first bicycle effortlessly, knew her homework after reading it through twice, but was thrown into disarray by cruelty (the huge blue moth we found impaled on a thick screw nail, and, as I pulled it out, her half-strangled cry as she fled; it oozed green and yellow and drifted away drunkenly). Caina called her 'the good one'. Myself she dubbed 'Francinha' – the little Frenchified one, who had her own ways and style of doing this and that. Bee, at the roly-poly stage, with her round face, round eyes, mouth a little open, trying to keep up with us, frightened of Romolo's deep rumble vibrating through the floor at night while Caina sat in the doorway doing her crochet till she fell asleep, was the 'English one'. My elder brother Charlie, with his dark good looks, curly hair, in-fectious laugh, the tease too elusive and self-contained to be teased back, he was her favourite. (She left him shares in her will.) Edward, the youngest, sweet-natured, neat, eager, observant, quick, who could dart on a pin slipped into a crack – he was 'snake's eyes'.

Caina basked in Father's approval. When he joked with her, she did a little bob, made modest disclaiming gestures as he praised her, smiling widely. He was saving most of her money for her as she spent so little – investing it to buy a little house and garden in São Paulo for her retire-ment.

Caina was indulgent with children. In her hands they were pliable and docile. She picked up, sorted and tidied up after us. She sheltered and encouraged the teased or awkward one, rather than take the others to task, but the offenders would soon want to get back into the accustomed warmth of her approval.

I took her for granted. As far back as I could remember, her warm African presence, the gentle beam from her eye, the set of her full mouth, her heavy, gentle hands peeling off my clothes, the feel of her plummy cheeks, were part of the warmth of the nest.

We had been invited to a children's party, with some sort of gala fuss, a faint snob nuance. For this special occasion Caina evidently felt that I needed a little beauty treatment – Lydia was a lovely child anyhow.

She washed my shoulder-length slippery hair, and while it was still wet she started to work on it. Beginning at the crown, she parted fine segments and, holding the strands erect, she plaited them tightly to the roots. I sat passive in a sensuous trance, while my scalp tingled and my head burgeoned with Medusa-like snaky plaits. These were allowed to frizzle well in the sun. Then Caina started to loose the crimped fila-ments. They sprang into electric life. A touch of the brush, and I was aureolled with a crackling halo of shimmering hair. I peered in the glass, meeting my familiar eyes and straight brows, a little lost in this fleecy wonder.

Mother came in to see us off. A cry of horror. She held my head

14

under the tap. My hair was dragged straight with the comb. In a few seconds, Caina's labour of love was undone. A satin bow was double knotted on a slippery strand, and I was presented as my ordinary self. I could not meet Caina's eyes.

This was the only time I remember her authority assailed.

Caina had of course been baptized. She had her bible. She used to lend this to Cassimiro, and in the evening, they would 'read' it together. Cassimiro would tempt Caina's appetite with young lettuces from the garden. He was a short stocky man with the broad stooped shoulders of a countryman always working on the ground. His nails gaped with black earth. All the fingers of his right hand except for his little finger and thumb were stumps, but he worked these two together so well turning screws and gripping, that they were almost as good as the full hand.

My brother shadowed him, bending when he bent, crouching at his side, talking away to the patient taciturn man, pestering him with childish nonsense.

When Jack destroyed a carpet put out on the line, it was Cassimiro who had to chastise him. I could hear his gentle rumble, warning the animal as he approached with a stick. Jack's tail would curl under.

Cassimiro was a solitary. He would not look up, under his thatch of burred eyebrows, or speak to you, unless you addressed him directly. His face and arms were a deep copper colour, but a tear in his shirt revealed a dazzling white.

His living quarters were over the stables, in a line of bare wooden rooms on plank floors. Some of them we used for our plays, with the big room over the main stable as an auditorium. A black leather trunk filled with treasures inspired the parts, gypsies, courtiers, Rudolpho and Orsino out of Louisa M. Alcott's plays, and of course Cinderella and the others. We pulled out pearl-encrusted stomachers, satin skirts, black velvet boleros decorated with sequins, white satin breeches, scarlet jackets with heavy gilt epaulettes, and huge curled ostrich feathers – relics of early São Paulo days in Mother's girlhood when family theatricals were a favourite pastime. With the doors open, the small rooms presented a variety of scenes. My sister and I doubled all the parts, the other children being too young to remember their cues. Two of the rooms wouldn't open. They shut in Cassimiro's private world. But I always felt he belonged to the garden, that was his home. When we were playing there and the warning, the sibilant rushing in the air, sent us pelting under the chasing arc of the rain, to reach the safety of the veranda before the wave broke, we would dimly discern, from our vantage, the

15

misty figure of Cassimiro, the genie of the garden, moving slowly in a sea of water.

Everybody joined in Carnival – three days' holiday before the beginning of Lent. We drove off in an open carriage with three sacks of confetti, pink, yellow and green, coils of serpentine and boxes of squirts with highly volatile scent that struck freezing and instantly evaporated. In the main square bordered with purple jacaranda, the battle was on, confetti deep on the ground, and carriages entwined with flowers and serpentine. As they crossed, they slowed down, confetti flying and screams as a freezing jet caught someone in the nape of the neck. The crowd milling round in fancy dress and dominoes joined in, and there was a free-for-all.

Later on, mostly in the garden, we had our grand water fight. It started with the exploding of coloured water balloons, and then the filling of everything, the bigger the better, from the tap or scooped out of the filled bath, and sloshing it at one another. I snatched the good-natured Mr Handyside's hat and emptied it on his head.

I gobbled up the unending pleasure of the day, eager greedy for the next, impatient of the night's delay before I could rush into the sun. But sometimes I woke in the night screaming, caught in the claw of a nightmare. In the trembling dark I would hear the approaching rustle of my mother's wrap, the sweep of her long nightdress. The halo of candlelight revealed her calm face and long black hair. She bent over me to hold a glass of orange water to my mouth. In the small horizon of my downcast eyes, her firm hand, mine on hers, her solid gold ring. The liquid went down in cool sweet sips, with the scented orange blossom bobbing against my nose. (Where in the middle of the night did she find the flower to float on top?) Composed, restored, I was content to be arranged in bed and folded back to sleep in the familiar room.

Another midnight scene. My mother believed that castor oil was easiest to swallow in the night when the child was half asleep. In the dark bedroom, father behind with a candle, she pulled me up limp and docile to drink a sweet spoonful of orange juice. My open mouth ready for more received the stinking viscid stuff well down the gullet, quickly followed by more gulps of orange juice. A few piteous retches and hiccups, and the dowsed bundle was buried deep in the bed, fitted again into the comfortable groove of sleep.

I fell in love with my music mistress. 'Fräulein' Göerke was Russian, and we spoke together in French. She was a small curved dove of a little woman with soft hair under a toque, her head a little too large for her tiny frame. Her twinkling divining eyes looked deep into mine, tender and amused, and melted my heart. She would pick my hand up by the wrist and make me drop it limp, then stroking down the fingers into a curve murmur, 'Courbe! Courbe!' ('Curve them, Curve them') like a little turtle-dove. Her strong active hands would ring and peal the piano into joyful sounds, so that I would be wriggling with eagerness to capture the magic. She encouraged my painful efforts, and assured my mother that I had promise.

I remember once when she arrived a humming-bird was imprisoned against a small fixed windowpane and together we captured it and for a moment the jewel lay limp in my hand before we freed it into the sunshine. I felt that she divined the inmost secrets of my heart, and I glanced at her and away with love and awe.

At the end of the lesson, she would take my hand, smile kindly and tell me that I was improving. I knew that good manners required that I should take her down the hall and show her out, but each time at the parting I was so overcome with shyness that instead I slowly backed out and slipped away, leaving her to find her own way out. Later, on board ship to England, my mother reminded me more than once: 'You promised to write to Fräulein Göerke,' but my feelings were too private and beautiful for a supervised letter.

Sir William Haggard from the British Legation would sometimes drop in, always accompanied by his great dane, Mimosa, an unnatural mother who devoured her puppies. He was a close relative of the Rider Haggard who thrilled us with his adventure romance, *She.* Sir William liked to call at teatime to pay compliments to my mother, and she invariably brought in one of us, as she said, 'to entertain him'. I remember my young brother carefully following up the clue of the black ribbon and dislodging his monocle. The last time he came was when Vovó was staying with us. He embarked on a long involved compliment to Vovó that lost its way and somehow linked her up improbably with French aristocracy. Vovó didn't quite follow – she was more familiar with written English. Mother translated. I looked at Vovó in her homely dark skirt and striped blouse, her grey hair brushed back into a little bun. It was a new idea to me that there might be anything aristocratic about her.

That evening the air was electric, the sky closed heavy like a lid. The storm crashed it open, tearing and ripping, shaking and thrilling us. Mother startled us with the most joyful, the biggest thunder-clap of all: We were going to England! ! Our Mecca! The hub radiating everything

17

important and new. We were to be absorbed, to live in it for good. The spring! London, theatres, books... I caught the infection from Lydia, her excitement, her sanguine certainties of the joys to come. Our new boarding-school!

No more just the two of us and Mademoiselle. Hosts of wonderful girls, a gymnasium, tennis courts, swimming pool, library. Midnight feasts in the dormitory! Prizes – silver cups for the high jump. Desks shining, full of drawing books, nature books, poetry books. Neither of us looked back to the boarding-school at Seaford, four years ago. The past was nothing to go by, our future was always different and delightful. The seamier side of school life I had exorcized in a long continued story, that I don't even remember telling, but that my sister said that she used to listen to absorbed.

On our very last night in Petropolis, in the hotel bedroom, opposite the mountain railway station, we were lying awake, too excited to sleep. Our house and its shrouded furniture were to be sold by auction. There was something in the passage outside... now it was at the door... trying to get in... Lydia tiptoed to open it... Trailing a bit of broken rope, flat on his belly, eyes closed, nose on the ground, Jack crawled in. We had abandoned him, but he had found us. With cries of joy we dropped on our knees to comfort and pet him. But he was abject, inconsolable. Piteously he licked our hands and faces, but he wouldn't stand up, he wouldn't open his eyes. The rough unbroken outdoor animal who bowled you over in greeting, the savage fighter – he was beaten. He crawled under the bed and stayed there, flattened, dumb. (Jack went to an aunt of ours in Rio, but an urban setting couldn't contain him. Finally, someone poisoned him.)

In the stabbing sunlight, we cut a path through Rio bay to the *Royal Mail* liner. We swarmed up the ladder. The hand-luggage for the cabins was piling up on the deck. My father was checking it with the steward. We were dancing with excitement, eager to discover our cabins, the top deck, the saloon, to explore the great whale of the liner.

Suddenly the ship gave tongue, shuddering an imperious note.

In the shelter of his straw hat, Father kissed Mother goodbye.

Mother's mouth went crooked.

A terrible doubt stabbed me. I felt a tearing of the roots... our garden... my books... Jack – our darling Jack...

My father's head vanished over the side. We were all leaning over

18

waving. He was getting smaller and smaller...he belonged to his own world. We would see him again.

Now my mother stood with her brood – five children, three girls and two small boys. She was leaving her country for good. She had to start her children in a new life – in a cold climate. In the group was the febrile Mademoiselle and the strong sheltering Caina. but for us there was the dazzle of the decks, the new sense of equilibrium. I quickly rejected, refused to recognize the appalling wound of parting. I was caught again in the present, important, excited.

The lift carried us down into the thrumming womb of the cabin. Caina unfastened the wall button, dropping down the basin and taps. She gave us each an apple to settle the unease travelling up our legs into our stomachs. She sat down and opened her black bag and took out a letter. Dona Ottilia had already read it to her. It was from Cassimiro. The priest had written it for him. It was short, formal. He asked for her hand in marriage.

'But we are going away!'

Caina was laughing a little. She put the letter back in her bag. She snapped it shut.

'You *will* answer it?' I was pleading for him.

Caina smiled. This was not her first proposal.

Too late! Poor Cassimiro – too late...he was condemned to be solitary, to walk alone in the rain...forever.

Mario, from the Argentine, the self-appointed leader of his little group, plagued us on deck and spoilt our fun.

But Lydia knew how to get even with him. You only had to return good for evil and the wrongdoer would be overcome. Remorse, 'coals of fire heaped on his head'. She had read all about it in a story. First of all she needed the largest box of chocolates from the barber's shop.

'For one of your friends?' Mother inquired.

'Not quite. But he will be. It's a secret.'

Mother compromised by letting her buy an outsize bottle of Pascall's boiled sweets – assorted coloured acid drops. The bottle had of course to be properly wrapped up in brown paper. The surprise of a present was opening it.

A formal invitation was sent to Mario to meet us on deck with his 'friends'.

Lydia advanced sweetly towards the enemy.

19

Mario measured her with narrowed eyes.

'This is for you from all of us.'

He took the bulky parcel and tossed it over his shoulder into the sea.

A howl of agony.

We craned overboard to see the last of our treasure.

'It was *sweets*!'

'Sweets? I *don't* think. Why was it wrapped up?'

'Because it was a *present*!'

We were yelling at each other.

'Do you think I am a fool, or something?'

'You *are* a fool to throw away a lovely huge bottle of sweets, without even looking at it.'

'*You* were the fools to wrap it up. Of course I threw away a dangerous parcel. You say it was sweets. I say you are liars.'

The experiment was over.

But it didn't alter my sister's convictions. She was committed to her world of ideals. It would have taken more than a little touch of reality to shift her base. I had been sceptical from the start. But was she *right*? I don't believe that after that Mario *did* pester us anymore.

The rumour went round that you could look into the steerage. The end of one deck normally closed off was open. Passengers drifted off to take advantage of the spectacle – like looking into the zoo. I arrived too late. There was only one man disappearing with a musical instrument. A deserted blackish deck, encumbered with functional fixtures.

Years later I heard my father talking to a business friend about the steerage on some line to America – herded, crammed in like cattle, with no service, appalling quarters, inferior food: 'If they'd only known it, the profit on the line depended on a capacity steerage, to carry the cost of the first class – service, state rooms, food, etc... Well they could have had the whip hand.'

At night, in my narrow bunk, I made myself small, aware of all those dangerous fathoms of ocean beneath me. The tilt, creep and drop, the soughing forward, were taking me further and further away from my home ... the garden ... the feathery pink caterpillars ... drenched violets ... the black earth ... the cradle of the rain at night ... the sweet exciting texture of childhood.

Night after night, I slipped back in my dreams to cling to it, to live again in the home we had stayed in longest and that I loved best.

We arrived in London just as the round may trees dotted in Kensington Gardens were turning a solid white and red. From our small family hotel in Lancaster Gate, Caina took us each morning into the park.

We had a craze for transfers. We dipped them in water collected in a little pail from the Serpentine, and pressed them on brown paper albums spread out on the grass, peeling off the skin to reveal a girl in a hood with a basket of rich fruit in purple, scarlet and winter green. In the afternoons we went to the Tower of London, Madame Tussaud's, Maskelyne and Devant, and matinées. Beerbohm Tree as a fruity Jacob in *Joseph and his Brethren* at His Majesty's, with an exciting tropical blue night scene where Potiphar's wife almost succeeded in seducing Joseph. A torture scene in *Ivanhoe* when the Jew was branded with a red-hot poker was upsettingly ambivalent about who indeed was the villain. Rebecca, more beautiful than the heavy flaxen Rowena, had to side against her Jewish father before she could come into the love interest.

In the autumn my Mother took Lydia, Bee and me, with Mademoiselle, to Switzerland, while Caina and the boys stayed with Granny in her cottage at Little Canfield in Essex. Our hotel overlooked the Lake of Geneva. For the first time we stayed up for dinner, with starched decoratively twisted napkins and grand iced puddings. Every day we chugged off in a launch to explore the lake, the Château de Chillon, Lausanne, Montreux, Vévéy. We climbed into coaches to take us to Chamonix, etc. The expedition I liked best was to Voltaire's home. Losing our way back, we found ourselves in an enchanted deserted village caught in the pre-glow of sunset, chestnuts shining in the rustle on the ground, and mysteriously not a soul in sight or sound.

Mother fixed us up for physical culture in a gymnasium two mornings a week. We used to cross the bridge over the lake stopping to drop a coin into the metal cup of the St Bernard, and to pat the soft cushion of his head. But one day my hand was arrested in mid-air by the man behind him: 'Don't do that,' sternly, 'you'll give him a headache.'

My mother visited shops, concealed, more like offices, in heavy buildings, and with practically no window display. Over huge wooden counters she examined hand-made lace and embroidery, made into fichus, collars, handkerchiefs. Afterwards we had tea with friable patisseries studded with wild strawberries.

We were not sorry on the way back to drop Mademoiselle in Paris – still morose and discontented.

Now we were all together again in a house in Surrey, at the end of a gravelly drive between strawberry trees. You stared out through French windows at snowy lawns and bare branches, and beyond to our own little dark wood, where there were to be primroses. At the back, past a courtyard and empty stables, lay a friendly copse, where, in the spring we would discover lilac bushes drooping with heavy wet scented bouquets.

This Christmas we had our first real Christmas tree. It was huge and branching. It needed a stepladder to hang the topmost glittering baubles and tinsel. Nets of golden chocolate sovereigns, red, white and pink marzipan apples and peaches and countless little dripping singeing candles that gave off an exciting smell. All round the ivy-swathed tub, the secret brown parcels waited to surprise.

We had a romping party with our cousins (the children of mother's eldest sister who, like us, had come to settle in England for their education). Hide-and-seek all over the house – except behind the green baize doors. I never ventured beyond them; I never discovered the kitchen or the cook. It was so different in England: the separation of starched aprons and caps, Miss and Madam. There were implicit rules for behaviour with servants – what was expected and what was not done. Like the cold weather it pinched and restrained you.

Granny came to look after the household while Mother stayed in London for a few days. (I believe she was visiting the Harley Street doctor to have a device implanted to prevent conception.) Granny, as I knew, was kind and comfortable. I had been to stay with her when I was seven and convalescing after measles caught at boarding school. I had felt important and grown-up to be a visitor on my own. A sophisticated traveller, my legs dangling over the stuffed prickly railway-seat, I had perused my comic newspaper, exulting in the daring cheek of Tiger Tim. I had looked forward to tea in Granny's garden with its canterbury bells, sweet-william and mignonette, and jasmine at the windows: Granny in her little cap, a cape over her shoulders and whaleboned front, presiding at the lacy white table, while I sat on the grass to eat buns, and perhaps strawberries and cream! Kathleen D'Arcy, Granny's silent companion, had trimmed the lamps and climbed the little ladder up to the loft to get apples. At breakfast I had remarked conversationally that I never eat boiled eggs. I didn't like them. 'Let me crack it for you, dear.' Granny removed the red flannel cock's head and took off the top. 'Lovely new-laid!' Was Granny deaf? I had to peck away at it politely.

Granny herself had a wonderful appetite and enjoyed good food. Mother ordered lobster and salmon when she came to stay. Granny took us to the pantomime, she laughed as much as we did. Her slipped whaleboned figure shaking and quaking, as though there might be another landslide.

In the New Year, Lydia and I went to a day-school near by. I learnt all about daily life in Anglo-Saxon England, and how to tell a Doric from an Ionic or a Corinthian column. I had piano lessons again. For my birthday in January my father sent me the best present he ever gave me – Walter de la Mare's *Peacock Pie*, that had just come out.

Fat envelopes arrived from Brazil, Mother sat absorbed, slowly turning the pages. She called us over to read little bits written specially for us, in a *Pilgrim's Progress*y sort of way: how he had to contend with the Giant Procrastination and the dwarf Sloth, who were standing in his way. I was a little touched at this attempt to interest us – though I had found *Pilgrim's Progress* dreadfully dull. Did he really mean to tell us something? Mother was a little evasive. Daddy, she said, had to work very hard.

The next letter told us that he was on his way to England! He was leaving Brazil – for good!

– 2 –

The Family: Vicar and Slave-owners

I NEVER got to know my father or to feel at home with him. No sense of consanguinity. Left alone together, I was awkward. Nothing to say. Only to make conversation. As I piece together a few facts about his early life, he remains in outline, a stranger.

His family came, I understand, from Yorkshire. I know nothing about them. I have been told that a relative discovered that they had originally been violin makers. Apart from Granny, his three married sisters and their children, the only English relative I met in childhood was the elderly maiden Cousin Connie, related to his eccentric miserly uncle Charlie. She called to see us at boarding-school on a Saturday afternoon, took us for a walk round the neighbouring streets, bought us a bag of acid-drops, and delivered us back at the front door in time for school tea. My father had a cousin Vivian, a solicitor who became Comptroller of the City of London. Another was a country doctor with a large family. And there was Horace, a sports cartoonist and croquet champion, author of *The Art of Croquet*, for long the standard work on the game. He and his charming wife Kitty called to see us in the fifties. And that is all I know of my father's family. He never got in touch with any of them except his own immediate family, when he retired from Brazil.

Grandfather died before my first visit to England. He was a C of E clergyman with a degree – or a diploma – in Divinity from King's College, London. Some of his papers have survived: half a dozen appointments to benefices in London and the Home Counties with a stipend of £100 a year paid in quarterly instalments. Later, on retirement, a chaplaincy of £250 a year in Surrey. The family were living, then, in quite a handsome house. Grandfather was supplementing his income by running a crammer's and taking in boarders, some of them well-to-do Indian and Persian students. He was many years older than his hearty Irish wife, Jemima Montgomery. An old tinted portrait shows her in early married life as a comely sober Victorian matron with calm eyes. As an adopted child she was probably more vulnerable to the cold bullying and iron discipline of her bearded Jehovah. He was a mean tyrant, stone deaf when he wanted to be, but when Father, as a little boy, whispered back from an errand: 'There's a penny change,' his hand was waiting for it. He kept his family short, and his own box of chocolates locked in the drawer in his desk.

Father was a dayboy at Christ's Hospital, the Blue Coat School, which accepted the sons of clergymen at a reduced fee. He learnt to play rugger and to tackle, the hard way, on an asphalt court. Up to London by train each day and home at night starving for his main meal. It was fetched out of the oven glazed to its plate – saved over from lunch. Granny was not allowed to indulge warm impulses towards her only son. A juvenile photograph shows him in his belted gown and upstanding collar, neat and bright, looking exactly like my youngest brother. Another photograph transforms our warm, comfortable Granny – then in middle age. Severe and magisterial she faces a lectern, eyeglasses on a dangling black cord, as if about to deliver a corrective homily.

Father's youngest and favourite sister, Aunt Edith, gave me once a glimpse into the family home. Alice, her clever eldest sister, was in love with a young lieutenant. In an old photo Alice poses elegantly in a Dolly Varden hat, chestnut curls and large limpid eyes, the curving brim held by a wide ribbon under her chin. Aunt Edie remembers her sobbing and pleading all night while Granny – entrusted with the grim task – urged her to do her duty and give up the handsome soldier for the little Scottish terrier, the wealthy solicitor. It turned out all wrong. It was the soldier who went to the top. The solicitor lost half his fortune. Aunt Alice, cold and worldly by the time we knew her, never forgave him for a house in the Boltons instead of Knightsbridge. She led him a dance, had no children, took a rest and a beauty cure in Switzerland, underfed him, and he finally succumbed to a trivial complaint in his late fifties.

Father was a clever and athletic boy, a good runner and fond of sport. By the age of sixteen he was well enough qualified to become a pupil teacher, and that was how he ended his schooldays. Then he was apprenticed in the City to the Commercial Bank of Sydney. He had in mind making his way abroad, somewhere in the Empire. But an opportunity cropped up in an exporting firm of coal merchants. A tempting salary was offered for a post in Santos – where there was a risk of yellow fever. Father took the decision. It was to be Brazil.

In the eighteen-eighties, Brazil had its attractions for a young man with the enterprise to stake his career abroad. It was moving with an ever increasing momentum into the modern nineteenth-century world of steam and power, railways, roads, ports, telegraph-lines, industry. It was attracting each year an increasing flow of immigrants, with the British already well established as traders and engineers. The British had built the 'miracle of engineering' the São Paulo railway; and the word for a sound contract was *palavra d'ingles,* the Englishman's word.

The British connection started when Napoleon invaded Portugal and the Portuguese royal family and the court, with the help of their British ally, took refuge in their neglected colony of Brazil, and ruled Portugal and its empire from the primitive tropical capital of Rio de Janeiro. Later, when Brazil was establishing its independence, Britain mediated with Portugal to avert war, and so gained another advantage in Brazilian goodwill; it also got special trading facilities with the new independent country.

I am not sure what year it was that father came to Brazil. If it was 1887, the elderly Pedro II of the Portuguese House of Braganza would still have been the Emperor. He was a mild, liberal, cultured man who would have liked to have been a schoolmaster if he had not been an emperor. He appointed a free-thinking Brazilian humanist as tutor to his Catholic grandson, and allowed a Republican paper to appear in Rio and publish a Republican Manifesto. He was the first South American to be known and respected in Europe, where he put Brazil on the map. When he travelled in Europe and the United States, he made cultural contacts with poets, writers, scientists – Pasteur, Victor Hugo, Longfellow, Whittier. He visited a Mormon temple, a Protestant Revival service, a Jewish synagogue – he was labelled 'a limited Catholic'.*

He had a profound admiration for Queen Victoria. His parliament – it is true a self-perpetuating oligarchy of landowners, professional and business men and churchmen, in a population ninety-per cent illiterate, poor and unenfranchised – professed a great respect for British democracy, and imitated Westminster customs and procedure. It is even said that in his time officials left office no richer than they went in.

The blot on his regime was slavery. Even Spain had freed her slaves, last of all in Cuba. An abolitionist himself, he kept no personal slaves, but was afraid of bankrupting the powerful landowners and upsetting

A History of Latin America, Hubert Herring, pp.843 and 844

the country's economy. In the seventies laws had been passed cutting down slavery at both ends: children born to slaves were freed (but apprenticed to their masters till they were twenty-one), and so were all slaves of sixty or over – what they could do with their freedom at that age is another matter.

If it was 1888 when my father arrived in Brazil, slavery would at last have been outlawed and emancipation celebrated with three days' public holiday and a burning of the shameful state records. If it was 1889, the army in a bloodless *coup*, more like a parade than a revolution, would have seized power and declared a Republic, the landowners standing by complaisant, the radicals and nearly all the country in support, the ailing emperor abdicating, declining a pension, retiring to Europe and dying two years later. There would be inflation – army officers' pay doubled – paper money printed, and, by decree, a constitution laid down based on that of the United States.

Whatever the year, Father would be approaching this new Latin country with the conviction that as an Englishman he had the advantage of a superior status. For was it not universally accepted that all things British were best? His British passport not only assured him of the rights that were his by birth but was also a recommendation for promotion. On his side, he would assume that it could be taken as a credential as to his strict Victorian standards of probity and reliability, his acceptance of the code that honesty is the best policy.

Father probably started off short of funds. He would have taken a second-class passage. But as a personable young bachelor who could speak the Queen's English, he would have been invited by the captain into the first-class for the social events, the dances, the concerts, the sports – deck quoits, races and the duel astride the parallel bars for young blades thwacking at each other with leather bladders – and the masculine horseplay crossing the Equator. It is unlikely that he would have indulged in the usual on-board-ship romance. Ambitious, forward-looking, schooled young in self-reliance, he would more likely have been putting in time with his Portuguese vocabulary and dictionary.

The only clue to his early days in Santos when he survived and was making good, are some yellowing photographs. The earliest shows the very modest set-up he crossed the Atlantic to join – six of them, apparently taken on the pavement outside their office: three Englishmen, two Portuguese of humble rank, and a black man. The senior is seated, hard eyes and a flowing moustache; father, arms folded, stands in a rather crumpled suit, looking as though, ignoring the present, he

27

gazes towards a future in which the possibility of failure is inadmissable. In the next, he is in a group with four other solid young Englishmen outside the boarding house where they shared bachelor quarters. Three of them died of yellow fever. Father staved it off, as he believes, with whisky and quinine, and plenty of exercise. An interior shows their sitting-room, 'like home' with its photographs and trophies, piano and card-table in a Victorian clutter of bric-a-brac, antimacassars, drapes, crochet. Now Father stands holding his horse's bridle, in a perched bowler, breeches drooping into high boots, looking rather like Laurel without Hardy – a comedy country boy. Then we see him on the sports' field in skinny running gear – like underwear – and black socks, toeing the line, hands clenched. In the background, trilbys and bowlers like the crowd in a Charlie Chaplin exterior. Finally, relaxed and handsome in amateur theatricals, run by the British colony, surprisingly contemporary in sideburns and a moustache, with a pretty parlourmaid in streamers.

By the mid-nineties he was securing a good independent position and had gravitated to São Paulo, which was becoming the economic centre of the country. Most likely he was still in coal, and that might well be how he met my maternal grandfather, who was president of the São Paulo railway, and came to be invited into the family circle, and to fall in love with the attractive young Ottilia.

I know more about my Brazilian forbears and their background than I do about my English antecedents. Vovó was only two generations removed from Europe. Her grandfather as a hidalgo in Portugal was entitled to certain privileges, including being driven in a coach by four black horses, but as he lacked the means to enjoy these, he emigrated to Brazil where he had wealthy cousins in Rio with attractive daughters who lacked suitors of their own class. He established a shop in São Paulo which did very well, one of the profitable lines being little medallions of the saints which had a wide appeal in a simple Catholic community. Once he had substance as a merchant, he married one of his well-to-do cousins. He then went on to buy land on a vast scale. He ended up with a string of *fazendas,* the honorary title of Brigadeiro and a street named after him in São Paulo. His eldest son, my great-grandfather, finished his education at Coimbra University in Portugal, studying law. He too inherited *fazendas* and wealth. He had been brought up in the liberal tradition of the family – the progressive cleric, Padre Diego Antônio Feijó, who introduced reforms in education when he was regent during Pedro II's minority, was a constant family friend. And so it was that my great-grandfather, after being favourably impressed by the German colony that Pedro II established outside Petropolis, took the decision to introduce free labour on one of his *fazendas*. He recruited workers from Germany and Switzerland, an experiment frowned on by his fellow-*fazendeiros* as unnecessary and uneconomic. The Swiss Baron Tschudi came to Brazil to see for himself how his countrymen were faring in the land of slavery, and was satisfied with the contracts and conditions of work. (One of these German workers ended up a coffee millionaire.) Great-grandfather was in his forties when his wife died, leaving him with a family of eight children. He married again, Great-grandmother Felicissima, twenty years his junior, slim, lively, aquiline. Maria, my Vovó, was the eldest of the new family of ten.

Vovô's forbears, of Dutch Portuguese stock, date back (according to the painstaking research of a relative) to early pioneering colonial days. They left the Portuguese colony in the Azores to settle in São Paulo, one of the earliest Paulista families. In the seventeenth century the family was related by marriage to a Portuguese leader of the Bandeirantes, the pioneering Indian-hunting frontiersmen celebrated as heroes in Brazilian history. This one was remembered as a kind of fierce Pied Piper, leading whole Indian tribes into subjection. He made his final pioneering expedition at a time when gold and precious stones were being discovered, dying at last, too stubborn to give up, still clutching a bag of green malachite believing it to contain emeralds. Great-grandfather was given the title of Barão of Piracicaba by Pedro II in recognition of the work he did opening up land in the neighbourhood of that Indian town. (All titles died out with the setting up of the Republic.)

Grandfather went to college at Nuremberg. An old photograph shows him sitting in a group of students smoking long pipes and wearing the little pill-box caps sported by their club. (Mother treasured his tiny old leather cap, tooled and embroidered with vine leaves, a cryptic initial and a question mark.) He came away without the Nordic status duel scars – in a Latin country these would have been considered barbaric. Tall, square-shouldered, fair-skinned and blue-eyed, he was sometimes mistaken for an Englishman. He had inherited considerable wealth and a *fazenda*. At twenty-eight he entered into an arranged marriage with his distant cousin Maria, my grandmother, at sixteen half-in and half-out of the schoolroom.

Vovó has left a record of her childhood in a slim paperback, *No Tempo de Dantes* (*As It was Yesterday*), published in 1946 when she was ninety-five. She had already written a *History of Brazil,* angled I believe

29

for the education of the young and published in 1932. After this she was persuaded to look back to the mid eighteen-fifties and sixties and record her life as it was lived in the small provincial centre of São Paulo, when candles were the source of illumination, the garden spring the water supply, horses and carriages the only transport, and when the empty streets echoed to the clang of the coppersmith. Vovó wrote her story still settled in her native São Paulo – a sky-scraper city of three million, with a half-hourly plane service to Rio, and a cost of living almost as high as in the USA.

Vovó's book was not designed as autobiography. An old lady of her generation would find that out of place, lacking in modesty. She was offering a social picture of the times, introducing the characters discreetly and anonymously: 'a little girl', 'the young bride', 'the mother', 'the Commendador B' (her father) on the assumption that they were typical of the period. At times she records in meticulous detail as though she was assembling material for a period room or a piece in a museum. The past is imbued with the innocence of childhood, the climate is all limpid, the only drink described as 'delicious' is water, the only reference to strong drink, the sugar-cane rum the slaves enjoy on the *fazenda* on holidays. It is almost a shock to find her accepting adult venality when she refers in passing to the custom, on a son's birthday, of granting his black mistress her freedom.

How typical her family was of Brazilian society is another matter. There is no hint of the easy-going luxury and sensuality we read about in Gilberto Freyre. It is perhaps hard to reconcile her sleepy, semi-feudal São Paulo with its aggressive role in Brazilian history. In her enclosed family circle she was quite unaware of contemporary ramifications in the world outside. It comes as a surprise to read elsewhere of the activities of the first Brazilian baron of industry, the Baron Mauá – whose role in Brazil has been compared with that of Pierpont Morgan in the USA – with his banking empire centred in Rio, with branches in London and New York, and his companies operating vast farmlands even beyond Brazil, who used his powers to finance and profit from a war against a neighbouring state (a war that Vovó refers to briefly with patriotic fervour), and who attempted to reverse the colonial economy and introduce tariffs to protect Brazilian trade – opposed by the *fazendeiros* and the English traders – Pedro II taking no part, more interested in studying botany and Arabic. Baron Mauá finally crashed and ruined thousands.* Not a stir or a ripple of all this 'modern' developing Brazil

*A History of Latin America, Hubert Herring, p.839.

30

intrudes into the old-time pattern of her enclosed patriarchal family rooted in the slave-manned *fazenda*.

In the preface to Vovó's book, Monteiro Lobato comments: 'With the spate of today's anxious uncertain literature, revealing the most disparate and confused tendencies, it is more than ever pleasant to shelter in the calm shade of a tree of the past ... Paulista society of today is offered a daguerreotype of what it was like before the immigrant invasion disintegrated it and left it in its current instability.' But Vovó welcomed the flow of immigrant workers as the answer to the labour problem after emancipation. She always hoped, believed that change would lead to progress. She did not want to put the clock back. In her nineties and widowed for more than thirty years, Vovó was living on a modest income in São Paulo. She looked back with deep affection, but no regrets, to the prodigality and the simplicities, the balanced harmony, the serenity of her early days, a precious legacy that the passage of time could never obliterate. Interviewed on her hundredth birthday, she was asked: 'Is it true what they say about you that you are a communist?' The deeply religious, liberal-minded old lady who had been giving her support to protests, pleas, manifestos against injustice in her country, stood her ground: 'If you think to support humanitarian and just causes is to be a communist, then you will say that is what I am.'

Vovó was born in 1851 in a barrack-size house in the centre of São Paulo. It was benevolently ruled by her dearly admired, strong, capable papa. A corpulent jolly man, fond of Latin tags and jocular quips, he adored his pretty young second wife. Their mutual happiness was reflected in the children – eighteen in all when the family was complete, including Maria's eight stepbrothers and sisters. Mama admirably managed her big household: the retinue of black girls, the menservants and page boys. A governess, French or German – but always known as Mademoiselle – was in charge of the schoolchildren. Maria's godmother, an elder stepsister, a dedicated Martha – affectionately nicknamed Dindinha – was entrusted to keep a vigilant eye on Maria and bring her up as a model little girl. The precious fountain in the garden was their only source of water, and the burden of fruit trees even a little girl was allowed to climb and enjoy. Beyond were the outhouses with cooks, gardeners, a mason, the laundry, and the craftsmen, a cobbler, a carpenter, weavers. They supplied the household with home-made candles, shoes for the daily barefoot menservants to wear with their blue and red livery, the heelless indoor silent shoes for the children, cloth and straw hats for work on the *fazenda*, and Kate Greenaway hats, stif-

31

fened with bamboo for the little girls. Luxuries, ordered from Europe, crossed the Atlantic in slow paddle-steamers: porcelain, tins of butter, and the tartan cloth made fashionable by Queen Victoria. On Sunday, in the devout procession of family and domestics to church, Maria in her new tartan skirt and taffeta tippet followed her elders all clad in solemn black, the page boy running ahead to chop down tall weeds sprouting in the cobbles so that Papa's 'trowsers' would not get too bedewed.

The stables housed the carriage and riding horses, with space for the pack-mules for the two-day trek to the *fazenda* in the interior. Mama in the throes of preparation, tied a handkerchief round her head to ward off a headache. Cutlery, linen, mattresses, candles and flour to be loaded on the mules, and the black leather brass-studded trunks filled with country clothes. Ready for Papa when he gave the word to be off. The children, the old and the sick travelled in the wagonnette; Maria as soon as she could hold her seat side-saddle joined the mounted cavalcade. The black girls rode astride in long blue split skirts. For the annual holiday there was another day-and-a-half journey tilting down the high tableland to the seaside at Santos. Papa at the head warned Maria to hug the mountainside to prevent her horse from rolling down into the mules' graveyard, sheer below through luxuriant forest trees, in the deep valleys where leopards lurked. The mist cleared and for a never-to-be-forgotten moment Maria caught a shining glimpse ... in the immense distance ... of the sea! Bathing, always before breakfast (just as it was for us at boarding-school). Sometimes it was still dark. Leafy branches had been hacked down to make two separate shelters. The girls unbuttoned and untied and slipped into long woollen shifts and sabots. The sun was rising as they ventured over the empty strand and into the running surf. 'First thing,' Dindinha insisted, 'to duck the head.' In the routine morning exercise, Maria straying on the vast beach shed shoes and stockings, the accompanying page complaisant. But her barefoot pleasure was spoilt by a deep sense of guilt – the habit of obedience so ingrained. (More than half a century later, a seven-year-old at boarding-school, I was forcibly ducked in the choppy sea at Seaford – not to prevent sunstroke but for some other nonsense reason. And at school at Eastbourne in the summer term we clumped over rocks at Beachy Head and splashed into pools in our solid walking shoes, unheard of to undo suspenders and pull off lisle stockings.)

Duty and order are the accent in Maria's home. Early rising for master and slave, and each one to his appointed task and in the proper place. Papa in his study with reports from and instructions to his *fazen-*

da, his correspondence with Hamburg, and his involvement in local politics. Mama at her sewing-table in charge of the women spinning and sewing. The children, after morning exercise, subject to a timetable with bells to send them in and out of the school-room. At morning break – promptly into the garden, for refreshment with bread and fruit. Punctuality and obedience implicit in the curriculum and punishment accepted as a necessary part of education. A blotted untidy page is pinned on a little boy's back. Maria, obliged as a punishment to murmur 'No thank you' to the figs and syrup at lunch, is quizzed by Papa: 'What, no appetite!' She hangs her head and a blush suffuses her cheek. (Just like the sensitive little Victorian heroines. It was disappointing to me that I was never able to summon up a rare interesting blush.) When Maria's little sister, handed alms for the beggar woman, bridles: 'Not me! I don't want to go near her, let the slave take it,' she is made to put on a ragged old skirt and shawl and take a tray round the dinner-table begging for her food. Maria, too proud to make excuses to the visiting tutor for her lateness, is punished with a ferule on her outstretched hand, while she conceals behind her back the hand gashed on a sliver of glass just after the bell went. It is good to be Spartan and to suffer in silence. (Just like Humphrey Miles in *Misunderstood,* who dumbly endured one injustice after another till on his early deathbed, too late, his parents weep for their wronged innocent little boy.)

Interesting to find that Vovó's childhood story – in spite of its vivid contrasts – has much in common in its sentiments and patterns of behaviour, with the Victorian storybooks that Granny used to send us in Brazil. The maxims and deportment that the island race cherished as their own insular perks and quirks are found to be just as alive and valid on the other side of the Atlantic in tropical climes.

In the afternoon, a carriage drive, visits to friends and relations, playing in the garden while Mama chats in the flowery arbour. Too boisterous little boys are sent indoors to write out their verbs. When it rains, music, reading aloud and embroidery. Sketches of flowers and fruit are formalized into designs and transferred on to linen with green-leaf extract. In the evening the whole family is united to take tea. Papa with Mama on his arm perambulates the room mulling over and laughing at the day's events. He takes to his armchair with his gold snuffbox and his scarlet handkerchief, and there, by the light of the heavy Portuguese candlesticks, he reads aloud a chapter of his favourite Sir Walter Scott (in translation). Maria, bidding him goodnight, kisses his hand. He strokes her head and blesses her: 'May God make you a little angel!'

33

But the little angel has a sharp eye. When the girls cluster round the piano while their bright accommodating German Mademoiselle sings, rather coyly, a sentimental German ballad, the eldest stepbrother, just back from college at Hamburg, leans over to join in. Mademoiselle embroiders the initials on his handkerchiefs. To the earnest Dindinha she is a paragon – as well as the piano and singing, she can speak French, cook and sew. She is too affable to give anyone a bad mark. It is conscientious Dindinha who has to do all the punishing. Maria observes the ardent moralizer indulging in sentimental vapourizing, languorous sighs; it brings out a little sarcastic smile. Dindinha, stung, is quick to reprove and punish. A little girl must never arrogate herself as the judge of her elders. But now she is met with a gleam of revolt, and pert rejoinders. Dindinha has recourse to the highest tribunal – to Papa! Maria must go and confess her faults or else for her coming birthday: 'This is what you deserve,' – and she is confronted with a table strewn with sand and weeds. In trepidation Maria shadows her papa. At last he notices her ... 'No more nonsense now!' She is absolved! She skips away. And now the mollified Dindinha, 'Because we love you ...' The birthday room transformed: a sparkling pink and white cake! a beautiful doll, a dear little bird's nest with tinted eggs.

Slavery Maria had always accepted as the natural order of things. She was surrounded from birth by the friendly African warmth – delivered by a laughing black midwife, whose only credential was experience. In her infant nursery – with the remembered satiny wallpaper of pink roses and blue ribbons – the black girls gliding in barefoot carrying a little silver brazier. They pinched lavender and sugar on the hot coals. Joaquina, Maria's black nurse, enchanted her with her stories: the pin dropped by the runaway, springs up into a protective forest; the little girl stolen in a sack sings in the streets. On the fazenda Joaquina takes them to bathe in the river, near the lake with blue water-lillies. She carries their wet clothes in a basket on her head. She peels and splits ripe sugarcane to quench their thirst, and she fills a shiny leaf from the spring, to let each one sip in turn. At night, Maria awake observes Joaquina spread her mat at the foot of the bed of the youngest. By the light of a candle-stub she carefully pinches out the fleas from her chemise, then she rolls herself in her blanket and, head under, curls herself to sleep. Good, kind Joaquina! (V.S. Pritchett in his travels in Spain tells how the Andalusian maid sleeps in the cupboard in the scullery.)

Back in São Paulo there is the excitement of the Corpus Christi celebration. All the family festive in new clothes. The menservants today in shoes and their livery, the black girls in bright starched skirts and blouses. At the last moment a touch of patchouli on the handkerchief. All the household – except Teresa, too old now to do more than doze in a chair and chew tobacco – are transported by carriage or follow on foot to a relative's house that overlooks the route to the church. The ladies, separated from the men, mingle to chatter and gossip in the ground-floor reception rooms. The children with their black attendants are up-stairs at the windows, and so are the kitchen staff and the domestics. The roadway has been strewn with leaves ready for the gold and silver procession. The youngsters are on the look-out for their little angel brother in his white and silver lace, feather wings and crowned with mimosa and white flowers – Mamma replaced the jewelled metal circlet, too crushing for his small head. There he comes! Stepping proudly in his satin shoes, shaking his false curls and his white wings. The decorated litters and the handsome panoplies go by, the children chirping and ex-claiming and Joaquina telling them the names of the saints and pointing out their effigies: St John with his little lamb. The sweet smoke from the swinging silver thuribles floats up to their window. And now the crown-ing moment as the bishop is carried past under his tasselled canopy. He raises aloft the host and all the spectators, on the balconies, the veran-das and at the windows, as one, sink to their knees. Maria is transported in the heavenly moment.

After the procession, the crowd throngs in the street for the secular jollity. Trays with bright paper-covered sweets are lifted up. The page boy runs down to bring back a largesse for the children.

Maria, when she grows into the schoolroom, loses herself in a world of books. She is living in them now, crying with their heroines, and, best of all, daring with her heroes. She was enthralled by *Paul and Virginia*, which she almost knew by heart, and now she is reading, in translation, Maria Edgeworth, Dickens, Scott, Thackeray; history too: Macaulay and Plutarch. Poetry is running in her head, Lamartine, Chateaubriand and the romantic Portuguese poets. She has read *Uncle Tom's Cabin*, and is beginning to think for herself, daring even to question.

On the *fazenda* she is aware of the contrast between the free life of the Swiss and German workers and the forced labour of the Africans. The Europeans leaving their cottages in the morning of their own free will and in the evening coming home covered in the good red earth, to their own fireside meal with the family. Their christenings and weddings celebrated at the big house with a present for the infant, a wedding-dress for the bride. But the Africans, roused at dawn by the bell,

35

escorted to work by the overseer with his whip, and at night locked into their *senzala*.

Their solace was singing and dancing. All through the night on holidays, and sometimes on Sundays round the bonfire in the centre of their quadrangle. But on saints' days there was a celebration in which everybody took part. Tree-trunks were dragged in by ox-cart to pile up in the wide space in front of the big house. A long table was spread with roast heifer, pork, preserves of sweet-potato, pumpkin and citron, and plenty of sugar-cane rum. The black children ran around playing, and then the whole company of slaves settled down to the feast. They raised their cups with the cry: '*Viva* the master!' '*Viva* his lady!' '*Viva* the young master!' Papa and the family sitting on the balcony acknowledged the toast. Everybody cheered as the saint's flag was raised, the pole twined round with St John's orange-red flowers, the emblem with the lamb painted by the local artist. A match was put to the bonfire, and the first insistent beat of the drum invited, impelled the dancing. They made a big circle and first one appeared in the centre and, with the ritual movement, stamping and gesturing and uttering the chant of invitation, summoned another, who responded backwards and forwards, making contact in the centre, and then another and another, carried forward by the monotonous beat of the drum. Maria didn't like the cries and the abandon of the men. But the women in bright blouses and flowered skirts (bought by those settled in married quarters with money from the produce of their little plots sold to the villagers) she found solemn and graceful, swaying and shaking in a style half-African half-Portuguese, handkerchiefs daintily extended at finger-tips. After sunset the fireworks spattered out, breaking into the night above the bonfire. The family and guests retired for their own spread – sucking pig, turkey, cous-cous, etc. And then to bed. But the dancing and the singing, the drum, the stamping and the sharp cries went on all night. When the great bonfire collapsed, there were still one or two left dancing round the red ashes.

Next morning all the Africans went to work as usual on the plantation.

This was the holiday picture, but there was another side. A culture that accepted that a young girl should be chastened with a ferule, would not flinch at the use of the whip and the stock for a slave judged to be lazy, thieving or a troublemaker. If the slaves escaped, they were hunted in the forests, and there was the collar with inverted spikes to punish the runaway. (In the seventeenth century, groups of runaway slaves succeeded in banding together to form the Negro Republic of Palmares, with its own ruler, justice and law and customs, chiefly of Bantu origin. It survived effectively for sixty-seven years, defeating all attempts against it, until, in 1687, in a last heroic stand, the 20,000 blacks were destroyed by a fierce force of Paulistas hired to come north and annihilate them.)*

Maria remembered an uneasy incident. One evening as the family sat at their eight-o'clock tea – the time when pleas could be taken to the master – the girls were startled by the clank of dragging chains. They exchanged anxious glances. The ominous sounds came closer and a tall black slave appeared in shackles. In a low hoarse voice he begged to be freed from his punishment. Papa answered hard and severe: he would look into it later. In reply to Mamma's pleas, he said that the man was a witch-doctor. He terrorized the others and was said to have caused the death of two of them. He kept in the *senzala* a store of fetishes: skins, teeth and poisonous plants.

As well as her household duties, Mamma was in charge of the sick. She was trusted as a healer. He had her box of homoeopathic remedies and her *Family Doctor* by Dr Chernitz. She dosed with medicinal teas and vermifuges, and applied poultices, hot plasters, fomentations. Sores were covered with heated banana leaves smeared with oil. She cut thorns out of calloused heels, lanced boils and abscesses – no disinfectant of course – arnica was used to bathe infected places. The seriously ill, white and black, were carried in the waggonette to the doctor in the nearest town.

It was after Maria had gone to her first dance in São Paulo – in a home-made dress, ribbon criss-crossed round her calves down to her satin slippers – and after she had been overheard by her godmother reciting – no, declaiming with passion – a love poem in her bedroom, that Dindinha, perturbed, confided in Mamma. Mamma consulted Papa: Was this the right time? Papa approached a distant relative, a cousin at some remove, with a son, Antonio, now twenty-eight. After discreet visits between the prospective pair, discussions and negotiations, Dindinha was entrusted with the mission. She came into the schoolroom, very important, to interrupt Maria in her study hour. Maria must set aside her French composition and listen to something of great moment: 'Your hand has been asked in marriage!' ... Maria remained dumb. 'The offer is from Antonio ... of good family, good character, well-educated, amiable, handsome ...' Maria was still silent. 'Well then?

A History of Latin America, Hubert Herring, p.233.

What am I to say? ... What more do you want? What am I to tell Papa?'

The trousseau came in two big trunks from Europe. It even included a black dress for mourning. Her betrothed put the diamond ring on her finger before Mamma and Papa. The wedding was celebrated at home, an altar prepared in a front room. Dindinha cried into her best embroidered handkerchief. The 'honeymoon', as was the custom, was spent in the bride's home.

Finally they left for their *fazenda*. The journey was broken at a relative's home on the way. The next morning sixteen-year-old Maria, enjoying her bridal freedom, was laughing and joking with boy cousins of her own age. One of them, for fun, offered her a cigarette. She was taking her first puff, when her husband walked in. He said nothing, but looked *very* grave. She never touched another cigarette. It was the end of her girlhood.

Arrived at her own *fazenda,* on that first evening, she took her place with her husband on the veranda, overlooking the company of slaves assembled below. Her husband introduced the new mistress. A great cry came up – the conventional religious greeting – in one voice from all those African throats. Her heart sank. If only she could answer: You can all go ... You are free! Instead she gave the ritual response: '*Para sempre* [for ever] – Amen.'

Now she had to run the household, tell older, experienced women what to do – she was useless at domestic tasks. She had to supervise the women spinners, to approve the finished balls of thread of the correct weight. Afterwards she found that some of them had been wound round clay and stones. The girl-mistress wept. Now she would have to punish too. But she learned from her mistakes. She was young and resilient. And she was no longer living in books. She had her own handsome hero, she was enjoying her own romance. As she galloped in the open country with her husband, her heart sang: 'The world is mine!'

This is the last of Maria's story in Vovó's book. In her closing chapter she describes the end of slavery, the final victory. She welcomes the new populous rich São Paulo, with its library and hospitals. But she regrets that in the greedy scramble for fortunes, well-being and happiness are lost, and, under the pressure of a relentless commercialism, old-time ethics. But she is still optimistic. She believes this is a phase, and she looks to a future for her dearly loved beautiful country when wealth will be divided more equitably and the only distinction between man and man will be that of heart and mind.

Vovó was seventeen when her first son was born – he grew up to be her friend and life-long intellectual companion. Every two years, there was a baby, till she had a family of nine. She was nineteen when the Franco-Prussian war broke out. From then on she took a lively interest in politics, keeping in touch with affairs, reading French, German and now English newspapers. (Later, she annoyed my father by criticizing the British government in the Boer War, championing the Boers.)

In her twenties, she took the courageous step of renouncing the traditional family faith of Roman Catholicism, and becoming a Protestant. She joined the Presbyterian Church, with its socially humble congregation. Vovó said about this: 'It was a terrible family scandal. I was a fool, wicked and conceited. But nothing shock my faith. On the contrary I felt stronger and freer.' It was her children's black nurse who converted her. 'She was an ignorant unlettered woman who could hardly read, but she had a great heart entirely dedicated to good and God. I was a devout Catholic, I used to laugh, but with great patience she insisted, showing me the Bible and giving me pamphlets ... I began to think that she was right, and that it was she and not my rich family that really followed Christ ... It became the great joy of my life ... and later others in the family followed my steps.' Her own slaves were freed when she was thirty-six, one year before emancipation.

Her husband took her on a trip to Europe – Brussels, Switzerland, Paris and London. On the London stage, she saw Ellen Terry, in productions of Shakespeare, and the opera at Covent Garden. She visited the Crystal Palace, she was thrilled to sit in the gallery at the House of Commons, but best of all she enjoyed the British Museum; she could have spent days there. London itself she found sombre, the buildings like blocks of granite, and the people solemn and busy – 'not like in my own country, happy and laughing'. ('They are no longer like this,' Vovó writes sadly in her nineties.) In the London streets, remembering Dickens, she was nervous of pickpockets and thieves. Grandfather laughed at her as a country-cousin.

Vovó, at that time, had a handsome town house in São Paulo, built for them by a leading architect. She was a good hostess and attracted a lively circle of Liberals, including a future president of the Republic. She kept open house for family and friends. She helped to collect considerable funds for the founding of a Samaritan Hospital in São Paulo for the care of the poor, and she became director of a maternity hospital where expectant mothers were admitted irrespective of religion, colour or legitimacy of birth.

But by the 1890s Vovô's considerable fortune was dwindling. Emancipation – though Vovô would never admit it because to her it was an unmitigated blessing – must have hit them financially. Vovó's health was poor, he was leaving more and more on the *fazenda* to the manager. There were bad harvests. An exceptional frost ruined the slow-growing coffee trees. There were lean years during the replanting and maturing. Grandfather, who had in the past chivalrously lent enormous sums to relatives on no securities, now needed money himself. He borrowed from the bank. But it never occurred to either of them that they could become poor. Vovó, always positive and optimistic, went on living in her accustomed style, with no check from Vovô. She was still ordering from Paris party frocks for her handsome daughters. A letter she wrote to my mother in June 1893 shows her quite untroubled and relaxed. She was on holiday with part of her family in Rio because her eldest blue-stocking daughter wanted to be with her English fiancé, who was living there. Mother and the rest of the family were staying on my great-grandmother's *fazenda*.

My dear Ottilia,
I have just read your little letter, and while the others are dressing (it's nine o'clock in the morning) I am going to answer it. I am missing you all so much my dear children. Unfortunately I can't come back as soon as I wanted to because Papa remembered that he must have some clothes, they will only be ready next week ... We have taken advantage of the bad weather to go shopping. But the last two days it has been lovely. Yesterday we spent in Petropolis, blue sky, warm sun, lovely countryside. With snow on the mountains it would be as lovely as Switzerland. I was enchanted with Petropolis, it is like a town in Europe, so clean and happy. We are very comfortable here, big light rooms, good food, good style and quiet, very much to our taste. Wright [her daughter's fiancé] was careful to make sure we would be very comfortable so that we would stay for a long time.
The two of them are quite carried away, lost, impossible ... when they are not talking to each other, they are gazing at each other, they do everything together, they are no longer aware of anybody else in the world. I think they would be quite happy to drop the rest of humanity into the sea, provided they two could survive and be together. You can imagine how Virginia and Maria take it; the first consoles herself with me, and the second drops hints, giggles and talks nonsense to Rosalina. Father very serious in the middle of all this. This is the family picture in our room. How different from my

good little Tilly, supping her dish of maize, taking her walks in the wild countryside, tootling on her horn. Stay like this just a little while longer my dear child! Not that I don't want you to be happy, but not just yet, just a little later on ... Maricota is no longer mine, she belongs to somebody else ... I believe they are very much in love. God bless them, and I do too ... I wish them every happiness, because we all behave in this silly way when the time comes ... Much love to Mother and all the children. I am homesick for my own land and especially I miss my children ... An embrace from your mother who loves you,

Maria

Mother was then eighteen, and had not yet met my father. I don't have to speculate about her in these early days because I have the fourteen pages of foolscap, *Just a Few Recollections,* that she wrote in her slanting handwriting when she was sixty-one, before an operation for cancer which she did not expect to survive. After thirty-eight years of marriage and motherhood in England, her house was now empty of children, her husband self-absorbed and cold. At this lonely time she looked back unsentimentally to her own tropical land and her own family, the roots that had nourished and sustained her.

I was born in 1875, one of 9, blessed with a very happy home, united and peaceful & patriacle, beside of enjoying of all the earthly blessings: of position wealth and breading. From early childhood I showed a marked inclination for nature and animals. I was never very fond of books, but could spend hours watching ants work, or a wasp build its nest of clay on the wall; I once watched it from beginning to the finish. It took 2 days to build it a round little hut about the size of my thumb nail. The eggs came first ... I used to keep boxes with catapellars so obtained some very fine butterflies ... I always helped my father who was very keen too; and sent to Germany many boxes of rare specimens ... I always had chicken & rabbits of my own. I was called by my gouverness (a German who was with us for 10 years) 'Poulet Noir'. At 4 years I was riding a pony by miself. At 15 years I had a horse of my own, a beauty, grey, the fastest horse of all the lot. My best friend was my brother, 11 months older and all his friends; my sister was two years younger, and to my idea then a coward and a cry-baby. I had a few girls friend all cousins, but I prefered boys company and used to wear my brother's cloths and do all they did. At 12

41

we had our first taste of cigarettes and I was very proud of standing better than many of the others ... I felt a little queer too, but pretended to enjoy a second one ... One year at the seaside ... my brother and I ran away from home ... with the idia of getting into a steamer and see the world, but when we tried to get on the largest one, we were questioned and somebody reckonised us ... We got a good hiding ... Every year we used to go to the *fazenda,* a huge farm where coffee was planted and also sugar-cane ... and fields for rearing cattle. We were always roused from our sleep about 4 in the morning and had a huge breakfast ... At 5.30 ... we caught our train and had a most luxurious compartment as my father was the president of the company ... we only arrived at the nearest town to the farm at 3 in the afternoon; and then we had 1½ hour by road, for this some went on horse back ... and the rest in a kind of convaiance, of american origin, called troley ... no spring ... the wheels were very tall and curved (as if the axels were to tight and pulled them in) this was made on purpose to cope with bad roads, and the drivers were real experts to avert disaster. About 4.30 we arrived at last, tired and covered with red dust, but we children very excited, were running all over the empty house trying to find the treasures left behind at the last visit. Mine was a horn and a large dagger knife that I wore on my leather belt like a man. We spent about 4 months every year in this place. At first it was run by slaves. [Mother was 12 when the slaves were freed, one year before emancipation.]

My father had 300 adults, they were looked after by a black foreman. All the married couples had rooms of there own and a kitchen. All the rooms were built like a great square and the entrance led to an open square where in the winter a huge bonfire was kept to warm the people. At night the square was locked. All the girls from 12 years onward, used to sleep in a special room provided to them in the owner's house or the manager's, and they did all the work and cleaned the place. At 5 in the morning a bell used to wake up the workers and the foreman led the men and women from the square to work, the feeding mothers were left behind and all the small children were left under the care of the nurse, who saw after their wellfare till the parents came home; they were taken to the brook, were they had their bath and a clean shirt given, they only wear one garment in the winter a wool pullover over it. The nurse attented to their feet and took out any diggers they might have rubbed their toes with a little parafin to avoid others. They were then taken to the main house, where, squated on the floor, each child had their food given in a tin basin with a spoon; it consisted of brown beans cooked with greens, rice and porridge made with corn meal; twice a week meat and for pudding boiled corn (whole) sweeten with brown sugar or pumkins cooked with sugar and everyday a large basin of curds milk and sugar. The black nurse used to play with them tell them tales about 5 in the evening they had coffee and milk and cornmeal buns, and sent to their parents at 5.30 when they returned from their work. The workers had their food sent to them: a special cart was made with 4 large boxes, one with beans and greens, another with porridge or rice, another with sweet boiled corn and another with pumpkins; once a week they had meat instead of beans, but they prefered the beans to the meat. Oranges was given freely to everybody. Along the roads on coffee plantations there were always orange trees to be found. As the workmen came home, the women used to go straight to their homes and the men used to go on parade in the yard in front of the house, where father used to call each one by their name see if they were well and then they would say all in one breath: 'Blessed be our Christ' which sounded 'Vasumscristo' and father would answer 'forever' and they were taken to their quarters. Any day they came home wet they had a drink of national rhum, which they loved. The reason of locking them up is to prevent them from running away, but this did not happened very often in the farms where they were well treated. Our slaves were pared, by father, but they were always consulted before getting married, every child was christened and the name of the saint day given to them ... I used to see the parade every day as I loved to hear the blessing sung by all in one word. The farm was run all by these men: there were mechanics (tought by father) who looked after the coffee mills, the water-mill for sawing wood, and the sugar mills, we had several carpenters, bricklayers, plummers, cobblers, taylors. Among the women: lace makers, weavers, cooks, sugar refiners, soap makers, in fact everything was made at home and the only think that was bought was salt, flour, parafin oil and disinfectant; many medecines were found among the plants. A year before the abolition law was passed, all Father's slaves were freed. They had wages for 1 year, part in money and part in food chits, as they had no idia how to cater for themselves. The first money was spent in shoes, but as their feet were too broad, never having worn shoes, they were carried most of the time, they bought umbrellas and most of it spent on drinks. ... One old black from Zambeeze had both legs very swollen and skaily,

43

poisoned by snakes bite in Africa ... his work was to make baskets out of green bamboo shaven fine and supple till it could be bent. These were to gather the coffee ... He was very amusing with his tales of Africa and tell us how he used to catch snakes. Another who was a cripple had to go every day fishing and provide us with daily supply; but this man was a bit shifty and when ever he cought a larger fish he used to cross the river by canoo and sell it to a neighbour, but as he was a cripple it was overlooked ... Daily life was most monotonous for everybody used to town life but for me full of wonderfull things, and I was told that if I looked so much at cows I would acquire their stupid vague looks, but this did not impress me in the least. At 7 in the morning the family had a cup of black coffee. Father used to go about and inspect the work in the different mills ... Mother had the house to look after and give work to the 8 or 10 maids under her care. About 5 or 6 of us, and a factotum, went of for a horse ride ... Those rides to me were heavenly ... generally I had the best horse which was a bit lively and wanted some understanding ... and my greatest delight (to me at 15 the essence of happiness) was when we reached ... a real prairie with no trees ... and I used to drive my horse at full speed till I was galloping, out of sight of the party, alone with my horse on an enormous spread of land with the field till the horizon in front of me and the lovely blue sky above. These were one of the few moments in life, of greatest happiness and joy alone with nature with all its beauty and peace ... It used to make me happy and contented for the day ... After dinner we used to sit on the veranda doing needlework, while mother read to us, some interesting book, as a rule she used to translate them from the german english or french, she did this very easily as she was reading. About 5 in the afternoon we used to go out with mother (the gouverness could do as she liked ...) for a long walk. I used to find all sort of treasures on these walks and we used to decorate ourselves with garlands of wild flowers ... We used to return tired and dirty ... the little ones after there bath had some milk and went to bed and others read, or played pacience till 9 or 10 when everybody went to bed. Now life repeated itself *every day* with no break or change and no visitors as we were miles away from any neighbours or any educated person. I must mention the great excitement of the day, this was when we got the post, the only link with civilisation ... a black boy ... used to ride every day to the nearest town ... and came back ... with our letters and magazines ... enough to go round for old and young: 4 daily papers, *L'Illustration,*

Fliegende Blätter, Punch, Revue des deux Mondes, les Annales, and *Poupée Modèle.* The papers gave us excitement and something to talk in the evening. There was a veranda on 3 sides of the house, wide enough for 4 people to walk abrest ... on rainy days as mother was a great one on exercise and used to take us in turn for walks round them. I shal never forget the most magnificent sunsets! vivest gold to the darkest blue, but I am sorry to say sunset in the tropics are very short but wonderfull. These verandas were a great boom in hot nights, where the sky was lit not only by beautiful stars, but enormous fire flyes and the glow of one gave enough light for one to read by, they give a faierie glow ... I was my father's pet and used to go about with him a great deal fishing or shooting ... partiridege shooting is most interesting ... Father was an excellent shot every time the bird came level to the gun, it was killed ... after killing one or 2 we used to go back home. Father took me several times to the vergin forest we used to fastened the horses at the entrance of the wood and then walk for ½ hour or longer to a place where a little open space was made and at the end of it there was a little hut made all of green leaves and just room for 2 people: in the open space some corn was put everyday and so all sorts of wild animals used to come at dark and feed. One had to keep very still in the hut. We saw one evening a heard of 5 wild boars and as they were making such row snapping their teeth I got frightened and spoke to father and they all scattered away before father could shoot any. I was never taken again. But I must say it was very frightening, very dark in the forest, now and then queer sounds in the woods all those boars so near with terrific teeth ! ! ... Father had lots of tales of wild life ... I could listen for hours to all his ex-pearaences ... After a few months of this primitive life it was great excitement to go back to town and civilisation where we led quite another life.

I greaw up till 15 years as a perfect child (no idia of grown up) and dispised every girl who had a sweetheart, as I thought this very efe-minate, ... my freinds were all boys, as my brother and I were in-seperable ... all his freinds boys treated me as equal. I once boxed the hear of one who tried to kiss me. We had a very gay time in town and besides several dances a month, and theater seasons, we had an at home, every thursday evening; we seldom danced, but it was very varied: music, acting, charades (some written by freinds and a kind of critic of our life where everybody in our circle was caricatured). Our salon was open to all the élite of São Paulo and full of clever and interesting people. My sister and an aunt of the same age were two of the best looking girls and one of the greatest attraction to visitors, my younger sister and myself were supposed to be children and treated as that. When I was 15½ my mother came to me, and after locking the door, very salamly told me that a young man (who used to live opposite to us ...) had asked me to marry him. I can't tell you what a bomb shell this was to me! I never expected it and burst out in tears; my poor mother was at a loss to follow my thoughts and only told me: if I did not care for the youth I need not accept. I felt if all my childhood had gone, that I was grown up and that I had to face the serious world! This made me very misarable and I felt self contious; till then I thought nobody ever looked at me with any intention. I asked mother to decline the offer and never to mention to anybody ...

... I went to my first dance at 16 ... My hair was twisted into a chignon on my neck, little wringlets round my forehead and a narrow black velved round the head. I thought that this was very coquetish, my dress was quite simple, but girls never dressed. The dance was given by a cousin ... in honour of one of her nephews who had returned from North America where he had been studying. My sister and aunt looked lovely and were the belles of the night. I thought nobody ever would look at me, but this did not concern me in the least, I sat down in a corner of the ballroom and wondered at the decorations people dancing. I did not dance the first dance nor the second and I saw my handsome cousin dancing with his cousin the daughter of the house. The 3rd dance instead of asking my sister or my aunt, T came streight to me and I had my first dance and I felt so shy as I thought dancing with the 'lion' of the evening everybody must be noticing me. After that I never stopped dancing and I had the great honour to have my cousin T for partner for the cotillon, who paid me great attention. It was after 3 in the morning when we left the ballroom. My head was still waltzing and going round the room, and for the first time I thought perhaps it was not so bad to be grown up, and to see people take notice of you! After that I went to all the dances and had plenty of partners and unfortunately broke too many hearts. I never wanted to marry as I always feared to be unhappy and never would have married my own compatriot, but one day an Englishman came my way and although I did all I could in my power to discurage him he would not give up and so I married at last to my 8th pretender. [Mother was thinking of the French word, *prétendu,* the intended one].

46

Mother writes calmly about slavery, but she is at pains to vindicate her family's treatment of their slaves. This was on the eve of emancipation, when conditions had greatly improved.

Richard Burton, the explorer, was British consul in Santos sometime in the eighteen-sixties, and he travelled widely in the Brazilian highlands where the Paulista's *fazendas* were situated, and in his book about it, he wrote: 'Nowhere, even in oriental countries, has "the bitter draught" so little gall in it, in the present day the Brazilian Negro need not envy the starving liberty of the poor in most parts of the civilized world.'

At any rate the Brazilians have never shared the delusion so popular with Anglo-Saxons, even today, of the ethnical inferiority of the Negro. In Portugal, of course, with its proximity to Africa, the Negro was no stranger, and at times in their history, it was the dark-skinned Moors who were in the ascendant. Some Brazilian slaveowners accepted into their households the child of a liaison with an African woman, educated him with their legitimate children, and made provision for him in their will.

The freedom Vovó gave my mother in a world of boys and in an out-of-doors life, hunting and fishing, and later playing tennis with unrelated young men, was quite exceptional in Catholic Brazil in the eighties. Girls and even women were strictly circumscribed and supervised. Vovó was an innovator. Eager, idealistic, an avid reader, absorbed in politics, she went ahead to welcome new ideas, and once her convictions were engaged, espoused them ardently and implemented them irrespective of social, worldly or personal considerations.

Mother could not share these enthusiasms. She was more interested in growing things and live creatures than in ideas. Practical and methodical, she had more in common with her engineering, sport-loving naturalist father. She loved and admired him best. In spite of her independence and individual tastes, she had in her nothing of the rebel. She was at heart a traditionalist who respected the accepted order of things. If she had married a Brazilian, she would, in her generous way, have conformed to the role that went with it, just as she adapted selflessly and uncritically to father's English way of life.

I suspect that Vovô behind his rather detached reserve, was more conventional and formal in outlook than Vovó. But he too was unworldly in his old-time standards of behaviour rooted in the assured continuity of life and fortune based on his good red earth, the rhythm of the seasons and the slow tempo of the hand-labour of slaves. In spite of the implicit contradiction, he was a Liberal, and a liberal-minded *fazendeiro*.

47

It was perhaps three years after her letter to Mother in 1893 that Vovó sent an invitation to one of her tennis parties to an athletic and coming young member of the British colony. Vovó's hospitality, her expansive goodwill, and the comfort and warmth of her family circle must have been attractive to my father as a bachelor in a foreign country, and especially with his own cold upbringing; and I feel that Vovô's contrasting dignified reserve would have appealed to him too.

The courtship started on the tennis-court. Vovó had the novel idea that exercise was good for girls and that young people should be allowed to meet openly on the tennis-court. She had persuaded her sister-in-law to install a court at the back of her garden, which adjoined Vovô's property in the centre of São Paulo, so my mother could nip through a gap in her own fence to her favourite sport. Not that it was quite like that in those days. There was often a seated audience of cousins, uncles, sisters and brothers, occasionally Vovó herself. In one of the old tennis photographs my mother sits, among family and friends, balancing her racquet against a long skirt that touches the ground. She has a tiny pinched waist, puff sleeves and a little flat upside-down flower-petal hat. Father stands nearby, arms folded; he is sporting a weeping moustache.

The photo of my mother with her family sitting on the steps flanked by decorative urns, must have been taken after her engagement because my father's arm falls possessively on her knees as she sits one step above him with her hand resting on his shoulder. She is in a dark high-necked blouse, her hair drawn severely back, only a few tendrils escaping; she looks absorbed, wrapt in her own world, dark eyes intense, very vulnerable. Father with a level gaze over a high collar, his drooping moustache shading his assertive rather egoistic mouth. Vovó in the centre with a grandchild on her lap, sons and daughters around, Vovô, white mutton-chop whiskers and white moustache, standing lean and dignified in the background.

On the marriage certificate, dated 14 April 1898, Father describes himself as a merchant. He is thirty, Mother twenty-three. For the first baby, father insisted on an English doctor. It was a complicated birth, after it Mother had puerperal fever. The Brazilian family doctor was called in. Father took her with the baby in arms, on a holiday to England. He wanted to show off his lovely young bride, now that he was successfully making his way. Aunt Edith says that it was unmistakable that father adored her. Mother and Granny, a widow now, took to each other at their first meeting. Mother met all the closer relatives, including the miserly eccentric Uncle Charlie. On a weekend at his house in

48

Southampton, Mother out in the garden first thing in the morning was delighted with the flowerbeds and the nectarines and peaches on the wall. She picked two for breakfast, and praised them as delicious to Uncle Charlie. He observed coldly that it was the head gardener's responsibility to provide fruit for the table.

Sometimes when she was introduced as Brazilian, there would be a pause, and a query hovering in the air. She grew a little impatient of this, and when, at the Harley Street specialist, there was an evident demur, she responded by unclipping her bag and taking out a photograph of a naked feathered Indian with a blow-pipe. 'My uncle,' she smiled, presenting it to him.

After London, they went to the Great Exhibition of 1900 in Paris. Then back to Brazil.

Granny kept part of a letter Mother wrote her two years later enclosing a silky curl in tissue-paper:

Dear Mother ... You have been very kind to write us such good long letters ... We are all very well. Lydia has grown and is pretty and strong, she is quite a companion for me ... She is full of spirits and an easy child to manage. Sydney thinks she is the image of Edith. I enclose a little curl of Lydia's hair ... Sylvia is a dear little might a perfect model, she *never* cries, sleeps the whole night, and when wakes she is always happy ... She looks something like Lydia only with very pretty dark blue eyes and long black eyelashes. I think she takes the blue eyes after my father. I had plenty of change this year, in May I was with the children a month at father's *fazenda* and in August a month at the seaside place called Guaruja ... We enjoyed ourselves very much ... Lydia was not afraid of the sea and Sylvia used to paddle too. We were staying there with some freinds which was much nicer than going to the hotel. Sydney use to come every saturday to monday. My people are all staying at the *fazenda,* they are coming next month to make the preparations for Rosalina's wedding [The sister who was the big attraction at the dances in Mother's *Recollections.*] She was engaged in August to a young presbyterian minister ... They are all very happy ...

My sister remembers St John's Day on the *fazenda* just as it was when Vovó was a little girl – the ox roasted whole, the flag-pole, the orange flowers, the bonfires, the fireworks, except that the great crowd of black workers, moving to the big drum beating out the rhythm of the samba, were no longer slaves.

Father had for some time been on a very friendly footing with the Scottish-Canadian managing director of a big Canadian combine with its Brazilian headquarters in Rio, and a branch in São Paulo. Mackenzie now offered my father a position with the company at the Rio headquarters, giving him the firm promise of a directorship in due course. Mackenzie was a big, spare, rough-hewn, down-to-earth man with that most valuable deceptive asset for a canny business man, a gentle voice and manner. Mackenzie was attracted too by our family set-up. He found Lydia with her flossy infant hair, dark eyes and eager confiding way, charming. He gave us both little trinkets each in a pretty silver box, hers round, mine square. When he went on holiday, he lent Father his handsome house and garden in Rio.

Father who knew that Mackenzie was looking for a wife, had the idea of inviting Aunt Edie to come and stay with us and help with the children. Father believed that Mackenzie would find her charm and auburn hair irresistible; he would get a delightful wife and a good hostess and she, a reliable rich husband. But he was too delicate to spell it out to her. Aunt Edie had her beaux in England, and, although she was fond of my mother, she was not much attracted by the prospect of family domesticity abroad. 'If he'd only told me,' she said afterwards, 'I'd have gone like a shot!' And our story might have been rather different!

Vovô was getting pressed now for repayment by the bank. He was negotiating the sale of his townhouse. With its size and central position, it was to be taken over for some civic function. Before the business was finally settled, someone confided the good news to 'a friend'. Another landowner in difficulty cut in and clinched the opportunity for himself. Vovô's valuable property went for a song.

Then it was the *fazenda*. Now he was leaning on the cautious side, when he should have waited, he sold. Neither of them had any business sense, the commercial world was outside their experience. Vovó adapted herself with equanimity to a modest style in a small house in São Paulo. All her daughters were married, her youngest son had qualified as a doctor and was specializing in the new X-ray. Vovô was now a Senator in the new Republic, his special interest land improvement and conservation.

Father had handled a major job in the installation of the tramway service in Rio, and for some time now he had been company secretary. Mackenzie had married a widow with an artificial manner and a grownup daughter (the one who came for a weekend to Petropolis and was

50

captivated by our governess, Miss Hume).

When Father saw us off on the *Royal Mail,* after we had left Petropolis, he was anticipating that it would not be long before his directorship
fell vacant, and he would reach his goal. He was confident, in spite of
the fact that his friend and sponsor, Mr Mackenzie, had moved out of
the Brazilian field and back to Canada to head a new development. And
now in the Brazilian office there were protracted delays and postpone-
ments – hence his letters to us about the giant Procrastination and the
dwarf Sloth.

At last it was finalized. The long-awaited pot was assigned. It went to
a well-to-do Brazilian. Father was jockeyed out of the key centre, at the
peak of his business career, and after his sterling and undisputed service
to the company. There was nothing he could do, but to resign in protest.
For him, the alternative was impossible. Both the man appointed and
the motive, he believed, were unworthy. The prize he had been promised and had worked for for years and with dedication, was lost.

But he had his plans. Calculating on the basis of the status quo early
in 1914, he reckoned that with the investment he had made over the
years, he could educate his boys at public school, send his girls to boarding-school, put some capital into a business in England – preferably
where he could play an active role – and still live in reasonable middle-
class comfort. At forty-four, an ambitious and able man, he made his
decision to move into the blank of semi-retirement – and now he had to
live with it.

– 3 –

The Rainbow Goes

LYDIA, Bee and I came into Mrs Barber's friendly chintzy drawing-room to be introduced. The centrepiece was her Indian elephant-trunk ebony-top tea-table, on a leopard-skin rug. There were silver rose-bowls and photographs – framed on the piano, and stacked three and four deep on little shelves circling the corner settee. I was to make for this with my pals on soporific Sunday evenings when we clustered round to be read aloud to. Mrs Barber, little feet comfy on a stool, steel-rimmed pince-nez pulled from a button on her bosom on to her fine-bridged nose, pursued the unending tangles of a blameless Marion Crawford romance set in the Baedeker-familiar 'eternal city'. To break the excruciating tedium, I would carefully extract from the very back of the shelf the most risibly provocative old girl preened in the fashion of yester-year and pass it on casually to a highly-strung friend. In the shocked silence, Mrs Barber's arched eyebrows would hold the weak vessel until, beckoned, she struggled up to subside resting against Mrs Barber's Sunday-foulard skirts, to regain composure and restore the evening calm.

I responded to the warm clasp of Mrs Barber's little blue-veined hands, but her grey eyes were remote, contained in her own world of Victorian certainties.

Mother had taken at once to the rather beautiful little Queen Victorian widow, always dressed in black or dove-grey. This was when she was making a tour of schools in the coastal resorts in Sussex. Father had decided that it must be boarding-school, he wanted the very best for his children. She found Roedean huge and impersonal. West Hill, covered in Virginia creeper, approached by a modest in-and-out gravelly entrance, with jasmine drooping over the porch, didn't look like a school at all. Mother liked the family atmosphere – only sixty to seventy

52

boarders, and a sprinkling of day girls. She recognized Mrs Barber as a woman of principle, and she could see that she was devoted to her girls. She believed that we would be happy and safe with her. Standards of education and hygiene she took for granted – this was England!

'I can have my own garden!' I had called out almost incredulously. We had spread out the rival prospectuses all over the sitting-room carpet. And now Mother had chosen, and we had decided on the same one too!

Father's boat docked at Southampton when we were all at Seaford, waiting for our first summer term to start. Mother had gone to meet him, and Granny joined us to welcome him home. We were staying in a white house, set in two equal halves, run by Scottish Maggie, English Miss Rand and North Country Miss Shannon – who took in summer 'guests'. At first we squeezed into one half, then we overflowed into the other, and by the time Father was due, we occupied it all. Opposite was a field where we pulled up mushrooms for breakfast, and where, for an exciting fortnight, a merry-go-round was set up, with turning lights and hurdy-gurdy music spurting out long after dark.

I can't remember much about the evening my father arrived home with mother. He seemed quite a different person. Perhaps he was, bruised and shocked as he must have been by the gravest disappointment in his life.

The next morning, I found myself alone with him, waiting for breakfast. I was at a loss what to say. He cut in: 'Get me the cards, I'll show you a trick.' By a fluke, even before he had finished, I had guessed how it worked. 'Let *me* try!' I begged, excited. My young brothers traipsed in, in their woolly knickers and jerseys. 'Choose a card,' I taxed the youngest. After some mumbo-jumbo, I set it out and prized out the right one. Cries of surprise. But my father turned away coldly, as if I had cheated.

For the first time since the early idyllic days of the marriage he was not going to be a weekend father with everything angled for his comfort and enjoyment, only briefly exercising his paternal role in dispensing treats and surprises. Now, after a year as a bachelor in a man's world and in the hub of business, he was finding himself in the centre of domesticity, and confined in a small holiday house. He was restless, cold, irritable; even the warmth of reunion was chilled.

Was it a few days or much later, when Father was away in London on business, that I overheard Mother in the next room, in a small hurt voice that I could hardly recognize as her own, speaking to Granny, 'There is *nothing* any more that is right ... everything Brazilian is wrong ... even my family...'

'*You* are right, dear,' Granny insisted gently. 'He chose you.'

The hot summer started early in 1914. At West Hill we blossomed into cotton frocks, plain, spotted and striped, with black or brown lisle stockings.

On the first Sunday of the term Lydia and I scribbled away on our new lavender writing-blocks:

Darling Mummy,

When we got her we had dinner [Lydia's euphemism for mince patties and chocolate custard, or 'cat's pudding' as the girls called it]. Bee went to bed while Sylvia and I unpacked. We had to take everything out of the trunk and put them away [this was the first time either of us had had to do anything of the kind – we were used to Caina's indulgence] ... We have from five to seven every evening for preparation ... We all think school is lovely ... Bee likes school awfully ... I and Sylvia are in the iii rd. form & Bee in the first. I have lots of things to ask you, will Sylvia and I have Latin or German? ... do say Latin. [No one ever took German – and the war broke out in the holidays. Mrs Barber's brother, Dr Plume, taught Latin. He was a pocket-sized, gentle, 'wicked uncle', in a black cloak, with heavy eyebrows and a Groucho moustache. He coaxed and jollied us along: '*Eram, eras* ... Are you getting ratty? Now, don't miss the bus ... *Omni* – got it?'] Are we to have geometry and algebra? Is Bee to have swimming lessons and are we all three to ride?

Darling Daddy [I wrote],

I have just finished tea it is an awfully funny meal, you don't have any plates only cups and saucers, the bread is about five inches thick & you eat it on the table cloth ... [Swarthy black-haired Annie, a terror in her kitchen, gave us an institution tea. Two huge kettles, one with sugar, the other without, spewed a disgusting mixed-with-milk brew innocent of tea-leaves. Oil-cloth spread grey over the white tablecloth; coarse kitchen plates were piled with bricks of bread. No jam – unless you brought your own; if you did, spooned some on to a hunk and passed the pot up the table, it came down empty. On Sunday there were wedges of floury grocer's cake or sandy seed.] I have not got any real especial friend so far, but I like all the girls ... Everybody says when they see my writing what a nice one it is ... [sprawling and

54

sloped – Lydia had a pretty regular hand]. There are two awfully funny American girls called Dorothea and Bernice who have to drink beer at their meals & Bernice calls herself 'the Great Beer Champion of America'. [Her soft drawl took me delightfully back to our American friends in Petropolis. The fresh appeal of the American girls in those days! From Jennie Jerome, and Henry James's heroines to Tallulah, and Bernice in her jaunty stiff white sailor jumper, always laughing. I was not shy to chat with the big girls when I was squeezed into the sixth-form table that first night. Dorothea and Bernice vanished at the end of the term with a bunch of older girls, leaving behind exciting rumours of naughty escapades, assignations, truanting when they should have been at early service!] I like this school awfully but still I will be glad when the holidays come . . .

Bee with five or six of the youngest children shared a bedroom next door to Mrs Barber's room. 'Tap on the wall if you can't sleep, dear, if you feel homesick, or not well, I will hear you and be in in a minute.'

Every morning at a quarter to eight, these little ones trooped into her, waking the old lady.

'Give me my hair, dear,' a long fleecy switch swept back over the thin parting. They gathered round for a little chat and a nice story until the breakfast gong went.

West Hill was a rambling, old-fashioned higgledy-piggeldy building. The girls' steep back-staircase climbed erratically leaving unexpected little shelving landings where practice pianos perched; more squeezed higher up in icy bedrooms. (In winter, I let the half-hour dribble by, hands tucked under my armpits.) Coke stoves warmed the classrooms and the all-purpose school hall. A hard court for tennis in summer, roller-skating and netball in winter. A grass count on a lawn bordered with flowery beds. The modest garden ending in a clump of poplars.

Mrs Barber had attracted a sprinkling of upper-middle-class girls. Their parents found Mrs Barber's gentle patrician manner much more congenial than the ambitious talk of spinster headmistresses in the big modern schools with their endless corridors, science rooms and laboratories. (Such a waste of time really. Cynthia would get married, and Daphne wanted to breed red-setters in the country – or might even go to India for a regimental husband. Meanwhile Mrs Barber's fees were reasonable, and that was a help with the boys at public school.) So that West Hill had a nucleus of rather blue-blooded, but evidently not moneyed girls, and this gave the school a certain tone. But Mrs Barber was not the worldly type to cash in on this. Indeed for a variety of compassionate and sympathetic reasons she accepted some girls at reduced fees, and two of them stayed on when their parents abroad had defaulted, because she had not the heart to refuse them.

Mariota Featherstonhaugh, one of the blue-blooded, had the slender bone fingers of the crusader's lady on the tomb. On a Saturday afternoon, she unrolled her family tree to tint the coat-of-arms. I went to stay with her in her grandparents' manor house in Sussex. We spent an afternoon gorging on peaches pulled from the walled garden. We couldn't get at the heavy long grapes dangling behind glass, because Feathers, the head gardener, had the key in his pocket.

In the big dining-room that evening the old man studied the menu. We were served with brown soup, boiled cod, and grey mutton. When it came to the dessert, the old lady, in the dim room, could not quite focus on the centrepiece; she asked for grapes. 'Not ready, dear, nor the peaches yet. Feathers has found us some pears.' He offered her a gnarled green handle of fruit. But her appetite faded.

In the snob atmosphere of the school, it was only well into the war that a big girl who by temperament and in her background had something in common with our English-rose governess, dared to admit that George Robey was her uncle. I soon learnt that a Brazilian mother wasn't *quite* the thing. And, although I immediately rejected this, her once unassailable authority was imperceptibly diminished. I remembered a little social blunder during our first winter in England. A girl at our local day-school invited all three of us to her home. Aunt Alice, staying nearby, made such a fuss about the eligibility and wealth of this new friend, that my mother decided, at the last minute, to dress us up in special new party frocks. Caina and a local needlewoman worked hard at primrose silk pleated foundations with transparent overslips trimmed with lace-crochet scallops. We arrived all prinked up, and wearing dancing sandals. But it wasn't a party. Only tea! I felt more uncomfortable and sorry for my mother and her mistake, than silly for ourselves. We had to romp indoors instead of in the garden.

I was living now in the storybook world of school come true. Joyfully exchanging conversation over the partition in the dormitory. Answering at roll-call 'One' instead of 'Here' when I broke a rule – even by mistake. You were on your honour! It was even amusing, out of church, to do all that kneeling down and standing up at prayers, and holding a little hymn-book. Girls and more girls dashing through the swing-doors. Colliding with heavy plaits that smelt faintly toasted, eyelashes like light paintbrushes, a smile behind a grille. New names – Dainty, Oenone, Jacinth . . . 'I'm going to call you Piepin – you can call me Phillimore.'

My Darling Mummy & Daddy,

Yesterday we went to a cricket match . . . It was our first team against a boys' school second team, we won . . . We had a lovely tea, I had three platefulls of strawberries! & some buns with sugar on them, unluckily I had to come away before the end . . . I am longing for the guild . . . we go for a picnic at Littlington in charabancs & in the evening we have a gorgeous dance, to which many boys are invited.

It was a programme dance. We bought white silk gloves for the occasion, and we had to lie down in bed and rest before it. No boys materialized, and Bee was the only one of us who had a comedy dance with 'a gentleman', but my enthusiasm was undiminished.

My Darling Daddy,

The guild was glorious, & millions of old girls came. All traces of lesson books were taken away . . . the floor was polished & everywhere there was flowers roses, carnations, ferns, lupins & millions of other flowers . . . the dance began at 8 oclock & went on till eleven it was simply lovely I wore some pink carnations . . . the dinner was lovely we had all sorts of lovely puddings & nice things . . . We were allowed to go and sit in the drawing-room, in the mistresses classroom, & on the stairs, during the intervales of the dance . . .

Saturday was our favourite day. First thing after breakfast, you placed your order for your own choice of four pennyworth of fruit and two pennyworth of sweets. By lunchtime it had all arrived, stacked on a trestle table. Plump brown bags of sweet cherries, fat gooseberries, melting greengages, ripe blackcurrants, garden plums. Smaller white bags with bars of chocolate cream or nougat, chunks of coconut ice, marshmallow, Turkish delight. Each separate bag marked with the girl's name.

Stretched on hot rugs on the lawn in twos and threes with our fruit and sweets and a library book we chatted and laughed, dangling our cherries over our ears and scrunching coconut in the sunshine smell of snapdragons and pinks. I curled up with *The Scarlet Pimpernel* – 'a simply ripping book', reading on and on into the long lazy afternoon. I see myself in the snap, squinting in the sun, my hair parted in the middle and hideously looped back with two fascinating slides.

By late teatime, the tired team came plodding back, the games mistress was red in the face. The important cricket match had been held up *half an hour* because the *bails* weren't in the pavilion. The pavilion I had learned the day before was an ugly brown shed with a shaky veranda, deep in cow parsley, that smelt pleasantly of bread and butter.

After prayers that evening, we were put on our honour to own up – the one who had taken the bails out of the pavilion. It was rather fun in a way. Only nobody owned up. 'No,' I said firmly when it came to me. I was praised: 'I like a straight answer.' Another new girl was bridling and hesitating. She had *seen* the bails. She was *almost* sure she hadn't touched them. The fuss went on again on Monday. Now each form was cross-questioned separately in their own classroom. Still nobody owned up. It was getting a bit flat now.

'What,' I finally asked a girl in the cloakroom, '*are* the bails?'

She stared at me through her glasses. 'The bails! They sit on the wickets, and when they fly off, you know you're out.'

What, those two silly little bits of wood left on the shelf, like something broken off a piece of furniture? We had been tidying up for the next day's match in the pavilion after games – the big girls bossing. It was my helpful contribution to pick up the two little pieces and to drop them into a basket of rubbish. It was too late now. I had only been a spectator, curious and interested in all the to-do and excitement. It would be quite out of place to step into the centre now ... I thought bails were big woolly things ... Lydia, of course, would have dashed straight in to own up.

Up to now adults had never offered themselves as the opposition. In our vulnerable childhood we had never been punished. With a tolerant, unpossessive and confident mother and a strong and loving Caina, there was no need for smacking, early bed, standing in the corner, depriving of pudding or sweets, etc. (I remember only one big pinch from Mother at a party in Petropolis, that quite took me aback.) She brought us up in her Latin tradition of mutual respect, so that we knew we had to be polite to adults – including of course our governesses, even the impossible Fräulein. Indeed adults were often attractive with their aura of experience, or with the sweet smell of money (as when Brazilian relatives dropped in on us from Paris, and there was much unwrapping of silky tissue-paper), or they were arresting for the enigmas they posed (like the man on fancy-dress-night on board ship in a low-cut black evening dress with a cigar in his red mouth, and the less attractive fat 'jolly' one in the frilly baby's cap, jumping up and down in his nightdress).

It was true I had hated the games mistress at my first boarding-school at Seaford. Small for my age at seven, I was treated by the big girls as a kind of puppy or kitten substitute, and picked up and squeezed and hugged till I squeaked in alarm. Early one morning when I was sunning myself on the beach, the powerful games mistress snatched me up by the slack of my bathing-dress, swung me into the choppy sea, deep-ducked me, pulled me horizontal and, cupping me into the spray, told me 'to swim'. Lost to all reason, blind and gasping, I clung to her like a limpet. In revenge for my humiliation, I made a big drawing of her naked stomach in cross section, two huge freckled arms hanging either side. Her undigested meal I detailed in bold crayon – yellow peas, green cubes of turnip, and red circles of carrot. This 'obscene' demeaning picture satisfied my artist's pride and avenged me. I displayed it covertly to my best friend, behind the shelter of the lifted lid of my desk.

But now, adapting to English ways, I joined the classroom game of seeing how far you can go. The tug-of-war that made the lesson-room a lively sportsground, injecting exciting tension. I was discovering that it was fun to be cheeky, and I admired the courage of girls who took the lead. I wrote home about a 'sporting' girl taking a dare and breaking the rules, assuming that they too would find all this admirable.

I tried to be cheeky with Miss Rootes, the senior mistress. She stood embattled, stocky and busty, with a light ginger moustache. The textbooks she used were no more than skeletons, factual timetables: king at the top, dates down the page relating only to names – a battle, a treaty, a Parliament. Her geography, just the same as in Petropolis with Mademoiselle, only now it was England. The lessons worked out rather like a crossword game. You had to scribble down the right word quick, before the next question. Then change over books and correct, cross or tick, so much out of ten. With no peg of reason or interest, nothing stayed in your head afterwards. Miss Rootes had a master-weapon. With her underhung jaw and through her crosshatch of uneven teeth, she could project a fine barrage of indignant saliva. She held me with her fierce yellow eyes, I backed and twisted, but she followed up, she got me against the wall. Cornered and bedewed, I had no alternative but to capitulate. A terror if crossed, she was quite a sport if you played ball with her. She would jolly you along, and even help you to marks on unprepared lessons.

The visiting music teacher, pink and balding, took the most advanced pupils. I was not up to his standard. The older girls he helped on their way with a bit of waist-squeezing and hand-holding.

I found that the practice half-hour dragged with scales and exercises, but vanished easily with a smuggled book. 'If you spent half the time practising that you do pinking and polishing your nails, we might make a start!' I tried not to exasperate my music-mistress still more by looking pleased at her unconscious compliment. I had done nothing at all to my pink nails – the very thought of filing and polishing them set my teeth on edge.

Mademoiselle was Belgian, a stately woman, rather like an affable Queen Mary with a fringe. Second only to Mrs Barber in status, she clearly had some special influence – all the little ones wore black pinafores like French schoolchildren. She seldom took staff duties and never left the staff sanctum for French lessons. We came to her. A peaceful haven, with the clock ticking on the crowded mantlepiece, the cat curled asleep. We sat round the woolly bobble-ended tablecloth, Mademoiselle at the head; she had sharp eyes but a generous smile. I was placed with an older group, but with little effort I could get nearly full marks.

Miss Charlesworth, the gym mistress, always on parade in her green tunic, set us an example in posture with her athletic stance. She translated the decadent slant of fashionable Edwardian woman with that provocative hour-glass tilt of bust and behind, into a healthy schoolgirl pattern. Knees clenched, her waist sharply indrawn, she projected a rigid behind and stuck out her blameless chest. We enjoyed swinging the clubs in time to the school-hall piano and we vaulted the boom and landed on or over the horse. Miss Charlesworth approved of the sporting breed, and could not resist a bracing tonic for those who funked it. It was in the following term – when the war fever had infected us – that Frances, the school butt, wobbled up to the boom, an amorphous jelly, and skidded to a shuddering stop instead of swinging up, with a hand on and legs over the top. Miss Charlesworth made her take the run again and again, but still she funked it. Dismissing her at last with a cold stare: 'You look *just* like the Kaiser!' Frances crumpled up in tears.

Mrs Edwards – the courtesy marital status conferred on her as a deserving female of a certain age – turned up once a fortnight, her yellow face poking out tortoise-like with peering metal spectacles, her gnarled hands clutching her holland bag. Ancient but undefeated she set about the ungrateful task of impressing on us the laborious skills and Victorian discipline that had ruled her life. ''USH! I *will* 'ave 'ush!' Invisible darning – under and over each separate thread, perfect herring-boning, hemstitching to border handkerchiefs – catching up no more than two or three threads – scallop finishing, etc. We never *made* anything, only coarse linen bags with our initials on to contain the increasingly grubby half-hearted picked and unpicked specimens. On her very last visit, she played her trump card: "Ush!' Her horny fingers were poking in her holland bag. She pulled out of withered yellow tissue-paper some clenched woollen stuff, heavily embroidered with yellowing fleurs-de-lis. 'Pass it round! ... Now!' – she was jubilant – 'You can all of you say that you've 'andled the Queen Mahree – the Queen of Roomahnia's petticoat!' (Queen Victoria's own granddaughter). *She* knew her place in the world of true blue, with a decent bob for royalty – even minor Balkan.

This summer term it was mostly tennis in the garden or cricket in the playing-field. A dusty walk down, and a slow-drifting afternoon. After I discovered the savage bite of the ball, I became a 'butter-fingers', content to be long-stop or deep-field, where I could daydream and suck clover.

Twice a week or so, we trailed down in crocodile on to the beach. The sea breeze ruffled our cartwheel ridged-straw hats, circled with ruched black velvet, and sent them joggling on their loose elastic. Down the hill, through the town and on to the front. First, the mock gaiety of the bandstand. All the dullness of conventional life caught in the tight clump of people, passive, wooden, staring at the sawing conductor, accepting the bangs and squawks as a makeshift parody of enjoyment. I was glad to escape towards Beachy Head, to clatter down on to the shingle, skidding over the stones in clumsy sensible walking shoes, to play ducks and drakes over the inscrutable grey sea.

We didn't bathe in the sea. A girl had been drowned years and years ago. If you wanted to swim, you had to make the Spartan choice to be called at 6.30 a.m., swallow a cup of tea and a biscuit, and, still sluggish, arrive in crocodile at the baths. The blue water in the echoing aquarium was mild but prickly. Too soon the whistle interrupted you – a boys' school was lined up and waiting outside. Virtuous and tested, you came back to breakfast.

Six horribly public downstairs lavatory-cubicles with open tops and doors revealing feet and ankles, were invaded in a communal rush whenever the tight move-about-and-sit-down game of the school timetable gave you a chance. A stampede with girls impatient and vocal to get in, bells imminent and a tension and hurry to get out, bowels spluttering, rapid stinks, freezing air pouring in from the high-up vents always open. It became a horrendous, noisome place to avoid. I dodged the main incursion and tried to cultivate unusual visits, provided I didn't have to make a childish hand-up-excuse-me exhibition of myself in prep.

61

After a while I found that I didn't need to go nearly so often, I was training myself to be constipated. Every now and then I got a dynamite pill from Matron, it clawed me in the small hours and sent me flying barefoot across the landing.

I don't know what impossible dream 'having my own garden' had conjured up as I read the prospectus. But it came down to a chalky rectangle backed by a privet hedge and ending on the path leading to the lavatories. I was advised to plant Virginia stock. I expected scented spikes, but a dwarf army came up, the insipid flower-equivalent of hundreds and thousands – no smell. I grew a tangle of nasturtiums and a few stringy daisy plants. It was too shady, nothing prospered; fuchsias out of pots slowly died, pinks mildewed, the prolific buds turning into empty husks, London pride that sounded big and bold came out in tiny shivery flowers. My garden was a sad failure, it served only now as fill-in for my letters home.

It was at this stage that the big parcel arrived. I unwrapped a wooden box with a fitted lid, inside, little niches and partitions filled with miniature packets of seeds, more in labelled pill-boxes, cards carried neat hand-written instructions, when and how and where to plant, in sun and shade. Dark shiny seeds like robin's eyes, flat grey discs, rectangular ones, and green and yellow pellets. Enough to bloom and blossom all the year round. The meticulous care, the methodical precision, the choice, paralyzed me, it brought out all the unconscious anarchist, the irrational muddler, the fits-and-starter, the impractical dilettante. The rewards it offered mocked me and my ugly garden. It was too immaculate to be tampered with. I replaced the lid carefully. I enjoyed possessing it beautifully intact.

On Sunday I started a thank-you letter, but it was flat and lame, my sense of inadequacy was crippling me. Mother had met the donor on board ship, and she had invited us to visit her. I had wandered round her bright flowery garden, exclaiming at the scent and colour. and Mother had embarrassingly referred to my enthusiasm for my own school garden, so that I had felt obliged to respond with mock fervour. After the lapse of a week I picked up the stale thank-you letter. But the more I tried to whip up my gratitude, the more something negative intervened, imposing its will to deflect mine and frustrate my efforts. The letter drifted into the following Sunday – and the next. Until, at last, I had to give up the attempt.

In the holidays after our first term, the war broke out. It meant nothing to me. I imagined the King would have to face up to the Kaiser with cannon and cavalry charges in some distant battlefield.

That winter we were in a house in Chislehurst, with a conservatory filled with faintly evil-smelling pots of calceolarias and cinerarias, a billiard-room used as a dining-room, and a butler called Spitter. The house must have been let furnished and staffed. Father, back from the tropics, was not going to put himself out in his own home in a cold winter, so, to Spitter's disgust, no one dressed for dinner. (At school we always changed before supper.) Now Lydia and I just washed our faces and put on satin bows.

Upstairs I could sit right inside the deep window seat. With the snow falling outside in the dark garden, I read *Dombey and Son*, munching my Christmas sweets. And then I found Kingsley's *Hypatia*, with its fascinating hint of the luxury and sensuousness of Roman orgies.

'Pass your sweets around.'

I stared back at my father, stung at the implied meanness.

'Pass them around.'

Woodenly I complied. We all had our own sweets. I licked mine slowly and they lasted longer.

Playing by the artificial pond, thick with ice, Edward had broken a piece of the ornamental balustrade and fallen in. Charlie took the blame. Edward was ill. Mother was in his bedroom all the time. The doctor told us he had double pneumonia. There was a screen in the room and a blanket hanging. As Mummy was looking after him night and day I was sure he would get well.

When he was convalescent, lying in his little bed, his snake's eyes tired and sleepy, I peeled one grape after another, carefully pinching out the seeds, and popped the juicy globes into his small beak, always open and ready for another, and soft to my fingers.

Partly inspired by *Hypatia*, and partly by the *Water Babies*, I was engrossed in painting a decorative water scene – tumbling infants and a rather daring bosomy mermaid floating in water-plants and flowers.

Daddy was leaning over my shoulder. I awaited his comment with pleasurable anticipation.

'That is what we would call a *dawb*.'

What *could* he mean? I found it at last in the dictionary: 'a coarse painting, badly executed, inartistic.' (I believe it was my precocious topless mermaid that offended him.)

I heard too for the first time a theme that was to recur again and again. I reminded him of his sister Ethel. Lydia had been her infant bridesmaid. In the photo Aunt Ethel was taller than her husband.

'She was afraid she was going to be an old maid. Poor old Herbert, he imagined that would make her grateful, easy to live with. That's where he made his mistake!'

I studied the photo. A strong nose and chin and a thin mouth, nothing like mine – and her eyes – a little too close together? Perhaps that was it – the eyes. It was supposed to mean you were shifty.

That January winter term we caught the jingo war-fever. It was fanned by excited horrified rumours that were whispered, about the atrocities of the Huns in little Belgium – 'Cut off their hands, and their breasts!' How was it possible, our own were so small. We shuddered. To embellish our letters home we copied crude cartoons of Tommy Atkins with his bayonet chasing Kaiser Bill and Little Willy, bulldogs and Union Jacks (the wide seam the right way up), and these replaced blackbirds nesting in blossom and robins on the twig.

'Darling Charlie, This is an union jack made of kisses. Do you see this awful-looking creature popping out of a submarine, that is a German who thinks he looks very terrible, but who really is a great coward & would run away if he saw an English ship.'

'Darling Edward, This is a picture of dirty Mrs Kaiser who is getting very cross because she can't get enough bread to guzzle...'

My best friend filled a page in my birthday album with three Belgian-flag little girls in red, yellow and black, a burning village and church spire in the background – 'Brave little Belgium!'

Father was doing his war-work in a ministry in Whitehall, and Mother was sewing, and rolling bandages with the local WVS.

We got the news that Uncle Edmundo at the front was missing. It was confirmed, at last, that he was dead. A first touch of bleak reality came to dim the heroism, when I heard Father say, 'He was a fool to have rushed into it at his age, and with his family responsibilities.' Aunt Maricota, Mother's eldest blue-stocking sister who had been so madly in love long ago in Rio, was left with three sons at Charterhouse, a girl at boarding-school and another at home.

Lydia was reading Ian Hay's *The First Hundred Thousand*. Father, with the new *Punch* propped against the coffeepot at breakfast, regaled the family with the latest Owen Seaman – 'Thomas of the Light Heart'.

> Facing the guns he jokes as well
> As any judge upon the Bench
> Between the crash of shell and shell
> His laughter rings along the trench

> He seems immensely tickled by a
> Projectile which he calls Black Maria

He mouthed the contrived rhyme with special enjoyment, and interpolated his own favourite schoolboy rhyme from *Don Juan* ... 'not another morsel, I've had enough to make a horse'll' – this quotation nicely tempered a respect for culture with a judicious philistine levity; we were to hear it again, and again and again.

> He whistles down the day-long road
> And, when the chilly shadows fall
> And heavier hangs the weary load,
> Is he downhearted? Not at all.
> 'Tis then he takes a light and airy
> View of the tedious road to Tipperary

> He takes to fighting as a game;
> He does no talking through his hat,
> Of holy missions, all the same
> He has his faith – be sure of that:
> He'll not disgrace his sporting breed
> Nor play what isn't cricket. There's his creed.

This final accolade for Tommy Atkins for playing the game as well as any public school officer, imparted a general glow of satisfaction. Lydia, her big trusting eyes on Daddy, was inspired to copy out these and other patriotic verses, almost filling an exercise book, adding her own favourites from Kipling, including of course, *If*. One of these poems, Ellen T. Fowler's *Song of War*, captured the mood of righteous fervour, carried later to the bellicose extreme of white-feather distribution to men out of uniform:

> England lay asleep 'mid the tumult of the nations
> While her sons beheld no visions, and her daughters dreamed no dreams ...
> So he roused the cannon's rattle
> And he called to them by battle
> And by noise and great confusion and by garments rolled in blood
> And her sons obeyed her call, and went forth in mighty numbers
> While the angel that had saved them
> Rode before them on a pale horse and the rider's name was Death.

I remember the opening lines of Owen Seaman's verses that Lydia didn't quote. This was on Bernard Shaw. It ran:

Supernal jester who in happier days
Amused us with your prefaces and plays

It ended something like:

And balm he offers to the nation's foe
While pouring vitriol on his country's woe.

I had already enjoyed snippets out of a Shaw calendar, and these led me on to dip into the Prefaces in the two volumes *Plays Pleasant* and *Unpleasant* which Father had on his shelves, and which had come over in our trunks from Petropolis. How could it be that this brilliant writer was pro-German?

Then there was Sir Roger Casement. Father had known him when he was consul in Brazil ... 'undeniable quality ... and a charmer too. Of course he was quite lost to reason when it came to Ireland. Quite mad on that score ... a tragic end.' This was another enigma. He also failed as a war-time patriot, and now he was hanged as a traitor!

Our cousin Richard, the eldest son of Aunt Maricota, came to military age. He had been in the OTC at Charterhouse, but now he was a conscientious objector. Father, much against his will, spoke for him at the Tribunal. Richard was clever, a little plump, and unperturbable. I remember him as amused and a little patronizing. He could, if he had chosen, with his mixed parentage and born in Brazil, have claimed Brazilian nationality. Partly because of this, and because his father had died in the war, he was exempted. He went on to King's College, London and got a good degree, and later he joined the 1917 Club.*

Term after term, and the excitement, the war-fever petered out. The

---

*In Gerrard Street, Soho. Entry in Virginia Woolf's *Diary*: 'Oct. 1917 Leonard Woolf bringing the 1917 Club into existence.' Quentin Bell: 'Leonard and other socialist intellectuals thought that it might provide a congenial meeting place. It very soon became the centre not only for the politically minded, but for a kind of second-generation Bloomsbury. The old pre-war Bloomsbury beginning to acquire a sort of mythical existence, to be admired and imitated or denigrated by younger people who were for the most part non-conformist in a nation at war.' *Virginia Woolf*, Quentin Bell, Vol.II, p 45.

picture of courageous romantic young officers daring death over the top, had turned into something sad and dreary – the long, long trail a-winding – sticking it out in the trenches, Ole Bill with his walrus moustache in his 'better 'ole'. We heard Father talking about DORA's restrictions, and that there was no more cricket, no boat race. The stalemate, the mounting casualties, and then poison gas, spread a gloom that had a subduing impact on us too.

We were feeling the shortages now at school. The hunks of bread at tea were grey and ropey, made of potato and bean flour – I found grey string folded in – they were topped with a smear of the too-oily, yellow, rudimentary margarine (later that was to be short too). Annie with her old-fashioned training and her standard homely fare, was quite unable to adapt to war-time shortages of fat and sugar, etc. Her attempts at barley rissoles, savoury oatmeal pudding, bean fritters, and unsweetened cornflour and rhubarb jelly and maize semolina, were quite horrible.

'I am sure Annie is doing her best.' Mrs Barber accepted it placidly.

I used to feel a little hungry most of the time.

One night I lay in bed hollow and wakeful, obsessed with the thought of the torn top of a jar of home-made raspberry jam oozing syrup, hidden behind my wide Sunday beaver in the hat cupboard high above my head – part of the booty waiting in trust for our midnight feast. At last the sweet temptation pulled me up on tiptoe – the wind shivering my curtained wardrobe – to feel silently in the dark – not to wake Lydia – for the sticky treasure. Safe in bed, I licked the top clean. A finger probed the crack just a little wider, for another drop. Against my will, I tore it so that I could dip my finger right in. And then I carefully scooped and dripped and licked on till I had extracted the very last drop and gobbet of nectar.

Bath night was every other night. Then as coal got scarcer, two baths a week, and finally once a week. Instead, a small jug of hot water for the nightly good wash-down. I shared with Lydia the end cubicle, exposed to the icy flow of fresh air from the high double-window in the corridor, open all the year round. Wrapped in my woolly dressing-gown over my flannelette nightdress, I curled in a ball, and slowly my legs and feet unfroze in bed.

The sea walks were the terror of winter, when I had the 'curse', or rather when the curse was trying to start. What had begun so easily and even unawares one summer holiday at Seaford, had now turned into a monthly agony. Matron refused to 'excuse me' from the walks. Mrs Mann, again with the courtesy title as a respectable elderly working spinster, and with no other qualification as a Matron, was in her element as a nanny, supervising the uncritical little ones in her room at their early supper, etc. 'Severe but we liked her,' Bee said. With the older girls she was grudging and suspicious. To me, she was a Grimms' witch – no flesh on her, a frizzle of grey hair, colourless eyes, and a puckered round O of a mouth drawn in perpetual distaste. The girls, half in ridicule, half to soften her, greeted her as 'Mannikins'. I found it impossible to be familiar. I dreaded her impervious stupidity, her power to wreak pain on me.

I set off in the crocodile, an unexpected bomb in my vitals, tearing me, dragging up waves of nausea. The east wind glazed my eyes, thickened my chilblained fingers into a mittened block, and then my feet. Grey stones, grey sky, grey sea ... In a haze of spreading pain I started to count my steps, trying to eke it out, to help me get back, to stay upright, to keep on walking.

In bed, twisting in the small hours, the knot at last untied. A hotwater-bottle was out of the question for a healthy young girl.

I changed my tactics. I asked Mrs Mann 'to excuse me' because I had blisters. She turned a suspicious snout: 'I'll have a look at them.'

In my cubicle, I tore off my stockings, grabbed the nail-scissors, and jabbed hard between my toes. They bled profusely. My ploy succeeded, but it was not an easy one to repeat.

One morning at breakfast I found I couldn't swallow. Mademoiselle noticed I was ill. Mrs Mann took my temperature. It was so high she said I must have diphtheria. I was to go to the sick-bay, a semi-detached a street or so away.

Carrying my sponge-bag and brush-and-comb bag (we had bags for everything – nightdresses, handkerchiefs, shoes, etc), a maid accompanying me with my dressing-gown and slippers, I made my way on a nebulous pavement in a receding prospect. It took eight dynamite pills, four nights running, to get my temperature down. (The result I suppose of my aversion to the lavatory routine). It was tonsillitis not diphtheria.

When I got back, the doctor recommended that every morning before breakfast I drink senna-pod water, soaked overnight. This was all right for the first few days, but after that it was a matter of whipping a runaway horse. But Mrs Mann was adamant. She had to see me swallow it. Now I became one big ache, hugging myself and reluctant to stand up, but still, every morning, the medicine had to be taken. After the holidays, it was dropped, and the following term I became as firmly constipated as before. Now I was landed with a problem that was to last for years.

That cruel winter we were in Seaford for the holidays. A unit of black volunteers who had been recruited from Africa were billeted in a camp on the downs. As we stood at the roadside with Caina, sad little military processions used to wend their way to the cemetery. The Africans in the exposed unheated huts were dying of pneumonia before they even reached the trenches.

Black soldiers strolling in twos and threes on the pavement smiled and greeted Caina. One of them gave her a letter. Caina asked Bee to read it to her. She kept it a secret between the two of them. It proposed marriage. In his own country, he said, he was an important person. Bee wrote back as Caina dictated. 'Dear Jim, I hope this finds you as it leaves me, in the pink. I am sorry I can't marry you. I can't leave my children. I love them too much. With much love from Caina.'

Caina knew the proper way to write a letter from her friends in Seaford who read her their own letters from the front. Caina, who loved joking and laughing, and whose instinct was to trust and like people, made friends with everyone – the policeman, the postman, the man behind the counter as she handed him her purse and showed him what she wanted, the fishermen on the beach. She couldn't resist stopping to buy presents, trinkets and beads, little toys, whistles and balls for the bare-legged children with their red hands in the wind. She was invited to tea in the back streets. Any wretched child in Caina's arms grew quiet and happy, unalarmed by her black face. One of her friends from a fisherman's home, Lucy, big and blowsy with red hair, came to us later as a cook with her baby – no husband.

Mother, who wanted to have everything just right for us, had us measured for side-saddle riding habits. I felt weighted down by the heavy cloth, and I hated the foolish gap at the back so that you had to hold the skirt round to hide your legs. Skewed sideways was awkward after legs astride. At first, at school, we had to put up with the indignity of being led on the snaffle, like beginners. The ride always followed the same pattern. We walked the horses endlessly through the streets, then a little trot up an easy slope, and on to the downs ... I had been told about the beauty of the downs. I gazed at it: sallow turf, dun curves, stark, colourless against a watery sky. Was this really beauty in England? More trotting and a brief canter, and then home again the same way. There were only two alternative rides. Sometimes more walking, sometimes more trotting, sometimes no canter. The wooden riding-master never yielded an inch, he remained dumb and distant.

In winter, my fingers thick and stiff with chilblains fused in their leather gloves on to the leather reins in a lifeless clamp. I had to melt and undo them painfully in the cloakroom under the tap. I wanted to give up riding. It was so dull.

Sunday at school was the dreariest day of the week. Church at eleven, and again in the evening. In Lent another evening service in the week too. The hollow almost empty church streamed with currents of cold air, sweeping down the stony naves and drawn up into the bony heights. The forlorn scattering round the central aisle – our sixty or so odd boarders, a small prep school and the straggle of the elderly faithful – were swallowed up, an insufficient sacrifice, not generating enough warmth to counteract the cold flow. There was no comfort, no colour to warm the eye – no friendly pews, no plush hassocks. Only rows of cheap, ugly wooden chairs, joined in a line by a slat under the hard seats. A flat kneeling envelope in faded maroon rested on the slat in front, but as you dropped down on it, your knees were claimed by the cold stone underneath.

In the six and a half years I sat captive each Sunday as the vicar dominated us from his pulpit, I never heard him say anything that could remotely touch, engage our interest, except for his bitter jeremiad at the end of the war. A big gaunt man, his voice and face spoke of a strong ambitious nature shackled and tormented. He was as it were howling in his own wilderness of disappointment and frustration but in a guise conventionally throttled into the harsh neutrality of arid dogma. We, his starveling congregation of children and old women, his scapegoats. My eye wandered, searching for some anchor of hope to focus on and find relief, and met only the blind eye of the gilt spreadeagle. The absence of any mutual involvement or sense of propinquity induced a kind of vacuum which atrophied even the power to connect in thought or daydream, reducing me to a small uncomfortable animal scratching its chilblains – much I suppose as captive creatures in enforced idleness are reduced in cages.

The miasma had a strange effect on the adolescent girls that summer. A big girl, during the hymn, turned white and began to sway. A mistress pushed her down and lowered her head. Then it was a girl in the row behind, and another beside her. That Sunday it was three, but the next Sunday there were six, and the following – with an extra mistress on duty – they could hardly cope. It was an epidemic. There was scarcely a girl left standing. Recumbent figures were carried out and left unconscious in the porch. Finally there was no room for another body. A mistress hastily liberated the remaining girls. We filed out into the sun-

70

shine. Mrs Barber in a stern bracing talk told the girls it just had to stop.

Sunday afternoon was the duty-time for the letter home. After the dreary seed-cake tea, and before evening service, we scraped the hard wooden chairs into a semi-circle round the sulphurous coke stove, its black chimney buried in the end wall, a basket-chair and stool awaiting Mrs Barber. She joined us, a purple volume clasped in her small hands, to embark on another castrated romance. Her gentle voice intoning the calm assurance that we, the young, were growing up to take our place in an ordered and confident society, and we were presently enclosed in a circle of contentment and repose.

In the back row, a block on my knees, I was still scratching round for something to write home ... 'The other day an aeroplane passed over and looped the loop three times. We went for a walk on the beach ... it seems a long way down & it is an awful drag up the hill ... This must be a dull letter but really nothing has happened at all, so I will just have to write rubbish ... I am simply longing for the holidays...'

One empty day, as a last resort, I decorated the green woodwork around our classroom stove with a red-hot poker – the wood sinking and smoking deliciously as it went along.

A few days later, Mrs Barber came in. We were alone together.

'Look at these dreadful marks, aren't they shocking?'

Together we examined them.

'Is it true that you did this?'

I assented.

'I am very surprised. I never thought you would do anything like that.'

I was a little surprised too. I turned over in my mind why I had, and found no answer.

'You wouldn't do anything like that in your own home?'

I agreed that I would not.

At this impasse, Annie went by outside, festooned with parcels and baskets.

'I must speak to Annie ... I don't know what we shall have to do about this.'

Gravely she left me. I heard nothing more. Mrs Barber was always tolerant and kind to me.

Much earlier on Mrs Mann had reported me to her for being dirty, allegedly with a grey neck. She had burst into my cubicle one freezing night to discover me in my woolly dressing-gown swabbing my face, instead of 'washing down' bared to the waist. Next morning, with the hot

71

water jug came the instruction to go along to Mrs Barber's room.

The well upholstered room was pleasantly stuffy. The old lady greeted me from her bed: 'You can have a nice wash here this morning, use my flannel, dear, the water's still warm.'

Reluctantly I bared my puling torso and, controlling my distaste, basted the limp rag and dabbed and sluiced myself gingerly.

'That's right, dear. Always have your wash-down night and morning, and then you will *feel* right.'

Mrs Barber, who was determined to do the best for her girls, was moving with the times. To get her school accepted as a qualified secondary, she strengthened her staff with a sprinkling of degrees, and finally added a laboratory and two more downstairs practice rooms with pianos.

I was going to the town hall now for art. (For my first drawing lessons at school, a sheet with a geometric pattern on a squared base was draped over the blackboard. First you had to make a framework of dots – ruler not allowed. Once the dotty scaffolding was in, you could link up to fill in the pattern, but this was never achieved, the dots took too long.) Now a small group of us were released from school for an afternoon. We started off a little tipsy at the prospect of freedom, more in the mood for adventure than work.

Our small group, marooned in a big outer room, was left to assemble easels and drawing boards round a dusty group of papier-mâché pyramids, cubes and squares. Nobody bothered much with us; an advanced class of art students was going on next door. We whispered and gossiped and ventured down corridors exploring. Finally one of us hopped down the stairs and out into the free world to buy sweets. One afternoon as we were chirping away a dark handsome man burst out of the inner room to reprove us 'for being frivolous' – I liked the accusation, it sounded light and gay. In the hope of provoking him again we dropped our easels and raised our voices. But this time it was only Mr Millington who came out. With his long white face, black eyes and waxed moustache he was like a kindly seaside Salvador Dali. He sucked violet cachous and was a conscientious objector. We grumbled that we were bored with geometrical shapes, and for a change he gave us Dante's head in plaster. I showed Mr Millington my Saturday afternoon drawings, including a careful copy of *The Soul's Awakening*, a romantic girl with huge pupils looking up in a ray of sunlight. (In Compton MacKenzie's *Sinister Street*, the hero undergraduate is given *The Soul's Awakening* by the mater and *Grouse* by Torburn by the governor for his rooms at Oxford.) Mr Millington praised my effort and commented in my school report that I had talent and must work hard in the holidays. But I never took him seriously.

Miss Rootes, the very last of the old brigade, left and her place was taken by Miss Turner, an angular gentlewoman with academic qualifications. Looking back, I picture her as a clergyman's daughter with a brood of brothers, brought up in a hard-working parsonage with the odour of sanctity and carbolic. Her nose, once tip-tilted and cheeky, now pinched, and the fun drained out of her big mouth, now too full of teeth. She was restless, eager to tackle and make a tidy job of organizing, rationalizing our higgledy-piggeldy ways that offended her.

'What are you going to do now?' she asked me. 'What do you do on Saturday afternoon?'

She had just heard my 'lines' – six for a rule, two for a late, two for an order-mark. We could choose our own lines. Scott was the easiest: 'The way was long/ The wind was cold/ The minstrel was/ Infirm and old.' Sometimes I chose something I liked: 'Haste thee nymph and bring with thee...'

'On Saturday we do what we like,' I told her.

One of the things we had liked to do when we first arrived was to improvise our own special enclaves of privacy – our wigwams – two chairs uptilted on the lawn, or in the classroom next to the stove in winter, draped with rugs so that no one could see in, and with plenty of cushions. The young ones still retreated into their own hideouts.

Her slender ankles and thin heels outside, and her stooping doubtful gaze, smelling a little laxity. What were we up to?

We were arm-in-arm reading a shared book, turning the page when the other was ready. Exchanging glances out of the corner of our eyes when the hero disguised as a highwayman put out his hand in the dark passage and encountered something soft, and there was a gasp and a rustle of silk. The best one was a book borrowed from a day-girl about an orphan heiress with a male guardian who had to buy all her clothes and prevent her from sipping eau-de-cologne, and who only discovered in the climax that he was really a lover and not a father.

We emerged from the wigwams for the camisole craze. A quarter of a yard of mauve, baby-blue or soft pink crêpe de Chine stitched to a deep-slotted lace insertion, threaded with satin ribbon and tying with a big bow in front. Glimpsed through a ninon or jap-silk or, best of all, crêpe de Chine blouse, this was just the thing.

Then it was drawing, with charcoal stumps dipped in pools of black powder, which made shading so easy and professional. Afterwards, the

73

operation of fixing the encrusted drawings, the ebony curls and kohl eyes, with a little spray that glazed them over with a yellow sheen. We tried smoking the stumps too.

On a cold rainy afternoon we would pack into the practice room with the best piano, sitting on the floor, sardined against the wall while Iris played to us – Chopin and Rachmaninov and more Chopin.

Sometimes we improvised netball matches on the hard court, and as we picked sides we brought in some of the promising young ones, to make up for the girls who couldn't be fagged to move away from the stove and their book. Bee wriggling like an eager puppy waiting to be chosen by her big sister. We enjoyed the fun and the informality of organizing our own game, and went on playing into the dusk.

Miss Turner latched on to the loose-end of Saturday, and organized our precious free afternoon away. Those who were not listed for official games would take proper exercise in a walk – and not droop about over the stove or curl up in wigwams. The outrage of a walk on Saturday shocked us all. For me, it was the end. She had pushed me into revolt. Now she was the enemy, and I could show no quarter.

It was a pity because she was introducing us to poetry: 'The slender stream, to fall and pause and fall did seem' – it took me back to Petropolis. She was enjoying herself also with *The Lotos-Eaters*. It was apparently all right in poetry for sailors to lie in a sensuous stupor 'propt on beds of amaranth and moly ... To watch the long bright river drawing slowly, His waters from the purple hill ...' She was eager and happy: 'You can see it all ...' she gestured, in full spate, 'you can see it in pictures ... in black and white ...'

'Black and white,' I echoed contemptuously.

'Well then,' – punctured – 'in colour – Sylvia!' She raised her chalky knuckles dramatically, 'You *destroy* life!'

For a moment that shook me ... My Mother's face close to mine, her eyes burning and tender ... 'Krishna, Vishnu and Siva ... I am now going to call you Siva – the Destroyer!' Why did she say that?

But I hardened my heart.

It ended up at last in a grand duel. I seem to remember I spent a lot of time banished to my bedroom. I missed the summer bazaar with its attractive stalls of home-made cakes and jam, garden flowers in tubs, and ewers overflowing with roses, sweetpeas, pansies, stocks, clumps of delphinium, its second-hand book bargains, and its platform that always promised that something exciting was just going to happen, ending up with a giggle at 'two awful old maids playing duets, awful little hoppy things'. I believe that I was even excluded from the examination room. I have no idea what the storm was all about, but I remember a compassionate glance from Mademoiselle when at the finish I was getting a little battered, but still holding out.

I had a terrible report, with a placid footnote from Mrs Barber: 'A disappointing term but I feel sure she will do better in the next.'

Miss Turner had given us up. She retired from the scene.

Our new form-mistress arrived with the intake of new staff.

She entered our classroom in a long stride. Lean and well-proportioned, her cardigan falling flat on the much-prized hollow chest. A rather melancholy Burne-Jones face with wide-apart well-set grey eyes, but a thin-lipped mouth and a strong jaw. Almost masculine hands.

She faced us in an unassuming business-as-usual manner, not at all as though this was the key opening scene, the testing time. We couldn't let it slip by like that. We tried it on: eager offers of fresh chalk, to stoke the stove, fill the ink-wells, close the windows, etc, officiously scampering around. She was apparently taking it all in good faith. But when she turned to write on the blackboard someone followed up with an unmistakable bit of cheek. She swung round, eyes flashing. My spirits rose. Unexpectedly she sat down. She stared at us in silence. Something almost tragic in the hard experience of the mouth. The fire died out. In a quiet dry voice she lectured us. She had not expected that kind of thing at this type of school. Of course there were girls too stupid to understand that learning meant co-operation, etc, etc. Everybody was listening. She went on, reasonable and easy, to tell us what she was going to cover in the term. It was up to us – hard and tight-lipped again – how we wanted it done.

The bell, a girl darted to hold open the door. She made no attempt to harvest any smiles or small gestures of goodwill. As non-commital and remote as when she had appeared, her lean behind vanished. It was up to us to meet her all the way.

How ridiculous the classroom-baiting seemed now. Why had I ever involved myself in such childish nonsense. I kept seeing her brooding eyes. The pathos of those big hands playing with a little piece of chalk ... so much strength ... and reserve. Her easy mastery of the situation. The vulnerable hint of cockney in the flat voice ... the contrast when her eyes were on fire ... her locked secret personality...

I could feel the pull, the attraction of giving way. Yet I was half aware that this, too, was childish nonsense ... to be resisted? But I didn't want

75

to be outside, in the cold. I wanted, needed to believe in something, to have a focus, to fill the hungry vacuum.

Surreptitiously I polished her red inkwell to a perfect whiteness.

We were now following the syllabus of the local Cambridge examinations. No more ping-pong question-and-answer add-up-the-marks and forget-it-all lessons. We had to cover the ground. New textbooks and set books; we made a little advance each week, and had a few 'taking-down' lessons at the end, when we were short of time. The blackboard beautifully covered in her neat interesting hand, that gave me a little thrill each time I looked up.

Then, for a few of us, it was down to the town hall to spill it all out, scribbling away at the papers. There were prizes too for Distinction, and coming near the top. We had to make our choice of prize books from one special shop. In theory you could order what you wanted, but invariably you had to choose off the shelves, as the ordered copies could never be delivered on time. I had to take a hideous purple leather Milton, only to discover after the award, that it was adorned with academy colour-plates of large complacent angels. I tore them all out.

Waiting at the steps up to the platform at the town hall on prize day, I felt self-consciously bunchy in Lydia's tight-waisted cast-off dress; inadequately flattened by Caina's little crocheted bust-bodice with its roses and clover leaves. I had to stoop my shoulders before stepping up into public view on the platform.

Now we had a demure self-contained neat parcel of a Welsh woman, Botany-Jones, who taught maths too. We picked our flowers from the border, and while she talked about inflorescences and stamens, we sniffed and played with them, and after drawing them, sadly dismembered them, to note the parts. It was all so attractive and interesting – the virtues of green colouring matter, breathing, taking nourishment from the air – that later at college I hesitated at first whether to take Botany instead of English.

The headmaster of a local secondary school, with a day-girl at ours, lectured once a week in the school hall on physical geography, decorating the board with attractive chalked diagrams of terminal moraines and glaciers.

I was keen now to get to the top, to win the regard and the attention of my goddess. In my imagination she had grown into a Juno of wisdom, a mysterious Sphinx, or at times a fascinating kind of King Cophetua beggar-maid, noble but unassuming in her hum-drum mistress's guise, and with that little flat accent. I brooded on her all day long.

I had written eight pages of flimsy block declaring my. . . (I only dared say) admiration, my ambition to get to know her, to talk to her. I wanted to ask her so many things. Questions that had to be answered: Is life worth living? What is the point of it? Did she believe in God? Wasn't religion just conventional humbug?

Folded in four, it bulged my pocket. I was still unsure of myself, reluctant to take the step. I was waiting for the right moment – which never came.

When she kissed me goodnight, a distributed favour as she was putting out the dormitory lights – she had her court now in all the older forms – I half detected a little wispiness round the thin lips, which I privately found disenchanting. It was a cold encounter.

No, I didn't want something physical in the dark. I wanted a marriage of true minds! The freedom of her oceans of experience. The consummation of understanding, of recognition and acceptance.

And yet? That dark starry evening, her physical dependence on me as I took her round and round the hard court, her first time on rollerskates, and she leant heavily on me, brought a precious ache in my wrists that lingered pleasantly, afterwards. And the moment before, when she bent to fasten her skates and down the V of her blouse in that mysterious concave I glimpsed another more intimate V – my goddess was human too!

She took us to see *Julius Caesar* at a matinée on the pier.

Shakespeare up to now had been a complete flop. We had learnt in Petropolis from our quotation book the murder and sleep bits: 'Sleep that knits up the ravelled sleeve. . . great nature's second course' – homely stuff, not like poetry at all – knitting and second helping. And now in the classroom we had done the casket scene in the *Merchant of Venice*. Once you got the hang of the involved charged lines, it was no more than fairy-story stuff, gold and silver and princes choosing, with silly rhymes stuck inside. Shakespeare was turning out to be just another adult sham imposed on us.

On the pier, we were in holiday mood, but I was expecting dull fare. Nothing like the pent charge, the explosion in Brutus' tent! The cry of the heart! The wrongs, the hurt, the shock of the fatal duel of will and temperament. . . I was Cassius – mean, right, passionate. But I knew Brutus must win – Brutus must always win!

As we filed out, the wind and the rain caught us. The weather was banging about on the deck of the pier, and I was in tune with it, and with the dark swirl locking and clapping below, rushing round the thickened

77

girders. I wanted to talk, to linger, to stay a little longer in the violent world of impact, with the shock of ideas, raw feelings.

But it was all over, it was ebbing away. As the cab relentlessly tilted up the last hill, I was thinking... the dull print... yet it was all there locked inside... and the key was you, you had to be aware, to recreate it.

Sometimes on Sunday evenings, our popular form-mistress would take a small group of girls away from the usual dead evening service, for a long walk in the dark to a tiny church hidden in the mysterious night of the park, past half-guessed weeping-willows and a stream and then through yews. In the pulpit, the vicar with his interesting dark monkey face preached a down-to-earth sermon that always promised to touch a more vital point that it ever really did. But we were all drawn together in a friendly intimacy, it kept you warm and relaxed, even if you were not sitting next to her. Walking home, in the rich silence, I would venture to voice something positive... to press a little nearer... to break the barrier, to turn the flatness of her voice into the deeper note that I yearned to hear.

Mother and father both came down for my confirmation. But I had to be in a kind of spiritual purdah till after the ceremony. I couldn't be taken out for the usual handsome spread at a big hotel on the front. I had to meet them in Mrs Barber's drawing-room, and chat awkwardly, suitably cut off, while the other candidates were engaged in subdued exchanges in family groups. Most of the mothers had come armed with prettily bound religious booklets, the *Little Flowers,* etc.

Mother tactfully extricated Daddy from this uncongenial setting: 'We will be going now. Would you like me to get you some little books in the town?' I shook my head. 'Then I'll get you a nice prayer-book.' (I came across it, in a dusty old pile, in its faded strawberry suede cover; the inscription in her slanting hand still makes it worth keeping.)

I had resigned myself to going through with the approved performance as a necessary step to becoming a senior in the school. Besides, attending early service gave you certain small privileges, not the least of these a good breakfast. For a few of us, Annie would rustle up fresh hot rolls and treacle.

I had a faint hope at first that we might get a new clergyman to prepare us for our 'spiritual coming of age'. He might drop some interesting hints about our adult initiation, something bearing on the vivid process of growing up. As it turned out there was no clergyman, nothing even about spiritual enlightenment, it was all catechism, and ancient Bible and order of the service. A visiting clergyman put in a hurried appearance to check up on our briefing, and then to extricate himself to take up his own 'class' which it was not convenient for us to attend.

My confirmation dress was Lydia's, handed down, heavily embroidered, and as usual too fitting. The last straw was the veil. I felt furious in the mock bridal array.

The bishop's hand landing on my head, skidded over my hair, displacing the veil. 'Clumsy old fool!' I muttered darkly to myself.

In my cubicle I was quickly shedding all my impedimenta, free at last to join my parents, to be secular – and greedy! – when I heard a small sound. I broke the bedroom rule and went in, two cubicles away. She was a big girl with a caustic wit. Now she was lying face down – still all in white – her head in the pillow, shaking and crying. 'Why... What is it?' I whispered. I could feel her disappointment, caught up in an emotional religious tangle, all the unchanelled adolescent feelings stirred up and left in the air – with no purpose, no answer – and no one had come to take her out.

Once a fortnight a tiny elderly woman, with a lorgnette, an imperious beak, and her attendant troupe of elegant pastel-clad young ladies, descended on us in our homely old school hall. They turned it into a kind of ante-room, a forcing ground for the crucial test it was assumed we would undergo in the world of fashion and know-how, to give us a foretaste of the competitive terrors and stresses of the ordeal when we 'came out' – to sink or swim.

The piano pealed a summons. We lined up to show our paces for the graceful swing-glide-walk round. Madame, pivoting on her tiny heels in her tight black gown, sent us off with a cockatoo shriek. Slender, tubby, high-low-waisted, plaits, frizzy, faithfully embroidered, or clever bought, hanging pleats and home-made tucks, ninon and muslin, flat sandals and shiny patent leather, fringes, dangling straight, looped, we circled round. Each of us striving either for merciful anonymity or approved grace, urged on by frenetic peacock cries. Down the centre for the formal bow, at just the right distance and with just the correct inclination of the head. All in line now for the curtsey... slow... all-of-a-piece... and UP!

'Everybody ought to know / How to do the tickle-toe', and the fox-trot and the Charleston with its shimmy, and the one-step and the quick-step variations. As it became correct and fashionable, we were initiated.

The young ladies, professionally perfect, led us down the room. We followed halting, slipping, picking it up ... Madame teetered up to a big shapely girl (my best friend) and singled her out in her smart frock as an example, accompanying her solo effort with approving shreiks: 'Kle-vah! Kle-vah!' while Celia plunged along scarlet and steaming, the cynosure of all eyes.

The voice and the ambience anaesthetized me, I lost my identity, I became no one, on the wrong foot, anticipating the wrong move – although I felt, I knew, I wanted to dance. Yet I was nimble and light, I improvised and camouflaged, and got by.

Lydia had remained a little aloof, detached from the competitive show-off, follow-or-lead game of school. She seldom joined in the current craze. Most often she was buried in a book.

She always led the way in reading. In Petropolis I tried *Kim* after she had read it, but found it incomprehensible. At school, while I was still enjoying adventure and romance, she was on to the classics in the school library and following up with the solid rows in father's bookcase. By the time I was devouring *Jane Eyre* and in thrall to the *Turn of the Screw*, she was discovering Saki and for birthdays and Christmases asking for one after another of Constance Garnett's translations of Chekhov and Turgenev. I felt I must work through *The Egoist* and *Diana of the Crossways* because she had, and as they were adult and sophisticated I enjoyed them.

But in other ways she never seemed to take the lead now. She was more reserved, less eager, a little remote, dreamy, but quite immovable when she made up her mind.

It was at Mother's special request that we shared a cubicle – much better if we had paired off with our own friends. She had a methodical routine for dressing and undressing, shaking, hanging and folding her clothes, a regular way of brushing her hair and her teeth. It used to drive me almost mad with impatience. Nothing deflected her, the cold nor the time. If the lights had gone out and she had not finished, she went on in the dark. She had to be satisfied that everything was just so and in the right place.

She had the placid gentle look, the classic face of the early twenties – round chin, firm nose and neat little cut-away mouth, big soft brown eyes and brown hair. She was friendly with older girls who were themselves half removed in imagination from the school world. She was without much effort almost always at or near the top of her form. When she did something well, it was done so quietly and unostentatiously that it was hardly noticed. She was good at the high jump. With her slightly hunched unextended run, she almost paused – and was over.

At the baths, she had set herself the hardest target; she made up her mind to dive off the top springboard, just under the roof. (I could only just bring myself to jump off the one below.) She stood poised, her arms raised over her head – my guts contracted. As she fell through the air, her legs flicked back turning her so that she almost went over into a somersault. I thought she was never going to come up. 'I just ricked my back a little.'

We were all swotting for the exams, but she went on reading.

That night she got into bed without following her folding and shaking routine. Her head was aching. She looked very strange.

'I'll get Mrs Mann?' She didn't answer.

Mrs Mann paid no attention. 'I'll see her in the morning.'

'She's ill. She looks *very* ill.'

'I'll see about it ...'

I was going to stay awake till she came.

Daylight. Lydia was flinging herself from side to side of the bed, her eyes blank, red round them and dark red spots.

It was cerebral meningitis. Father was coming down from London with the specialist. Mother was on her way. The school broke up a week early.

Bee and I went home.

She wasn't going to die. The specialist had given her the serum in time.

That autumn term we went back without her.

'Dear old Hag ...' I wrote to her when she was convalescing. (Seventeen was getting on for twenty – verging on middle age.)

Two terms later we were all back at school together again.

> Over there, over there
> The Yanks are coming
> The Yanks are coming
> Their drums rum-tumming
> Everywhere ...
>
> And they won't go back
> Till it's over over there.

For a short while at any rate there was a feeling of optimism in the air. (Although before long it was 'backs to the wall' again.)

And now a delightful pair came into our world of school – Captain Moore and his sister Dorothea. The two of them complimenting and probably contradicting each other could today in their mildly freakish idiosyncratic English way create a delightful zany sequence just by walking into a Monty Python or Barry Humphries programme and engagingly caricaturing themselves.

He was a doctor, and had been invalided out of the army, the RAMC I believe, after being gassed. Tall, lanky with a ruminating jaw and an air of concentrated abstraction, of always being somewhere else. He never looked at you, he was concentrating on the next sequence after the one engaged in, so that as he half-talked to you, he was occupied with what would next fill the space you were in. As a result, today I cannot see him properly. He is headless and anonymous. I see his boots and putees and his khaki coat, and I can feel his friendly head-in-air impatience to pass on. She is pattering in his wake with her forward slanting gait, improbably disguised in a navy blue uniform and tricorn hat, following him with her prominent vague eyes – a white hyper-sensitive face and questing upper-lip – determined to keep up, to be worthy of her warrior brother, and of her guider's uniform. Yet she was conscious of her own fey qualities and her own reputation as the successful author of a popular series of stories for schoolgirls. She herself the eternal schoolgirl, with radiant ideals, prepared to dare anything – ignoring timidity and shrinking – every new idea irresistibly a winner.

Mrs Barber had great faith in Captain Moore's modern up-to-date methods as a doctor. (He offered us a good cure for chilblains, in water activated by a mild battery that gave you pins-and-needles as you held your hand dipped in it.) He was becoming her John Brown, now that she was ageing and growing very frail and tired. She was getting to rely on him, and follow his advice.

We all joined the guides – in spite of the hideous uniform – attracted by the pair of them, and by Dorothea's enthusiasm – for the fun of it. Improbably, I became a patrol leader. (By then I was captain of netball, a runner on sports day and fairly senior in the school.) Our patrol was always bottom of the knots and other competitions. My second-in-command, a capable practical girl, accepted my inadequacies with amused and unperturbable good nature.

Even drill, with our informal erratic Guider and with Captain Moore as officer-in-command, was never dull. Dorothea had a nervous trick of tapping her cheek with two fingers, in concentration – or in panic – when her brain refused to connect and she was sending a frantic SOS to

82

her big capable military brother for the next word of command.

Lady Baden-Powell, on her way to a local function, dropped in on us for a flying visit. We were all in our guide uniforms lined up on the hard court being drilled by Captain Moore. Dorothea confidently stepped out to take over, and to demonstrate her and our expertise. But the gallant mood was slipping, her fingers were fluttering to her cheek. Her shrill 'Form Fours!' came before we had even numbered. We all had a go – but Captain Moore saved the situation with his 'As you were!' Dorothea, with downcast eyes, did a little Mickey Mouse trot down the ranks, hands behind her back, pretending nothing had happened.

Dorothea thought up grand enthusiastic guiding projects for our Saturday afternoons. That summer she planned the attack and defence of Jevington, a paper-chase to Hampden Park and a grand rally at Polegate. But no tiresome details were ever worked out. It was all left to improvisation and 'initiative'. The guiding projects muddled and sorted themselves out in amiable rambling, with nobody quite knowing where everyone else was or what they were doing, but all of us, according to temperament, either engaged or pleasantly relaxed. The essential point in everybody's mind, that at a certain time and a fixed place we all met for tea.

I enjoyed the long summer afternoons of freedom – the objective the distant but not intrusive goal. High on the downs with the larks singing, or near the sea with the confidential chatter of the seagulls and the rising plaint of one of them, sailing high, in repeated despair. I would drop into a crease with some cover to shed my hot bloomers, and cool off in the heavy tunic, the air around full of the invisible thrumming of insect life, crickets snapping, grass vibrating, the flat turf flowers exuding honey in a determined effort to survive in their bony foothold. The charm of the downs, the bleached English Quaker beauty, grown real to me now that tropical colour and exuberance was only a memory.

We would skirt ploughed fields and break through little woods, and at last, making our objective, surprise, from the rear, and capture a 'trench-full' of assiduous defenders, all facing the other way. Dorothea eagerly chalked up victories – claimed by both sides. Every venture an unqualified success. We settled down to tea at trestle tables on the grass by a cottage, or in a thatched shelter in a friendly tea-garden. Captain Moore approached, head-in-air, festooned with Brownies anchoring him, claiming his attention, while he dipped deep in his pockets to see if there were any more sweets.

The season ended with a grand jamboree. All the local contingents

83

assembled in the sports ground of a big prep school. In the lee of the big tent, sheltering from the high wind, I waited impatiently for my sweet-peas for the flower-arrangement competition. Only ten minutes before judging, Dorothea arrived breathless: 'Two shades of pink,' she pleaded, fingers on her cheek.

Salmon and pinky-mauve! Wincing I pricked them out tastefully into Annie's brown earthenware bowl. Balancing my careful effort, I stepped outside the flap of the tent, the wind snatched and I was left holding the empty bowl. I had to go pouncing down the field after them. Now I jammed them all in anyhow, broken stems and bruised petals.

They were all assembling for the grand march past. At the last moment, a great flag on its pole was presented to Dorothea. The honour had fallen to our contingent to lead the way. She looked round wildly – and caught my eye. I could, I found, just about hold it in the approved awkward handover grasp. The band struck up the Robber March from *Chu Chin Chow,* and we were off.

But I had reckoned without the wind. It sent me teetering and wobbling as though I was drunk. I began to feel hysterical ... But now the banner fell slack, and I came on smartly. I was almost level with the saluting base, when the flag whipped up again, it flailed round, caught me, and wrapped me fast to the pole. I thrashed about blindly, plunging and staggering, I was fearful of upending and pole-axing the Lady Mayoress.

Pom – P O M – Pom – Pompa-Pompa – P O M – Pom – Pom ...

I was holding up the procession.

Someone broke ranks, and began to unwind me ... she took hold of the flapping end and I struggled with the pole; at a jog-trot-twosome we made it past the stand. And that was my exit from the guides.

Father was spending part of his time in a factory in Putney that produced gramophone records. He had hesitated between two companies, the larger one called Columbia only wanted a sleeping partner, so finally he invested his money in the smaller one because he could play an active part as co-director.

The war, rising prices and taxes had changed his plans and his style of living. He still had to put his boys through prep and public school, and to place them in their professions. He had intended to buy a house somewhere socially attractive in outer Surrey, but he finally settled for the town, thirteen miles outside London, where he had spent his youth.

It was rapidly impacting as a suburb, the High Street growing longer and longer, the copses and fields on the London side soon to be torn up and bricked over, first by ribbon development, and then in a general sprawl closing over the green patches and linking into Greater London, the big houses scattered in his boyhood in the surrounding countryside, where he and his sisters had been invited to dances and parties, long since vacated. All except one where the elderly tenant still invited us to her at homes, to her tennis and strawberry teas, when her great-nieces were staying, and my mother to sewing parties for charity when she was alone. Apart from her, only a few remaining contacts, and those elderly – an old maid with her companion and her parrot.

But, although we had no local friends or contacts because of our absence at boarding-school, we were still content in the holidays with our own society, and with school friends and cousins coming to stay. Family tennis, bicycling and picnics, first to bluebell and primrose woods, and then to gather hazelnuts or blackberries, Mother joining with us. The suburbs were convenient for father. He could run up to London on his motorbicycle or to the local golf club on the downs, to get his round and his afternoon bridge.

Father brought from the factory some of the records. The first ones were small black cylinders that revolved on their axis and played on a machine called, as I recollect it, a phonograph. Now the company was only making the flat discs. My favourite was 'Cavalaria Rusticana'; 'The Watchmaker' and 'The Whistler and his Dog' were not bad. But the rest – 'All Coons Look Alike to Me', 'Ka-ka-ka-Katie', 'Maggie! Yes Ma? Come Right Upstairs!' were terrible – coarse raucous voices, and a grinding tinny accompaniment rattling away too fast. A laughing record painfully hacking and retching chilled us into embarrassed silence. Father was unperturbed. The records were intended for consumption by the masses.

As it turned out, the masses wanted, along with their biggest aspidistra, the biggest and best voice, and it was Caruso who had to be heard in every front parlour.

I was beginning to grow out of my unrequited calf-love at school. It was my best friend and confidant who, when she herself confided in me, finally brought me down to earth and resolved it. She was two years older than me – the big shapely girl that our dancing mistress favoured. She had the vivid delicate colouring – white skin, sea-blue-green eyes, soft limp red hair – that made people in London stare, and a superior 'pure' high-waisted figure, solid, with perfect little inverted ice-cream cones that compared favourably with schoolgirl bouncing buxomness. She had, too, a Scottish backbone of granite, a decided jaw and a high forehead.

She had been looking forward to going to college, but now, that morning, a letter from home insisted that she ought to stay with her elderly mother who had developed angina. On Saturday afternoon, letter in hand, to get support and consolation for renouncing her dream, she sought out my goddess. She quite simply walked up the stairs, knocked on her bedroom door, and entered Eden – achieved instant intimacy. I listened with jealous attention. They had sat on the bed together, and had a long, long talk. She had been consoled with an arm round her. She was embraced, the little ice-cream cones tenderly pressed against her, and she had been kissed. It had been beautiful.

In the cold, rejected, with my Aunt-Ethel lack of appeal, I experienced not only a dwindling of love, but of friendship too. The fatuity of my undelivered letter, idiotic questions – God and life. Pretexts, nothing more. Anonymous bunches of roses, hovering about, living in hope, waiting on events. To be positive, to know what you wanted and to take it. I could never do that. I needed a catalyst to resolve my ambiguities, to give me motive power. I was fated to remain outside and ignored.

When my friend left two terms later, I had a long letter about more conquests. A dance at a country house, sitting out in a bedroom upstairs – wonderful, wonderful kisses, dance after dance with the same exciting young man. A goodbye letter afterwards from the Junior Carlton, he was going abroad.

School was flat and dull, and now emptier than ever. Lydia, too, was leaving soon. She showed me Daddy's birthday letter:

Dearest Lydia:

Just a line to wish you every happiness on your eighteenth birthday. When the next one comes round you will be a 'young lady' far from school discipline ... I have had plenty of golf and your mother has been playing croquet for some tournament or other for charity ... Tell Sylvia her letters are models of English literature, but a little too much modelled on the more lately introduced short-story school. Tell her that perhaps a course of study of the earlier 18th-century writers might induce her to change her practice in this matter and she might

86

give us then a somewhat more lengthy and elaborate epistle. I find myself owing to either lack of practice falling into Sylvia's error, coupled no doubt with the always resounding echo of war, which seems to deafen the mind to all other thoughts or sound waves ... I am glad you are bathing again, it is such a fine exercise and very good for straightening the back, if you get enough of it. Mother has I believe sent you 5/- and I now enclose p.o. for 15/- to make it up to a £1 ... My best wishes for a happy day and still-happier year, from your loving Daddy.

Father, once high and undisputed in my estimation as the key benevolent centre of the family, now seemed to rule us from the outside, separating himself from the warm centre where my mother was the focus. I was beginning to feel cold and estranged towards him. He asserted his authority not only to diminish me, but at times her also. Now, I could ignore and discount his criticism, I was indifferent to his tone of sarcastic persiflage, but I was becoming increasingly indignant at his highhanded dismissive attitude towards my mother. Lydia and I both knew that Mummy's 5/-, measly compared to his contribution, was all she – the most generous person – could squeeze out of the housekeeping without having to ask for more.

It was well into the following term when we got the news. Our Latin master, Mrs Barber's brother, was scrunching by on the gravel outside, when he stopped, put his head in at the school-hall window to call out : 'Armistice signed!' and grinning walked on to the front porch. Dr Plume's suppressed elation triggered off the girls. They cheered, grabbed one another, whirling round, dancing, laughing, they jumped up on to chairs, a pandemonium of jubilation – suddenly stilled. A small figure stood in the doorway: 'NOT the way to behave! ... This terrible war ... all the men who have died ... we should be praying ...' She was recovering herself but still severe. Later on, she would let us know about the celebrations. I had never seen Mrs Barber so out of touch with her girls. Had her own husband, I wondered, died as a soldier?

That evening we went down to the front for the celebrations. I had the curse but I had chosen to drag out because I felt this was something I ought not to miss. Fairy lights sparkled on the bandstand (taken down afterwards), patriotic music – but no singing. In the dark I was doubled-up tilted over the railings. Bee found it exciting and moving: firework stars exploding in the sky and at the same time in the calm sea. Every now and then at the zip and crackle I raised my head to seize a fragment, a brief moment of the occasion.

Father got the news in Whitehall: 'My dear Children, So the end has come at last ...' When the maroons went off, he joined the jubilant throng jamming the streets. He slipped through Cox's Bank into Northumberland Avenue and on to Piccadilly Circus. Taxis carrying thirty, 'an American officer with his trousers tucked up to his knees dancing about on the top' as it moved along, 'and a hundred other curious exhibitions of joy'. At Buckingham Palace, the King inaudible, the Guards' band playing 'Land of Hope and Glory', 'Tipperary', 'Keep the Home Fires Burning'. He took two wounded officers out to lunch.

Mother, left alone in the suburbs, came up to join Aunt Alice and stayed the night.

Next day, Father was beside the royal coach on its way to the thanksgiving service at Westminster Abbey. The bells ringing out for the first time. Big Ben striking again.

The armistice terms are all in the paper this morning, and the army will have to be very busy seeing that the Germans faithfully carry them out. I am afraid things will remain unchanged for a long time yet as regards rations, high prices & necessary economies, but there should be no more deaths which is the supreme consideration ... My best love to you all with feelings of heartfelt thankfulness that this heavy cloud which has so long overshadowed our lives is now dispersed. From your loving Daddy.

That Sunday the vicar gave his end-of-the-war sermon. Tall and forbidding in the pulpit, his blameless surplice drooping on his gaunt frame, he warned, almost threatened us: 'Those of you who are growing up ...' He was directly addressing, implicating us! We, the young and unimportant, whom year after year he had ignored, obdurately preaching over our heads. 'For you, and for every single person listening to me today ... Nothing will ever be the same again ... the England we have known has gone forever ...'

His voice, doom-laden, had the fearful knell of conviction, killing the future. The war was stretching out its dead hand to drain and defuse and to subject us all to an iron discipline. We were to grow up in a world cold and joyless, too squeezed out and exhausted to allow alien vulgarities of colour, fire and excitement.

A visit to London for the photo
(author seated on right)

Lydia and I

Mummy in 1920

Daddy in 1920

Mummy and delicate baby Edward in
Tonbridge

Mummy as a young woman in Brazil

Daddy in Petropolis

My Vovó happy with her book

Our dear Caina

Rio de Janeiro. Our governess Miss Young,
Lydia, Bee and I

Vovô's house, São Paulo

My Blackbirds patrol at West Hill

Charlie and Edward aged five and seven

Lydia posing as a vamp after Noël Coward's *Hay Fever*

Charlie at Haileybury

With the Lena Ashwell Players

Betty and I by the sea

Holiday in Brittany – Bee, Edward and I

The Dundee company on a trip to Gleneagles

Ronald in a period play, Bristol's Little
Theatre

Ronald in the Twenties

Lena Ashwell's company on tour in York

Ronald, Harold, Bee and I, stopping for a drink on our ramble

My darling John when I first met him

Molly pulled me into her form photo at Silverthorn

Molly, Hector, John and I, drinking at the pub

If I had only understood. It was to be just the opposite. The England he mourned would have had little comfort in it for me. An England of 'splendid' cultural isolation, proud of its philistine insularity, its hierarchy, its rigid class separation, its squirearchy, its conventions and formalities. A masculine-orientated society, dominated by a public school tradition that segregated boys from tender youth to young manhood, engaging strictly masculine loyalties, and isolating and relegating girls and women to complementary, subservient roles. It was the war that swept in a liberating tide of change. If the disaster of a decimated generation of young men was to condemn some of us to be single and childless, it was the explosion of woman-power taking the place of fighting men – in factories, on the land, in the office and in the hospitals – that established a precedent that was to free us to lead our own lives, and not droop and wither condemned as superfluous because we were single and childless. Einstein's relativity and Freud's psychology were to shake Victorian certainties and absolutes, and the Russian Revolution to split the social atom. It was the former draper's assistant, H.G. Wells, who was to show the shape of things to come.

But my sixteen-year-old reaction at the time was only superficial. The popular line was jokes about land-girls, and the 'Young lady called Bright / Whose speed was much faster than Light / She set out one day in the relative way / And arrived on the previous night'. The fashionable Freudian cult was Couéism: repeat, Each day and every day I am getting better and better. Finally the Russian revolution meant no more to me then than flags moving uncertainly on distant frontiers. But I did later on – I was still at school in 1920 – through my own juvenile disenchantment, share something of the disillusion of the young at the end of the war, their once naïve enthusiasm shocked into early maturity by the ceaseless senseless battering, the bloody stalemate of trench warfare. And now these alienated young were expected to forget it all, and to fit into conventional patterns, and go along with the evaluations and the complacencies of civilian life. At any rate the Victorian concepts of duty, loyalty and sacrifice no longer stood for me as virtues or imperatives, but instead as meriting wariness, and suspicion of imposing chains and abusing trust and simplicity, deserving only a harsh respect when authority could enforce their observance. The poetry and the books came out later – Wilfrid Owen, and Robert Graves, in his *Goodbye to All That,* a hero to me then.

As for the post-war invasion of continental culture, I absorbed it, unaware even that it had occurred. When I saw *The Cherry Orchard* I

89

would have found it difficult to understand why in 1911 half the audience walked out, and *The Times* found it 'queer, outlandish and even silly'. I could drink in colour reproductions of Van Gogh's *Sunflowers,* Manet's *Bar at the Folies Bergère,* of Gauguin and Matisse without suspecting that this was 'unmanly art' which filled a lifelong academician with shame and 'terror that the youth of England, young promising fellows [exclusively masculine of course], might be contaminated', and which another critic described as the 'gross puerility which scrawls indecencies on the walls of a privy'. This was when the exhibition of Manet and the Post-Impressionists opened in London in 1910. Even E.M. Forster confessed that 'Gauguin and Van Gogh were too much for me'. And it was the provincial Arnold Bennett with his vulgar quiff and his regional accent who saw 'the tragedy . . . that London was too self-complacent to suspect that it is London and not the exhibition which is making itself ridiculous.'

Victorian morality with its piety and its purity that was reflected in Mrs Barber's creed, and in her choice of anodyne etiolated literature, was now a dead pattern, irrelevant to our needs. But in the maze of adolescence, relics of Victorian mythology, unconsciously imbibed, added to the confusion, creating a personal problem in the awareness of sexual feelings that 'ought to be dormant' or non-existent. At home, in the family circle, sex was for me instinctively taboo. It must remain a private guilt, an unmentionable secret.

When my mother took me as a teenager to have my eyes tested by the knighted Harley Street eye-specialist, she sat at one end of the long consulting-room, her grave profile bent over *The Lady.* He took me to the window at the other end and leaning back against it, he toppled me over his legs to fall awkwardly against him, and while he examined my eyes at face level, his breath on my cheek, with an expert masked hand he scooped down my blouse. I found it numbingly impossible to ravish the decorum with a cry or a struggle. It just couldn't be happening! 'And now,' he murmured in my ear, 'the other little fellow.' The effrontery of his assumption of my complaisance! My body's treacherous response. Furious, I did nothing. Impossible even to tell my mother. On the next visit, she was amused at my vehemence in ridiculing his absurd suggestion that I wear a monocle in place of occasional glasses.

In prep at school, when I was busy checking up interesting passages in the Old Testament with the help of a dictionary, I found Mademoiselle's eye on me. She detached herself from her desk and did a wander round – to find me innocently reading St Mark.

90

'Replace the dictionary on the shelf,' she said smoothly, 'if you have finished with it.'

She knew!

So did my mother when she found me slumped deep in the armchair with Maupassant's *Une Vie*. I had read more than once the virtual honeymoon rape by the almost stranger husband of his innocent convent-bred girl-bride ... *'Une jambe froide vélue glissa ... il la posséda violemment.'* My mother stood in the doorway her dark eyes on me. She didn't look at the book or say anything. When she had gone, I slipped it back in the bookcase, and joined the others for rummy in the sitting-room.

Une Vie was to prove too strong meat, too powerful to stimulate indulgent masochistic fantasies. With the terrible stamp of reality it scarred my memory indelibly. The prurient priest probing in the confessional the unhappy girl who wanted a child but whose crude husband now preferred the country maid in the attic. And later on, the ex-urban fanatic priest punishing the peasant children he surprised in a circle round a whelping bitch, and then savagely kicking the animal, disgusted at its shameless fertility.

In our immature confusion and with the social pressures of what was done and not done, we were always conscious of our innate feminine disadvantage. It was taken for granted that sex was a masculine prerogative and that acceptance was the feminine role. Masculinity in itself conferred status. It was *she* who had to make the grade. *He* was already as it were a member of the club. And he was remote too. He had been conditioned from tender years to accept and like segregation, and the code that went with it. He had been initiated through its pains into its privileges, to take and then inflict punishment – fags and beating – not to deviate, to make his fellows' likes and dislikes his own, to affect a contempt for work, and to find in sport a way of life, of good style, good form, and elegant amateurism. Sport was morally cleansing too. A good egg took a pride in healthy abstinence and found emotional outlet in fellowship, loyalty, team spirit, hero-worship and very often Greek love-friendship.

Girls were negligible if they were plain, risible if they were unsexed suffragettes or blue-stockings, huddled into women's colleges at the Varsity – the traditional preserve of golden male youth – 'perspiring and bedraggled' as Compton Mackenzie described them in *Sinister Street*. Just as bad, and to be shunned and denigrated, if they flaunted their charms, provoking a fellow's lower nature. It was more manly to indulge in a good red ratting with sticks and terriers in the shut barn.

91

At the Varsity, when mothers and pretty sisters and cousins were invited to Commem or May Day, gallantry and good form in the punt or the ballroom would be all that he would be taxed to deliver, and if he snatched a kiss behind the pillar on the stairs, a prompt apology for 'forgetting himself' could dispel any stirrings of hope of an engagement. The duty of marriage was a distant threat. The suitably decorative face better contained in a silver frame in a man's room with his other trophies than offered too close in an awkward personal encounter.

Lydia had a letter later on from a Cambridge undergraduate in which he kept on addressing her as 'old chap', and urging her to send him a full-face photograph 'showing your eyes' – more like a publicity agent than a hopeful lover.

I remember the dismissive glance of a schoolfriend's Olympian elder brother, godlike in his officer's uniform, relegating me, like the maiden in the *Indian Love Lyrics,* to 'Less than the dust beneath thy chariot wheels/Less than the rust that never stains thy sword.'

Girls were expected to be pretty and attractive but not too conspicuous, to be sensible and plucky in a tight spot, and to behave unemotionally rather like a good little schoolboy, and above all to remain cool, unaware, undisturbed. Bright, with a high clear treble, even a little empty perhaps, but never brainy.

A novel set in pre-war and wartime England that ran through twenty-one editions from 1917 to 1920, *Sonia – Between Two Worlds* by Stephen McKenna, gives an idea of the emotional climate of the period, and what the reading public could accept and enjoy in popular contemporary fiction. 'Only one voice in the world held as much music in it, low and vibrant, setting my nerves a-tingle ..' The speaker, a man, is NOT referring to a woman, to the Sonia, conventionally featured in the title – but to the fascinating hero, David O'Rane, who consistently upstages her. Sonia, the wilful spoilt darling, is only the foil; she has to be whipped round the ring, forced to shed her glitter, and be subdued into a good little brown wife. The glamorous O'Rane is not the period stock hero – the exquisite Mayfair nut with chambers in Half Moon Street, or the rugged Sahib or Bwana of adventure – but a modern creation, a charismatic outsider. The bastard son of an exiled Irish peer, with 'great dark eyes', a transatlantic accent, thin shoulder blades, the 'bodily grace of a girl' and fingers 'hard as steel cable'. (This epicene dominating type appears again in Ethel M. Dell's bestselling romances, slender in his breeches and carrying a whip.) 'Raney' in boyhood, after knocking around the world, homes in on England to make for the best the country

92

has to offer – a public-school education. Raney takes his beatings, makes the grade, emerges a good egg into an England 'utterly demoralized – from the government that flings millions about in fancy social reforms to the mill-hand who wastes shillings a week on cinematograph shows and roller-skating rinks . . . Nobody cares for anything but extravagant pleasure . . . That revolution's coming all right.' Sonia is flaunting herself in the Cordon Bleu Night Club in a skirt slashed open to the knee, arms and back bare to the shoulder blades, no gloves . . . She goes still further, compromising herself with a cad on the Continent, and gets caught up in the war in enemy territory. Raney risks his life to rescue her. On the long journey back he breaks her will. He leaves her in England to go into the trenches. He is discovered in No Man's Land crucified with bayonets – stone blind. 'What does a kiddie do when he's hurt?' He goes back to Alma Mater as a housemaster. 'The laddies call him the Black Panther . . . they simply worship him . . . ' Sonia ventures: 'If I can help you by body or soul in any way any time . . .' she drops on one knee and kisses his gloved hand. At last Raney gives in. 'Perfect contentment shone in her brown eyes.' They were married in Chapel, the Corps formed a guard of honour. On Speech Day it was all just as it always had been, including 'a diminutive malefactor publicly birched across the back of the hand'.

I was convinced that I would never get married. I was an outsider. I could never take on the approved pattern, measure up to the eligible girl. My voice was too emphatic and full of feeling, it could never climb into the happy, vapid carefree treble. My eyebrows were too strong and dark. I didn't like my face or my figure – tiny high breasts and long slim legs were infinitely superior. I was at a loss in the mysterious art of making myself attractive. Much younger, I had made tentative efforts, squeezing my foot into a 2½ instead of a 3, breathing in when my waist was measured, practising winking – which I heard was naughty and fascinating. And my reactions were off-key. It wasn't only my lower nature that wouldn't let me off as unaware and unconcerned, I lacked good form. I was incapable of the instinctive Anglo-Saxon assurance that treated all domestics, waiters, porters and servicing staff as necessary accessories, who knew their place, and only came alive when relating to US, and into our world amusingly at times in the jokes in *Punch*. The affable condescension in the phrase, 'denizens of the kitchen' – used in childhood by Virginia Woolf's brother – so inclusive and dismissive, would never have occurred to me. I was always aware of them as people – their hands and eyes, their coldness or warmth.

Miss Vernon, who was psychic, with beautiful dark eyes and an occasional tic that made her eyeballs swivel and her earrings vibrate, read my hand.

'You will marry in your fifties ...'

'When I am *fifty!*'

'*IN* your fifties ... After your marriage you will come into your own. When you are seventy ...' she hesitated.

'Seventy?' This was too much. I dropped my hand. I never heard what she was hesitating about telling me.

My last term at school. (It was 1920.) I was alone in my glory now. All my best friends – older than myself – had left. I made tentative gestures towards younger girls whom I had previously snubbed or ignored, but they were happily fixed up in their own groups. I found myself uncomfortably isolated.

> Darling Daddy & Mummy [Impossible to break away from the childish formula] It's not much fun being head-girl, all I do is ring bells from morning to evening. I think I shall strike. I don't see why the head-girl should do all the fagging, it's an idiotic idea ... The new mistresses seem very dull and are all ugly ... the music mistress looks rather like a washed-out jackass, she has the most idiotic smile I ever saw. Matron is really rather decent and most awfully good-natured ...

I felt detached from the school scene, I had discovered as head-girl the deceptiveness of being 'in the right' and exercising authority, and the gap between what mattered in school and what counted in the grown-up soon-to-be-ours world outside. It was brought home to me when I caught the sixth-form girl cheating. Fluffy hair, oblique inviting blue eyes, a fully-accomplished bosom – she was too old to be involved like this! However, summoned before our schoolgirl court, she struggled to carry it off. When I called her bluff and she stood tongue-tied and humiliated, absurdly it was I who began to feel in the wrong and mean to have exposed her. I divined her dilemma. With her newly found grown-up status she had opted out of the keen competitive schoolgirl stakes with its jealous rules, to find herself losing face and position in the form, and had been tempted to try to redress the balance. But now, isolated and labelled a cheat, today's rather silly schoolgirl –

94

maybe tomorrow's big success – took on an unexpected lone dignity. I let it all peter out inconclusively.

I was supposed to be swotting for my entrance exam to Royal Holloway College, residential and deep in Surrey, somewhere near Virginia Water. But as Mrs Barber was so ill, there was a devolution of duties among the senior staff, and I was finding myself working on my own – no one else was taking a college entrance. Left to my own devices I wandered with my books from room to room.

Latin was my worst subject – I had failed in it in the exam – and now I was to have a new coach to replace Dr Plume's friendly old-time drilling. I found the new master sitting in his overcoat in the deserted classroom. The stove had burnt low. 'You look cold,' he said kindly. 'Shall I warm your hands?' He offered me a large open sandwich of hands. But I was not a little girl, to be treated like that, and he was so disappointingly middle-aged and avuncular. I stared stonily ahead. Unruffled, he opened the grammar book.

I was drifting towards college with no clear objective – teaching, of course, out of the question. I pictured college as a collection of choice spirits – not unfledged schoolgirls like myself – with talent, intelligence. I saw myself sitting up to the small hours in some dark study drinking in illuminating talk about things that mattered, ideas coming alive at last, not locked up in books. Up to the present, books were my only source of knowledge and information. The adult world, respected in my Latin childhood as a reservoir of wisdom and resources, had failed. Now most often it posed a barrier, with either a compromise or a clash inevitable. My father off his pedestal, my own mother vulnerable. Strictly speaking, it seemed to me, life wasn't worth living. There was no point in it, nothing to believe in, no worthwhile objective. Religion, society – adult shams – each bolstering the other. Religion professing everything and meaning nothing. Society paying lip-service without the slightest intention of putting precepts into practice. 'Holy' marriage blessing an orgy of sensual delight that outside it was condemned as guilty and ignoble.

The ambition of every girl leaving school was to have a good time and then get married. If I managed to scrape into college, at least I would escape for a while, postpone both these fearful prospects. Comparing notes after the Christmas holidays, I had found it difficult to keep my end up – their evening theatres (my queuing in the afternoon for pit or gallery), their glamorous dances, exciting partners (my boring old men of forty and schoolboys). The horror of my first dance! The gaunt public hall. Ancient screens, out of the lumber room, erected round the dance floor. But every time the iron bolts grated open in the vestibule, winter rushed in clipping my ankles and running up my too-white silk stockings, and pimpling my arms. The hostess like a white rhino making over the wooden floor streaked with french chalk, rounding up vanishing males for her large white daughter, sheltering with her empty programme behind dusty palms, and surrounded by hard empty chairs. Now the lady back-tracked to grab a strong-looking boy – and surprisingly introduced him to ME! I understood why when the band struck up. He pounded forward as if on a route march at dawn. I skipped away, but every now and then – against the music – he caught up with me and trampled on me. Outraged, at last I broke away and glared at him. 'Sorry,' he mumbled, and grappled with me again, and now he directed himself sideways. I had to run madly backwards not to get left behind and overturned. In the hallway at home afterwards, satin shoes scuffed and stained, rebellious and disenchanted, I caught my father's eye as he emerged from the sitting-room to greet us – commiseration and humour – a rare moment of rapport that I have never forgotten, and that I cannot remember recurring. Lydia, as always, was serene and unruffled.

I had to bundle up my books as a class was moving in. I took refuge in the dining-room. The infants by the window were chirping away in a reading lesson. Impossible to concentrate. Now they were babbling a rhyme. I went off into a long daydream smoking my pencil: '... Dépossédé des airs son poids le précipite/ Dans les neiges du mont il s'enfonce et palpite' ... 'Mountains on whose barren breast / The labouring clouds do often rest' ... 'Beauty is truth, truth beauty' ... 'I'm going back / To the shack / Where the black- / Eyed Susans grow / I love you so ...' London at night all violet and mauve with exciting dark intervals between the glimmer of lamp-posts (the glamour half derived from Compton Mackenzie's exciting contemporary *Sylvia Scarlett*). A romantic encounter with 'a man' – something between the impeccable enigmatic 'Colonel of the Nuts' with a humorous twist to his mouth, and the unconventional bohemian artist with understanding eyes.

London and the theatre were my only source of thrills. Maurice Chevalier a swaggering soldier in red and blue, with the model girls swinging behind him:

Ah-n ooen zey wau-k wizzay ow wan-der-foole
Ah-n ooen zey tau-k wizzay ow grrran ...

Doris Keane in *Romance* in black velvet and pearls, Basil Sidney the young cleric, faltering and succumbing to her white arms and bosom in a curtain-swoon on the purple sofa. Dorothy Dickson frail and cooing in her Southern drawl: 'Awnly, it's lawnly, in Kalooah / Naow that you-ah / Nawt there.' (George Robey and Violet Lorraine in the *Bing Boys on Broadway* I found shop-soiled and middle-aged – not at all funny.)

Lydia as usual led the way. She introduced me to the Russian Ballet – exciting clashes of music, movement and colour – Picasso settings in magenta and orange, brown and black, purple and pink (before that, colours always had dutifully to tone in or match); to the grown-up sophistication of Somerset Maugham; to the wistful charm of Barrie; and to modern stimulating plays like Clemence Dane's *Bill of Divorcement* and Shaw's *Pygmalion* – with Mrs Patrick Campbell (old now, but compelling, magnetic) and Aubrey Smith as Professor Higgins.

Towards the end of my last term, Mrs Barber died. Tender-hearted Bee wept. 'Don't think of her as lying in her coffin,' Miss Vernon earnestly advised her class, and now Bee couldn't imagine her in any other way. But for me Mrs Barber was now as remote and archaic as a delicate ivory figurine. I was shocked when her brother, Dr Plume, taking prayers, broke down and wept, '... a wonderful woman,' he mumbled. That was NOT the way for a man to behave.

When I left boarding-school (the Mecca we had dreamed about, longed for, in Brazil!) I had chronically infected tonsils, I was constipated and my hair was falling out. I was convinced that the only colour my complexion could stand up to was beige, and that for me it had to be the lone hard way. No rapturous dances and long long kisses. I would have to paddle my own canoe, rely on myself, and make the best of it. I remembered how on my thirteenth birthday I had learned and accepted my sombre fate. In my party frock, the centre of attention, opening my presents, I had turned in excitement to my birthday book to discover my own very special fortune. 'January 21,' I read out, all eyes on me, and with growing disillusion: 'Follow your own advice, and abide by the result.' The cold knell of truth. Pink icing, lacy frills, make-believe dreams – all, all vanishing. It was a flat sober future that was waiting to claim me.

Caina was going back to Brazil. She had made up her mind. In winter her rheumatism was getting worse. She still liked to do the ironing – jabots and fine pleats and tucks, and she could get stains out better than any cleaner. 'How do you do it?' I asked her when she gave me back a spotless white dress. 'Cold water,' she assured me. But now her children no longer needed her. The boys, her last charge, grown independent since prep school; Bee was her last resort. They went arm-in-arm to the cinema – when Mother could scratch up enough ninepennies out of the housekeeping, the boys went too. They watched Charlie Chaplin, Fatty Arbuckle and Buster Keaton. Caina shook all over in soundless laughter, tears running down her cheeks. (I had the bad taste to be bored by the frenetic Keystone comedies, and Charlie, I thought, was furtive and a little sleazy.) Caina brushed Bee's hair at night, ran her bath and sat waiting to swill it down afterwards. In the morning she was there to do her hair. 'I can do it myself,' Bee exclaimed. Caina burst into tears.

Mother's widowed elder sister was taking the family back to Brazil now that her three sons had qualified with degrees and could make their way there. This was the right moment for Caina to join them and travel with them.

She was going to live with Vovó. Her niece was occupying her own little house in São Paulo that father had bought for her. Uncle Raphael, Caina's first charge, was now an X-ray specialist, and still living with Vovó – officially. He had his own establishment where with his French mistress he spent part of his day – and night. But in the small hours his chauffeur drove him 'home', and he always woke and breakfasted , and often lunched, under my grandmother's roof. When he was a young man Vovó had discouraged his love match with a first cousin, so he had remained single. 'That woman' was now a permanency, and eventually he married her – a charming person Mother found her, meeting her when she was elderly.

Four years after Caina had left England, our cousin Jayme, on leave from Brazil, told us that Caina had had a stroke. Uncle Raphael was looking after her in a private room in his hospital. Lydia who was now earning money as a typist sent her a long cable that cost £5. Caina was conscious when it was read to her. Three days later she was dead.

– 4 –

Four Years Hard

STRIDING down the carpeted library, kicking up the long skirts of her evening dress, Ellen Higgins headed the procession into dinner. On her muscular bare arm, the daughter of a former graduate bent attentively to her booming bass. Her stocky figure in a square-cut black *décolletée* with jet beads, and her heavy rather coarse eighteenth-century head of a magistrate with its masterful nose, full hard mouth and peremptory eyes, giving an effect almost transvestite.

Two deep, either side, we stood waiting, all the way down the handsome high-ceilinged library, with its opulent book-lined shelves and massive fixed tables. I was in my new black marocain sheath that slipped on loosely, straps pinned to my sloping shoulders. My hair that had been shedding so much at school kept up by an intricate skewering of invisible hairpins. I was caught up in, but instinctively alien to, the others – the raw material of tomorrow's staffroom – eager, conformist, earnest, the occasional bland face of future authority, the shiny, pasty, awkward buns, lank hair, plaits pinned round, high necks, long sleeves, maroon velveteen, grocer's blue, winter green.

The lecturers going past, all women, all resident, had spinster stamped in their bearing and their faces, the torch of learning waxing dull and heavy, elderly to middle-aged. One or two raw recruits, still to be broken in.

At the tail, two-by-two, we folded in to wind our formal way into grace in the vast dining-hall. With a clatter we got down to homely soup, meat, two veg and pudding. 'Eee you've a foony uxsn't!' A sharp face from the North challenged me. I was odd-man-out at my table. This was a new angle for me!

Royal Holloway College was a big rather grim joke. A monstrous raw

99

Victorian pile – the replica in crude brick of a French château – it was stuck all over with pepper-pot turrets, pinnacles and mock parapets. It was upstanding in an island of balustraded stone and cement, fronting an empty vista of playing-fields and tennis courts. Its grounds extended for 200 acres and included a sunken covered-in swimming-bath. The vast rectangular building enclosed two grassed quadrangles, and housed 200 women students, each with a separate study and bedroom. It accommodated a handsome library, an ample parquet-floor picture gallery furnished with Victorian canvases, and a chapel.

The ugly clamour of its bell broke out relentlessly before breakfast, nagging on and on – no respite. Footfalls outside responded, conforming obediently, more and more of them, hurrying past my door, tracking down the long, long corridors.

The edifice was a monument to Victorian trade and philanthropy, from Holloway's Pills, his offering to the New Woman, a torch of learning. No man except the visiting clergyman allowed to sleep under its dedicated roof, a few miles away he also founded a handsome lunatic asylum – for both sexes.

The crushing weight of the place! Its solid complacent assertion, its comfortable ugliness. A standardized commodious mill accepting into its endowed maw the unfledged, the immature, ready, hungry to fill the open suitcases of their minds with a good cramming. All jostling now in the competitive quest for that key to gain entry to future security in the scholastic niche.

A dead end. A no man's land. A prison! Never for me!

I fronted Miss Higgins in the corridor – mannish long coat, shirt, tie, ankle skirt and boots. Her Principal's challenging eye, her authoritarian tread making nonsense of my secret thirst for intellectual ferment, sparks and fire, turning all this into will-o'-the-wisp nonsense.

In the wide amphitheatre of the lecture hall, indifferent to the result, I scribbled away, indulging in long purple passages in my 'comments' on Shelley 'all fire and air' and Keats 'all stillness and quiet'. (It was Keats I loved, Shelley privately bored me – the interminable similes in his 'To a Skylark', 'Like a high-born maiden' – ridiculous!) My hair started to dribble down as one hairpin after another slid from my bent head.

That summer we had been on a family holiday to Westward Ho – golf for my father – Celia, my best friend from school joining us. The private house advertised comfortable accommodation in its own grounds and a tennis court.

The whole fortnight was veiled in a fine shimmer of perpetual drizzle. The first night a drip on my forehead woke me. I put up an umbrella and moved the chamber pot to collect another spot darkening the carpet. At breakfast was it marmalade or apricot jam? Hysterical tennis, the threadbare lawn knotted with plantain and strewn with the windy detritus of fir trees, every ball bouncing askew.

In a hired car we discovered the countryside. We bounded over huge boulders and slumped into potholes. At high tide the sea came surging and frothing, clattering the great flat stones in alarming snatches. We bathed when it was flat and shimmering, with seagulls stalking awkwardly over the empty sand. Mother, economizing, utterly lacking in vanity, still wore her ancient serge bathing dress, pants slipping over her knees, great heavy tunic with pockets and a belt. There was some argument, I stamped off, her light laughter followed me mocking, down the beach, turning me into a silly girl again.

In the wet early morning Celia and I went splashing down the winding lanes four miles into tiny ancient Appledore. But the Lundy boat was already into the estuary. A fisherman shouted and waved and rowed us out. We were hauled aboard. The scruffy little captain kindly offered us his look-out cabin, cosy with a stove, to dry off. In our bodices and knickers, we were squeezing out the soaking cotton – when in he walked! I was nearest the door, and he made a grab at me. In concert we screamed like angry starlings, and he did a quick exit. By the time we came back on deck, warm and dry, the boat was well into the wind and the choppy sea.

Off Lundy beach, we had to drop into rowing boats. A few grown boys in the surf halooed and beckoned us on. As we pitched towards them with lifted oars, they rushed out to haul us in and deposit us, soaked parcels, on the beach. They had been waiting a fortnight for a boat to take them back to the mainland.

Hungry now, a group of us made our way up the causeway towards the hotel that squatted low behind tamarisk hedges. We were promised a communal lunch. Now Celia wanted a bath. A maid showed the two of us into a neat hotel bedroom, gave us big towels and collected our wet clothes. They came back delightfully toasted.

In a bare white room, like shipwrecked mariners, we sat round one long table to eat up a welcome hot soupy stew and pudding. All we had between us was half-a-crown, Celia and I gave this as our share, and for the hot bath and bedroom.

101

We roamed the windy island, feeding our soggy sandwiches to the birds. On the beach the tide was up and the boat at the causeway. There was a scare that it was too rough to go back, but at last we were all stowed aboard. Apart from the boys and us two, everyone took refuge below, tin basins handed out as they went down.

The boys gave us chocolate that tasted of petrol lighter. I entwined myself firmly into the ship's rail. No need for a tin basin, the sailor grinned, 'Strew the decks!'

As we ploughed into the rough open sea, I let myself ride with the boat – swooping down and down into the trough and up again sailing into the sky. The boys were laughing and staggering round the deck. We were young and free – I was too exhilarated to be seasick.

At home, Edward was in my bedroom, waking me, waving a piece of paper: 'It must be a mistake!'

Halfway down the small print – my name . . . 'awarded a scholarship in English and French!'

My letter. Addressed to me. My father had opened it at breakfast.

The 'darling Daddy' of the school letters had been no more than lip-service for some time. The goodnight kiss a painful duty. The daily clash inevitable, dreaded.

Father had found his niche. He was now the cock of his own little walk. In the sporting cartoon of his golf club he had pride of place at the top of the page, next to the captain, the sitting Tory member, a knight, soon to become a peer. His friendly rapport with the local big man gave Father an incentive in fund-raising activities for the local Conservative Association. He occupied his energies in local government, first a councillor, then an alderman, a JP, and finally the Chairman of the Borough. Most days he left after breakfast and came home to the evening meal.

His homecoming clouded the day for me. My peace of mind on a see-saw, ready for the electric storm to break if I dared to speak out, or look what I felt.

It it was sunshine and we were at tennis, he genially, humorously purloined a racquet from Bee or Lydia and, Olympian, stepped into the game. He played to win. (Unsporting!) I shared instinctively the public-school ideal of amateurism – unaware that it was already dying, dead, battered after conscription and the other brutal facts of life in the 1914 war). He popped a ball just over the net. (Cad!) Mother, plump, in her forties, tried hard to race for it. He stayed in the game just long enough to clinch it. Spoiling all our fun in friendly laughing rallies, just for the sake of winning!

If we were whiling away the rain with a game of bridge, he stood behind my chair and pointed out the card I must lead. Mother had won the call and was playing the hand. She hesitated a second and pulled out a card from dummy, losing the trick. Father snorted. She ended up three down.

'I had a lovely hand.' She was still enjoying it retrospectively.

'Lovely hand! You had no *business* to call three hearts – WHY WILL YOU ALWAYS OVERBID?'

'Sidney, how *can* you – I had the queen, the king, the ace . . .' Mother eager, impulsive, defending herself, her splendid cards.

He cut her down contemptuously with a didactic postmortem.

'The way you played it, you were lucky, you were *very* lucky, you didn't go down FOUR!' He always had to blast and wither and spoil the fun.

Mother said nothing. She was always making allowances, finding excuses – it was only his back (strained years ago playing tennis) or his indigestion or more recently his nervous breakdown. His gramophone company had gone bust in the post-war depression, Father had been unable to override his senior partner's ill-judgements and extravagance. Maybe Lydia's illness and Granny's death and, most significantly, the dramatic rise in income tax played a part. He had gone through a stage when he would explode in erratic sudden rages, accuse mother of extravagance, of this and that, shout, make a scene. He had settled down now, recovered his balance.

Father dropped disgusted into his armchair. Now he was going to take us through his round of golf. His authoritarian over-emphatic tone revealing his recent irritation made listening in itself an act of subservience. He took us out of the rough, on to the pretty, avoiding the bunker, instructing, commanding attention as though we were an idiot audience. (I developed the faculty of switching off, going deaf.) He paused in the delivery, mouth hanging open, to note if a particularly telling point had got home.

'What a tremendous drive!' from Mother.

'You've missed the *point* – COMPLETELY. It was *not* the distance AT ALL. It was in the face of the WIND – the EAST WIND.'

'I see, dear. Now you must be starving. I'll ring for dinner.'

'*I'm* not starving. It's *you* the one that's always ready for your food. I seldom am.' To have a small appetite and be off your food was evidence of heightened sensibility and a superior nature. 'I had a final round with young Rivers,' he continued. 'He plays a lovely game.' He

103

was smiling again.

Lydia looked up. Rivers was one of the very eligible local bachelors, much sought after in this time of male scarcity. It never occurred to Father to invite him home and introduce him to his attractive eldest daughter.

Lydia with her classical placid good looks, big gentle eyes, her eager devotion to her father, her tidy methodical way, home-bound, affection-ate, conformed exactly to my father's picture of what a daughter should be. When she left school at eighteen, he insisted she stay at home. No question of college – after her illness – nor of learning to type, as she had begged. (Yet she had been fit enough to go back to school for the last two terms.)

Now she was eating her heart out with absolutely nothing to fill her day. No local friends. Mother was as cut off as she was.

She copied out from Rupert Brooke's diary: 'The worst of solitude – or the best – is that one begins poking at his own soul.' It was an ideal-istic necessity to her to feel cherished, to admire her father, not to admit his negative attitude, the bars that caged her, so she blamed herself for her *malaise*. 'I have no moral courage, no ideals, no standards, no reli-gion. I want the first, I wish to want the next two, and the other I don't even wish to want.' She attributed the vagaries of adolescence – dreami-ness, lassitude, vagueness, indecision – to weakness of character. With Victorian self-recrimination she concluded, 'I never try to resist tempta-tion to laziness . . . I have no energy and am fearfully petty . . . I have no interest in anything not personally connected with myself or my friends except books . . . I am self-centred and very selfish.'

She made resolutions and critically noted her failures: 'To read the papers and form an opinion on something twice a week, also to eat no chocolates for a week (3rd to 9th inclusive). To try to stop daydreaming . . . To get up in good time in the morning. To read some good books: i.e. French history, history of the world, Meredith, Carlyle, Ruskin, Darwin, Politics.' She listed the books she read and her opinions on them: 'Rose Macaulay, *Potterism* – a clever witty book about some very modern young people.' 'Sir Edward Cook on *Literary Diversion*: A good book well written . . . I was fearfully bored and disliked it in-tensely.'

The emptiness of her days was reflected under headings – things to 'Make, Darn, Arrange, Mend'; 'Measure green tammy, try new tennis balls, thread ribbon in nightgown, mend thin camisole, make night-dress-case.'

Father gave her no pocket-money, so she couldn't join a local tennis club, besides with our own tennis court why should she want to do that? She had no dress allowance. All our frocks were made by the local dressmaker. Pattern books pored over. Long sessions standing as dummy in the stuffy little room. Her dry fingers and sour breath as she eased the neck. Afternoon frocks with a fatal gathering thread at shoulder and waist 'to allow for the figure'. Bunchy, all wrong, an apology for what should be concealed, only guessed at behind the exciting flat drape. Evening dresses were more successful, patterned silk from Liberty, georgette from Selfridges, *diamanté* straps and a big creamy rose pinned on, or feather trimmings fluttering at the hem. But we longed for smart ready-mades, stylish three-piece suits, etc.

Old-time strictures about plain serviceable morning dresses – still our rule, smarter only in the afternoon – meant nothing at all to the thrusting young suburban society. Flappers with a predatory keen eye to advantage on the masculine front were chic all the time, even for a brief outing for groceries; heels, hair and lipstick as presentable as when we went to Ascot. That Ascot 'treat' was a huge disappointment. We were familiar with the hugger-mugger fun of the Derby, bookies shouting, welshing, oranges, gypsies, a cloth spread on the grass for our picnic lunch, and clambering on top of the car – hired or a friend's (Father still faithful to his motorbike) to cheer the close clump of horses spurting round Tattenham Corner. But then Father offered to take us to Ascot! Mother set us all up with new dresses. We arrived on the scene all prinked up to find ourselves ... on the wrong side of the fence! Jostled, twisting our ankles over the rough ground, one hand on the crinoline hat, we only observed the world of fashion long-distance through field-glasses.

We used to go to a funny little tailor in a side street in London for our coats and skirts. (Shocking to stand revealed in a petticoat, yet because he was a tailor nobody seemed to think it funny.) Ordinary clothes, cardigans, walking shoes, etc., were ordered on account from the Army & Navy. A few more accounts in London, but to go up for lunch and shopping, choosing hats, gloves, etc., was expensive. Much more practical to shop locally for cash – but there never was any – only the ominous: 'I shall have to ask Daddy.'

Father was prepared to pay accounts and bills without too much remonstrance, to make out cheques each month for the tradesmen's books, it was ready cash that raised the storm. Each month Mother laboriously checked each item in the books against the spiked greasy invoices that Cook pulled off meat, groceries, vegetables delivered at the

105

back door. Mother's lips moved as she added up farthings, carried over the pence ... 'Oh Lydia! No, Bee, I mean *Sylvia*! Never mind darling,' (she muddled up all our names, but as she loved us all equally it didn't matter). 'Go and tell Cook I haven't finished yet. For lunch she can warm up the mutton with gravy. I will pick some beans.' 'You mean, *I* will!' She took it for granted that we were all at her willing beck and call.

Unquenchably optimistic, she tackled Father as soon as he came in. She never waited for the opportune moment: relaxed with his detective story, mellowed by his evening glass of whisky. There was a little autocrat in her, too, under her always gentle manner. She was only asking for the children, for herself she only needed to do justice to the occasion and to him.

The storm broke. *Always* asking for money ... encouraging the children to spend ... the *same* story ... extravagance ... *no* idea of the value of money ... Her deep gentle voice placating, her eager warmth: 'the children' ... His cold disdain, rejecting her. Her voice rising high – not in temper, hurt, appealing to him. Waves of hatred flooded me. I raged in silence. At last I couldn't contain myself, I hazarded a word. He turned on me, eye and voice charged with venom to silence me with the smart cut of authority. The clash left my heart racing. If I couldn't speak, I could look, radiate my contempt.

Mother spent absolutely nothing on herself. Summer after summer in that bouncy little battered mushroom straw. 'You *can't* wear it!' Mother insisted, pursed her lips in a funny little *moue*. We walked five miles back from the dentist. She even made us travel – all dressed up for Mrs Maxwell's at home in Mount Street off Park Lane – by the cheap dawdle of bus and tram instead of by train to Victoria. The room was full when we arrived: immaculate willowy youths, bearded older men, an elderly lady with a slipped figure like Granny, who turned out to be an Austrian or was it a Russian grand-duchess? An exotic glowing girl-half-child with shiny chestnut curls decorated with cherries – Elissa Landi – the centrepiece, attractively moving round the room with a basket of flowers, a half-innocent child Nell Gwynne. She recited a little poem she had composed, or somebody else had composed, and everybody clapped. In the small talk about Surrey – 'Up by car I suppose?' I tactlessly let out no, by bus and tram, labelling us as eccentric as if we had arrived by camel.

Mrs Maxwell was the divorced wife of Father's wealthy American business colleague from Rio days. We had called on her first in London when she was living in a mansion in Kensington's 'Millionaires' Row':

one spacious living-room leading into another, open fires against mild central heating, florists' arrangements feathering white in the alcoves. Marian cosseted, insulated against germs, begging her mother to be allowed the thrill of a trip on the underground with Lydia and Sylvia instead of the boring old car or taxi. When they paid a return visit to our ugly yellowish-brick suburban home, Mrs Maxwell talking to Mother was surprised how she managed to put up with life in the suburbs, assuming, taking it for granted that Mother really belonged to, would be in demand in, her own smart lively world. It was a salutary reminder, after Father's belittling and denigration, that Mother, plump and middle-aged, still had an attraction in her own right. Mother shrugged with a little wry smile.

Father demolished Mrs Maxwell too. She was only a barmaid when Maxwell married her. Stately, handsome, mad about culture, the *grande dame* had absorbed the barmaid, if indeed she had ever been one.

I had to steel myself now to approach him for the goodnight kiss. Repulsive that cold negative face, the angry Adam's apple. Mother didn't welcome my championship. It only made matters worse. However churlish and cold he was, however sarcastic, however much he made her the butt of jokes with a raw edge, she never accepted that he really meant it. She was always ready to be on his side, to support him. She never said a word against him, she only wanted me not to annoy him, or provoke him. Indeed once when I had riled her and she wanted to scratch me, she said: 'You are exactly like your father!' Mother's erratic English that we and our friends enjoyed, exacerbated him. A riled schoolmaster, he snubbed and corrected, repeating with an ugly mouth more than once what she *ought* to have said. Mother unruffled: 'Don't get so impatient, Sidney.'

The toqued suburban ladies at afternoon bridge passed over in polite silence her foreign lapses when she spoke of the 'harbour' in the garden or invited them to use the 'towel-face' as Violet, after clearing away leftover dainty sandwiches and cakes and removing the embroidered cloth from the green baize bridge table, proffered to each seated lady in turn a finger-bowl and fringed napkin to dip and wipe her fingers. When mother was in her muddled English mood, Bee would rally her as Gladys, 'to pull her foot'. Mother was amused and half bemused, what had she said wrong?

It was through Mother's bridge ladies that Lydia and I were invited into Mrs Dorley's hospitable circle, with its lounge, toilet, serviettes, pardon and excuse me, to meet the local 'likely lads' and girls, the

friends of her son and daughter. Rules were just as strict in this suburban clime as in the public school strata. Girls must be bright and pert,
'have something to say for themselves'. Males could be dumb and taciturn by virtue of their sex, provided they kept the rules of polite behaviour. No clever show-off talk, serious subjects taboo. Anything outside the common-or-garden run of back-chat or persiflage died a natural
death or was promptly squashed with friendly jeering. A student with
brilliant scholarships had to put on a perpetual silly-ass act to make himself acceptable, an unflagging turn, sitting awkwardly, and making him
at last as dreary as the rest. We were very moral and correct. We darted
and shimmied over the polished lounge floor, laid bare, furniture
against the wall, the couple nearest the gramophone turned over the record, wound up and dropped the needle on the latest dance-band tune.
Mrs Dorley, fat and cheerful in the background, stage-managed the refreshment interval with liberal helpings of claret-cup, stuffed bridge-
rolls, fruit-salad and cream.

We made up parties for subscription dances at the Masonic Hall, sitting out on hard chairs round the floor or in the refreshment room. My
steady partner was Cyril, a lanky youth with fuzzy hair; not that he fan-
cied me – we hardly ever exchanged a word – but because I could follow,
and was light and easy to manoeuvre in his runs and swings and crazy
footwork. I accepted him as you accept an umbrella when it's raining.
The only one with any sex appeal was Bernard, small, dark, good-
looking. He showed me how to hold a cigarette and taught me to tango.
He had a bit of a crush on Lydia. Riding home late on his motorbike
after a dance he crashed head-on into an unlit parked lorry and was killed instantly.

My only thrill was when a stranger – after observing my gyrations with
Cyril – cut in and monopolized me for the rest of the dancing, and the
brief coming and going of contact, the expertise of twinned movement,
the sweet insistent beat, turned on the mysterious current linking us
both. Inevitably he eventually joined his party and I mine – 'My Sweetie
went away/ And he didn't say why ...' I never got a follow-up letter as
Lydia and Celia did – from the Junior Carlton. It was very unlikely my
partners were ever members of any club.

I got off the bus with my suitcase at the top of Egham Hill. Everybody
had been so pleased and surprised about my scholarship, I had to stifle
my misgivings, accept my 'good fortune'. I had attempted no other

entrance. School had advised I was most likely to get in there and 'feel at home'! I had accepted this as I was helplessly ignorant of any know-how or contact in the big outside world. It had to be Holloway after all!

A young woman was getting off the bus with me, lugging a lumpy Gladstone.

'Are you going to the college?'

'I'm a maid there, Miss.'

'I see,' I smiled. We walked on together and I could find absolutely nothing to say to her. The green baize door had long separated me from the easy familiarity of Petropolis days.

An unkempt man crossed over, hesitating. She let him take her bag and, although we were almost there now, I had to let him have mine too. He dumped the luggage just inside the big gates. We still had to carry it down the long drive up and curving round the massive building. Grudgingly, I gave him a generous sixpence. She fished in her purse and took out – a shilling!

As we jogged on lugging the cases, 'He's unemployed, Miss.'

'Such a short way . . .' I was excusing my meanness.

She looked at me: 'You wouldn't understand, Miss.'

But with her example, I did. And I have never forgotten.

Before the ritual procession into dinner, we were milling around, lost and strange. You had to have a partner – and eventually you had to fix up someone for every day of the term! Another competitive programme to fill up, but without the dance refuge of the cloakroom. The girls doing science were fraternizing, the North Country girls getting together in cheerful extrovert groups. Faced with a clump of arts students, the short cut was the familiar one of accepted speech, the vowels pronounced in the same way! Moira grabbed Audrey, and I took refuge with Dorothy. The foursome perpetuated itself.

As a scholar I was entitled to a larger more attractive study. Rather late, I applied for the numbered selection available and finally tracked these down in the vast plan. They all faced on to a quadrangle: an out-look on to a rising brick fortress studded with eyes – the rectangle of grass in between no mitigation. I went back to the registrar. All the scholars' studies facing outwards, she told me, had now been allocated. A moment of panic. The annihilating weight and size of the place, its static deadness, its orderly dull finality. The extending anonymous corri-dors swallowing, digesting you, leaving you thin and flattened. I couldn't face this for three years with no outlook, no escape – I couldn't stand it even for a term!

109

'I don't care how small or how high up, I must have a room facing out – and *not* on to a prospect of sports grounds.'

I got a small study overlooking the tops of the pine grove. The bedroom, instead of being opposite, was on the very top floor, and cramped by the crazy super-structure, an elbow of wall jutted out screening the light from the too-high window. No bathroom on the top floor. But in my study I could recover my identity. I could squeeze myself to sit on the windowsill, overlooking the tops of the rather silly little 'pine grove', and as light faded, be absorbed in the mysterious flow of the night – a distant owl – the power and ambiguity of the dark flooding in, to start up a little thrumming of the violin, a faint tuning of the orchestra of youth – to escape in a half-sensuous daydream.

I had only a few possessions. I was not acquisitive, and I had not developed any special tastes to indulge. Striped linen curtain and cushions. Lydia had given me the idea of a Japanese print and told me the shop in Charing Cross Road. I turned over a pile of sheets and selected a savage warrior with drawn sword, an austere patterning of grey stripes, a sober design in black, while and blue. An Indian tea-caddy, my flowered tea crockery, china ashtrays, a tall pottery vase with bech leaves from Virginia Water – some property in the soil turned them vividly ochre, cherry, bronze and viridian all on the one twig.

But even in here I was intruded on. My small study was hogged, half-filled with a regulation-issue monster Victorian desk, coarse, assertive. Too big to throw out. It towered high, its shelves and pocket drawers ascending into a great knobbly crowning mantlepiece, all decorated with pie-crust edging. I turned my back on it and worked at a little table facing the grate with its fire-lighter and scuttle of coal. I filled the big drawers with the coal I didn't burn, to use on some cold working night. The desk table top was piled deep in books, muddled lecture-notes, slipping, interweaving – illegible anyway. In the profusion of little drawers I was eternally hunting and losing small useful objects, pencils, rubber, ink, matches, cigarettes.

My father had given me £2 for the term. One pound went on the omnibus college subscription for the river (cheap fees at the boathouse that housed our own two skiffs and outrigger), and for tennis, lacrosse and hockey. The last two I never played. I was roped in once for a corridor hockey-match and inexpertly raising my stick I struck the bent head of a gentle girl with a high forehead bound in brown velvet – I can still feel a flinching in the guts at the red gash. Tennis – I may have played four or five sets in four years. The distant stark courts clinically exposed were not inviting to me. I was used to garden tennis. The buzz and smell of flowery borders behind fine netting, deckchairs, home-made lemonade, somebody's brother being a silly ass to the accompaniment of the gramophone, hunting in the vegetable garden for lost balls, pulling raspberries and blackcurrants. I never could serve overarm.

The remaining pound for bargains in second-hand textbooks, the dramatic society, cigarettes, and cakes and crumpets for tea and cocoa parties (wines or spirits of course undreamed-of and forbidden). Conventional little parties of four or five the approved way towards social contact. No communal student or staff rooms, everybody hidden away in their own study.

There was a special prim barrier the first year had to break through. You waited hopefully, anxiously, for your first invitation to tea from a desirable third year in the swim, rather like an adolescent in America would wait for a social date from an eligible boyfriend. Another expectant, even perhaps in that segregated world, longed-for moment was the proposal (so-called in fact!) when a senior student offered to call you by your Christian name, and hopefully followed this up with a dinner date. I was still waiting for something to drop into my pigeonhole.

Audrey and Moira had been invited out to tea together. They set each other off, complementing and contrasting. Audrey, the acceptable English country girl, vivid red hair, freckled, neat, sunny. Uncritical hazel eyes, a breathless happy gabble of conversation, academically quite at sea (she came from her boarding-school untested, because her sister had been an RHC graduate), shining at hockey and tennis. Moira, very dark, a little exotic. In an American campus she would not have been unusual. A touch of Red Indian? Or Mexican? Or maybe Jewish with a little Middle-East? Here she was striking. High cheekbones, a sculptured mouth and jaw, black eyes a little slanting under a dark fringe and thick clubbed hair. A tailored figure and legs, elegant hands and feet – always stylish. Etched as hard and clean as the recurring figure in a strip cartoon.

Dorothy and I fell together more as a friendship of convenience. She was a big comely girl with a womanly bust and behind. Anywhere but in England in the twenties she would have ended up the comfortable mother of a contented family, but now she might well turn into a capable organizing secretary or a spinster headmistress. I was too vehement for her smooth middle-of-the-road temperament, but we compromised. I liked her calm. Maybe she found me stimulating. The foursome suited us both.

111

The day started with the chapel bell wrenching me out of bed for compulsory attendance. Half-dressed, in gown and mortarboard, I streaked down four flights, down the narrowing perspective, the interminable panting length of the vast building, turning at right angles – the goal ahead in sight – to make it before the tellers, either side of the steps, retreated and the double doors shut in my face. Respectably swathed in my gown, marked present, I collapsed into my scholar's seat in the left galley, to get my breath back, and, with the victorious rise of the organ, to feel my anger swelling at having to kneel and conform and be a child again.

Unusually early one morning, I witnessed the challenge between two college leading ladies, to the tolling accompaniment of the chapel's final summons. Rowena, aptly named, a towering Gothic maiden nearing retirement, occupied the treasurer's flat in one of the turret excrescencies (with its own lift). Huge and handsome with fiery hair, her massive cheeks still showing white and pink, she was a Boadicea to stand up to Ellen Higgins. Her easiest approach to chapel was along a quadrangle cloister and through a glass door opening into the internal corridor. For some mysterious reason this access was forbidden to students. Rowena towering behind the proscribed entrance came into view as Ellen, striding level, observed her trying the locked door. Rowena signalled imperiously that the key be turned to admit her. Ellen wagged her finger in a verboten negative. Baffled, Rowena signalled her displeasure in eloquent dumb show. Ellen flourished her hand to direct her the long way round, and strode on. Rowena (ignoring me as I hesitated) swung round majestically and sailed back. She did not attend chapel that morning.

Nine o'clock chiming, Audrey, Moira, Dorothy and I, in a row in the lecture theatre. Attendance at lectures, nine to one, was compulsory. The college curriculum was based on the assumption of an eight-hour working day. Four hours in the morning – the afternoon conceded for sport and exercise – two, after tea, and two more after dinner. The output of essay, the recommended study, set work subject to check, was based on the eight-hour schedule. This left no time, no freedom to venture on one's own, no leisure to sample and evaluate the handsome library. This served only the utilitarian purpose of yielding up this or that volume as required for background to the essay, current study, etc.

I never succeeded in subjecting myself to this eight-hour discipline. The day after I had handed in an essay, I was flat and lazy, looking up all the quotations I had failed to track down in time, mooning about what I ought to have put in. Relaxing at last with a handsome prize volume of

Henry James – dull gold lettering sunk in immaculate white calf covers, thick parchment pages. The illusion of opening a virgin copy to escape into the expensive precious effete world of American heiresses and dilettante lords in Rome and Venice.

Miss Taylor came sideways down the steep steps of the lecture theatre, elderly, spare, with a high projecting stomach, like a medieval shrew mysteriously enceinte. On the dais now, sharp eyes over her pince-nez, sparse hair parted in the middle, she called the roll:

'Abramovitch?'

Ghastly pale she rose, near the back. Black ringlets, staring eyes behind glasses, gaping mouth uncertain but unyielding. What was required of her?

We were all turning round. At last, she answered: 'Present'.

The harsh tortured voice, the way she always rose to her feet, the alien face struck each morning a strange chord – was it terror or pity? I can see her still today – isolated, strange among the assorted assimilated pack of comfortable Anglo-Saxons, carrying in her arresting personality the faint echo of the shriek of the pogrom, the body bleeding on the ground, thudding hoofs, the bent back of endurance, the will to survive.

She was of course the subject of contemptuous giggles. Was she a vegetarian or was it only the Kosher strictures? She would get regular food parcels, said to be greasy, and her plate was piled high with a pathetic mound of floury potato. How did she survive? I never exchanged a word with her.

I was a vegetarian for a few short months. I had read in the *London Mercury* a poem in stabbing *vers libre* on the Stock Yards in Chicago. The conveyor-belt of slaughter, the big animals despatched and hanging, still warm, bleeding and smoking, dismembered, portioned, processed – a routine red hell. It was easy enough to keep it up at home, but here ... before long hunger overmastered my scruples.

The roll called, Miss Taylor opened her Roman history notes. (She had handed me back my last Latin exercise marked 'delta minus minus'. 'If you were a schoolboy you would be *whipped* for this!' She bit the word vindictively.)

For an hour we were condemned to forced marches with the Roman legions, league upon league, always in a neutral blank of fog, no local colour, no life, no distant vista, no prospect of resolving the strife. Campaign after campaign. The spotlight only on the signpost with the Latin name and date. Miss Roote's arid history but blown up with an academic proliferation of colourless factual detail. A grey pullulating antheap of past activity ceaseless, senseless, defying the scribbling pencil. All the trees in the wood... Which wood? Where were we? Was it Calabria? Sicily? Lombardy? The voice pecked on relentlessly, wound up to accomplish its stint.

After Roman history, English literature, followed by English history, ending with French literature. Like the 'taking down' lessons at school, each lecture was strictly utilitarian covering the syllabus chronologically (the total coverage for the term divided by the number of lectures, and potted into an hour). But the aural method was not tidy and leisurely like copying from the board. The lecture ran on uninterrupted from the unbreakable record in the head, released year after year, the face set in endurance or bright with the mask of mutual endeavour. It flowed on, spilling over us, sousing, swamping, running away, leaving a bog stuck with miscellaneous facts, broken ideas, half-grasped theories, interrupted categories. All this mess would have to be salvaged, cleared up later on – out of a book.

Miss Honey put in her markers, closed her notes. She moved solidly off the dais and up the gradations of the theatre.

Released, we flapped our cramped wrists, the expertise of running along with the pencil our only way of passing the time. Relief struggled with resentment, the frustration of four lost hours.

I was dimly aware too of what in some cases must have been the long slow defeat of these women, the lecturers themselves, the victims of the impossible boring system, which they too had endured, and now in their turn were obliged to impose on us, to drain and defuse, day after day.

The senior English lecturer, Miss K.S. Block, small, trim, alert, close on retirement, had been one of the pioneer torch of learning young women, with the achievement of a career won against the Victorian odds of personal sacrifice. For her, with her penetrating eye and perfect self-control, the torch still burnt bright. She had achieved an equilibrium that one guessed had cost Spartan dedication and self-abnegation. Maybe, as an ambitious young girl the prospect of finding life, academic satisfaction and independence in literature had been more inviting than submitting to Victorian matrimony with the opportune curate, doctor or lawyer and a predictable future of child-bearing, the silver, the linen, the mutton, the cook, the maids, mending, sewing. At any rate she had emerged very alive and undefeated.

Her delight in literature was evident in her lectures, beautifully composed, sensitive, percipient, with the gristle and muscle of hard thought and intelligent appraisal. If only she had had them printed – or even

114

duplicated – for us to mull over at leisure, to let the evocative descriptions, the adjectives, sink in, and yet not lose the next bit.

She was a little too perfect and rare for me. (Like Mrs Barber a delicate ivory figurine of the past.) She turned me into a clod.

On an early dinner date we were talking about Windsor or Richmond Park, and in a gauche remark I actually referred to the 'deers'. She stopped in her tracks in the procession, horror behind her glasses: 'A scholar! How *could* you!'

Miss Pick, the mathematics lecturer, trundled her heavy body in a barging liver-trot down the corridor carrying her canary in its cage, her red helmet of hair a danger sign above the blank of her inward-turned face. A baleful glare at a group chatting and laughing – a breeze of youth in her wake. (Why don't they go into their own studies if they want to laugh and chat.) She would have liked, as at boarding-school, 'No talking in the corridors.' Choleric, ready to snap, she was endearing only to her canary, talking to it now on her way back from the pantry. How long had these two lived caged together?

Interesting, and a little chastening, to get a glimpse of Miss Taylor and Miss Pick twenty years earlier, when these lecturers whom, sadly, we saw as antiquated and repressive, were in their own way playing a part in the struggle of women to lead their own lives and reject the conventional subservient role. Hilary Spurling's biography, *Ivy When Young,* tells how Ivy Compton Burnett came to Royal Holloway College at eighteen in 1902 to study classics under Miss Taylor. Marion Pick was a student a year junior to her. In her first novel, *Dolores,* Ivy used RHC as a model for her women's college, and based several of her lecturers on the originals in Holloway, including Miss Taylor and Miss Block. In her prime, Margaret Taylor as head of classics apparently outshone all the other departments. She directed an impressive production of *Antigone.* As Miss Butler in *Dolores,* she appears as a martinet in her fastidious scholarship, and a fierce champion of women's rights! Marion Pick – whom we saw as surly and solitary – reveals in her unpublished MS, 'Social Life at RHC, 1887-1937', that at the age of eleven, reading a serial in *The Boys' Own Paper,* the revelation came to her that through academic life 'I could be independent, and absolutely free of the need to marry'. She escaped the drab lot of a country parson's daughter by winning in 1903 a scholarship into RHC, and she came on to the staff as a lecturer in mathematics in 1911. 'When I entered college,' she commented, 'uplift was the keynote.' She was coolly critical of the 'excitable wayward emotionalism' which flourished among the college's religious

115

societies. A group photograph of the staff at RHC, published in Hilary Spurling's book, shows all the lecturers as youngish women. Miss Taylor is slight and skinny with a severe high collar and a deprecating smirk, Miss Block, demurely pensive in pince-nez – too early for Miss Pick to be on the scene.*

If you felt lost in the vast anonymous building, you were still more alone when you ventured outside it, coming down the stone steps into the grounds, crossing the wide paveway that circled the dominating building, and down more steps from the stone balustrade into all that open space in the lower ground, advertising your solitary status. You needed another body to fill you out, to give you some human context and support. At this stage the foursome was a necessity.

Moira had come to college recommended by her grammar school. She and her brother had been brought up by maiden aunts with some comfortable fashion-business in Swindon – millinery I believe. She always had more pocket-money than any of us. She had the vital confidence, the impetuous need to dominate, and the gift of creating her own atmosphere and making things happen. The college was her theatrical set, the lecturers comedy figures or wise counsellors, the rules to be ignored or observed, the wall maybe to jump over – according to her mood. But it was all no more than a backdrop, a setting for the action – that was the thing – action. It resolved everything, and she decided and stage-managed it.

She hooked her arm in Audrey's and dragged her off. Audrey good-natured, accommodating, her perfect foil and companion. A backward glance at Dorothy and me to summon us imperiously to join in, or to dismiss us promptly if two was enough, or again to coax and cajole if we were unwilling. Thwarted, she clouded over suddenly in a black temper, fierce as a naughty child. Indeed the child in her was alive and demanding, determined to get its own way, and when it succeeded, turning at once into high spirits – vivid and attractive with infectious tee-heeing high childish laughter.

She was at first, and at times, suspicious and doubtful of me and my approach to life. A realist, who could value, pounce on a bargain, cope, organize things her way, she was afraid I might be a spoil-sport, queer

*Ivy When Young. The Early Life of I. Compton-Burnett 1884-1919, Hilary Spurling, Victor Gollancz, 1974. Ref. to RHC in Dolores, p.146. Ref. to Miss Pick, pp.153, 154, note 2 p.297. Ref. to Miss Taylor, p.156, note p.157.

her pitch and perhaps even want to cut in with Audrey – her property! (Audrey and I have indeed kept in touch through all the years.)

She tackled me, eyes narrowing: 'You look' – accusingly – 'as if you abused yourself?'

My pallor due to constipation and infected tonsils, my then thin wispy hair identified me with the 'pernicious practice'. Interesting to find that the with-it grammar school girl from Swindon subscribed to the Victorian bogey-theory that the masturbator carries his own discernible stigma!

Sir William Acton the propounder of this seminal theory had researched and written on sex and disease and was an accepted Victorian authority – he also ran a large successful medical practice. He describes the typical masturbator – male, of course. 'The frame is stunted and weak, the muscles undeveloped, the eye is sunken and heavy, the complexion sallow... the boy shuns the society of others. He creeps about alone... if his evil habits are persisted in, he may end a drivelling idiot or a peevish valetudinarian.'* Worse still: 'an awful risk... if carried far enough... early death or self-destruction.'**

One wonders how many sickly children, pathetically admitting to the universal practice of masturbation, had to struggle on in ill-health their real malady undiagnosed. Fascinating that this same doctor, after studying prostitution in London and other big English cities, published findings so liberal and advanced that they may well have been one of the factors to spark off G.B. Shaw's *Mrs Warren's Profession.* He wrote: 'If we compare the prostitute at thirty-six with her sister who perhaps is the married mother of a family or has been a toiling slave for years... we shall seldom find that the constitutional ravages often thought to be the necessary consequences of prostitution exceed those attributable to the cares of a family and the heart-wearing struggles of virtuous labour.'† Again: 'Prostitutes maintain their notions of caste and quality with all the pertinacity of their betters. The greatest amount of income procurable with the least amount of exertion is with them as with Society the great gauge of position.' 'The better inclined class of prostitutes become the wives of men in every grade of society, from the peerage to the stable.'†

Moira evidently found my reaction sufficiently robust. Before long we were laughing at the comedy aspect of the matter. She confided that she

---

*The Other Victorians, Steven Marcus, Weidenfeld & Nicolson 1969, p.19.
**Ibid., p.17.
†Ibid., pp5-7.

first got 'a funny feeling' sliding down the ropes in gym. At my school we hadn't the advantage of all that modern equipment!

But she was still wary. I professed to be her peer worldly-wise. She wasn't convinced. She had to find out how far my general knowledge extended. She put me to the test with the story of the drunk in the Ladies-Only compartment... 'You flatter yourself, Madam; not sticking out, hanging out'; 'Do you see the point?' She stared hard at me to detect any vacillation: 'hanging... sticking?'

I am not at all sure that I did, before she herself made it explicit.

By the summer term I was beginning to know the ropes. Bed on Sunday till late morning. No chapel bell till eleven. (It was assumed that everyone would flock in, attracted I suppose by the visiting clergyman. But no check to see that you did.) Breakfast was never cleared away promptly. I could raid the deserted hall for delicious curls of cold bacon, toast, pats of butter, dollops of marmalade, for a lazy breakfast in my study.

No bicycling allowed on Sunday, and this put the river out of bounds all that long leisurely day. In any case cruising on the river was hedged round with tedious formalities. First-year 'beginners' had to be officially checked as capable of swimming three lengths of the small covered baths in the grounds before they were allowed on the river at all. And even then there was no question of getting into a boat with your friends when the spirit moved you. You had, in advance, to 'make up a crew' with a set number of 'moderates' and one 'efficient' to balance the 'beginners'. Until you and your friends could pass funny sculling, punting tests, this was the only way – canvassing around, booking ahead – turning it all into a formal boring business. You made the best of it, bumping over the field to the towpath, thermos, cakes and cups rattling in the basket over the handlebars. I believe a skiff cost us sixpence an hour.

Moira had the idea of hiding our bikes on Sunday by a low part of the wall. After Sunday lunch, we threw them over, after them ourselves, and pedalled away on the road to Staines. There we chose out-riggers (not allowed by our college boating club till you had passed some ridiculous test of expertise). I pushed off wobbling and swung in circles – to Moira's mocking laughter – and then nearly jammed going under a bridge.

Moira turned the forbidding red-brick prison into a kind of St Trinian's, and we became silly schoolgirls again. After a party ending perhaps at midnight with muffled laughter in the corridor, a ghastly

118

spectacle appeared silently, framed in the pantry doorway – Miss Taylor in grey-striped flannel dressing-gown! Outraged and incoherent: 'There are *limits* – even... even – to decency!'

As the scholar, I took the rap, or maybe it was for cutting lectures or being late for chapel. I was summoned to appear before Miss Higgins.

Lectures must be attended or I would not be allowed to sit for finals. Chapel was a founder's obligation. I wouldn't like it, she suggested, if she had to send a bad report to my father. He had brought me along from Waterloo for the entrance exam, and had evidently made a good impression, as he generally did with strangers. She was building up a Victorian concept of a devoted father-daughter relationship. I fell in with this, and I was dismissed with a caution.

Moira's tall brother came down for a dance in our parquet-floored picture gallery. Moira insisted on Audrey as her partner in the procession to dinner, so I went in with him. Only four or five other men appeared for the dance in the big gallery with two hundred girls. Fun to be dancing with a man. He was much milder, more placid than his sister.

As suddenly as she decided on action, Moira would drop St Trinians and turn into an assiduous student. She put on her glasses, shut herself alone in her study, frowning at the slightest interruption.

I was preparing too for serious swotting in Roman and English history – essential if I was to make it in the Intermediate. Getting close now. Four subjects in this first dull hurdle, before the start of the interesting honours course in English.

But I couldn't concentrate. Although we were on the top of a hill, there never seemed to be any wind. The air was stagnant, relaxing. My head felt as though it was full of warm porridge, and as if my throat couldn't swallow. I was too tired to run to chapel. I didn't want any breakfast. I couldn't get out of bed.

I had acute tonsillitis. They put an elsan commode in my ugly bedroom. I couldn't bring myself to use it. I staggered into the long draughty corridors. My temperature soared. They transported me down to a ground-floor room. At last my throat subsided. I dozed and recovered.

I was taking my first tentative steps in the grounds to find a seat in the sun, when the doctor called, so they told me afterwards, to check whether I was fit to take the exam. Finding my room empty, he left without seeing me. Now it was up to me. I knew I hadn't a hope now that I had spent the fortnight for revision in bed. But as I was on my feet – and in those Spartan days – I didn't see how I could get out of it. It was only when I sat down in the lecture theatre, limp and light-headed and found I could not concentrate, that I realized I had been a fool to make the attempt.

When the results came out, all three of us – Audrey, Moira and I – had failed. I had come down in history and Latin. Miss Block called me into her study for what I thought was to be a friendly little tête-à-tête. My English and French paper, she pointed out, were not up to scholarship standard. I gave a sickly smile. But the Latin and history were so bad – did I listen at lectures and take notes. I responded, off-guard, to her personal interest by replying very frankly. I had no idea that as a college governor she was investigating and getting first-hand information to present to the board. I made no attempt to make a case for myself, or to admit that I had been unwise to sit for the exam. I was certainly not fit enough to do myself justice.

So they took my scholarship away. It had evidently been a mistake after all! It had pulled me into the college against my will and now I hadn't the motive power to get myself out. Supine and unenterprising, I stayed put.

All three of us were going to take the exam, next year.

None of my family, no one at home uttered a word of reproach.

We went on a family holiday to Dinard in Brittany. The exchange was so favourable – a franc worth about tuppence ha'penny, I believe – that we could enjoy ourselves extravagantly compared to England. Our hotel, up the hill from Dinard, was full of English visitors.

Croissant and coffee in bed. Into a bathing dress and ankle-length wrap to walk down the treey road on to the beach. In and out of the warm water till lunch. The American girls, light-hearted and confident attracting the boys on the sand. A tidy frock for the afternoon spent with Mother window-shopping in the boutiques in anticipation of a final purchase (she would find some money for each of us, after in her turn extracting it from Father). Tea and patisseries under a parasol on the pavement. Sometimes we took a vedette to cut through the blue sea to a St Malo that defied change behind its medieval ramparts. Narrow ancient streets crammed with overhanging shops full of curious pretty tourist attractions – Quimper bowls, peasant bead markers. The gutters running yellow and stinking, dropped straight down the sluice into the sea – not far from the bathing beach. Excursions down the Rance to Dinan, and to Mont St Michèle. After dinner, coffee and liqueurs at the little café down the road. Madame la patronne in carpet slippers joking with Father as he settled up for the party. Parents back to the hotel for bridge, and we walked down the hill in evening dress to the casino. You

120

could dance all night on the strength of a citron pressé, and sit out over-looking the sea running in the moonlight. Champagne cocktails when we roped in an older man to join our juvenile impecunious group. (I found a curled old yellow press cutting about the High-Life Casino, Dinard. 'Le grand gala costumé un succès sans précédent.' Lydia is mentioned as a winning Pierette.) Back at midnight, occasionally later, after eggs and bacon at a bar. A friendly freemasonry among the English visitors. A violin playing in the moonlight in a café garden with tubs of hydrangeas, and we were invited in by a man, who turned out to be Oliver Baldwin, and his guest, Anton Dolin, just come from his per-formance at the casino theatre. The fun was all very innocent and English. Our parents quite content to meet us next day on the beach or at lunch, unless they too came out for a session of baccarat at the casino and we all walked back to the hotel together.

Second time round now with the Intermediate lectures at college. Stuck again in the lecture theatre, and the voice going on and on. Growing older every minute – time rushing by. I should be finished before I had even started. To have to sit there accepting – the sex that has to submit. What young man would stand for this? Clogging the sap. The fountain that no longer rises – a groan burst from me. I turned it into a cough.

The term before the exam we heard of a student tour to Vienna at reduced fees. But after the fiasco of my scholarship I felt I couldn't even raise the matter with my father. Audrey and Moira were going.

Vienna, they told me, was a dream – picture galleries, the palace, the Prater students, coffee-and-cream to the orchestra. Audrey decided she wouldn't come back to Holloway. She fixed up a job as a receptionist at the YWCA in Paris and met André. He was a young veteran of the 1914 war, blue-blooded, attached to a travel firm catering mainly for Americans doing Paris – André apparently one of the attractions. Audrey fell head-over-heels, and rushed into an engagement.

After passing Inter, Moira had enough of college. She took up a job at the Times Book Club. Then she went abroad, married a good-looking lawyer attached to a big firm, and she settled in Canada.

Audrey brought her financé down in the summer term to show him off. Solid and blond in white flannels and French brown and white shoes. He stretched supine in the boat, weighing it down, letting Audrey, Madeleine and me do the sculling. His glance had briefly measured and dismissed us. He stared up at the sky; quite enough, he decided, to give us the privilege of towing him along. Audrey a proud little wren had a formidable cuckoo in her nest.

Madeleine was taking English, and like Audrey she was unacademic, she hoped to scrape through. She confided in me, her Simple-Simon round blue eyes wide in surprise, her plump cheeks bright pink, that for a moment in Beryl's study she had been almost frightened: 'I had to run away or I would have been caught!' Beryl, lanky, square-shouldered, her lean attractive face deeply lined when she smiled, had coaxed her – just as she was leaving – her hazel eyes mocking: 'Come back Madeleine and be maudlin with me!'

In our shut-in emotionally empty world, schoolgirl crushes began again, and lesbian tendencies discovered themselves.

This first year in English was heavy going – dull Anglo-Saxon beginnings, long tedious Middle-English romances – no daylight till Chaucer. There was the grim Old-English set-saga of *Beowulf*. The text was turgid enough, but it was stuck, embedded in an incrustation of glossaries, emendations, alternative readings – more notes than text. Turning to these was to uncover a honeycomb crawling with the maggots of old men's pedantry, a nauseating proliferation – no end to them.

But the biggest chore was philology – as much time to be spent in finals answering questions on this as on the whole sweep of English literature. We had to trace modern English back to its continental roots, ultimately lost in hypothetical Indo-Germanic grunts.

Our lecturer was very young. I imagined her as the wood-cutter's youngest daughter (turning the peasant story into feminine guise) come to make her way. Big, raw, vulnerable, she gabbled away as though a spell had been put on her to spill out so many thousand words on pain of banishment back to her distant village. She was disgorging at record speed meticulous details of vowel changes, diphthongs, etc. Either every word had to be recorded – or nothing. When we all started sighing, and all the pencils had stopped, she was young enough to respond. She broke off in full flux...

'*Can't* we get it out of a book?' I implored her.

No book, she assured us, covered it in sufficient detail... and there was so much *more* of it... She was winding herself up again – it *had* to be this way. We were all caught up together in the treadmill.

We had no separate tutorials. Miss Block handed back our essays to us all together in our English group. I had dropped all my purple passages since Inter days. Early on, in an essay on eighteenth-century poetry (in a collection set for Inter), I had indulged in a rather fanciful piece

122

about the vogue for personification giving one the impression of wandering in a grove full of heavy statuary, etc. Miss Block in the big lecture theatre was handing back the essays. She kept back three. She read extracts in praise from the first two. Then – mine! I am sure her criticism was fair and constructive, but she withered me as effectively as if she had been cruel.

The set work piled up, there was never time to graze in the library – discovering, getting sharp first-hand impressions, making one's own evaluations. It always had to be the predigested, regurgitated lecture. However selective, discriminating this might be, it killed the impetus, gave at last a feeling of surfeit, nausea. I never managed to organize my day into the tidy prescribed eight-hour routine. Every fortnight or so to catch up with the set work, I had to work through the night.

It was almost 4 a.m. and, the essay done, my brain flickered low. Leaning on the mantlepiece, I couldn't drag myself away from the warm ashes in the fireplace into my cold bed. I met my empty eyes in the glass, stranger's eyes. They held mine. I sank deep into them. Mindless. I slipped out of my body. I was floating above it... free...peaceful... a distant danger alarm warned me... to come back... before it was too late... Unwillingly, painfully, I pulled away from the fluency, the power in the glass... Now I was tenanted inside my heavy body again, tired, afraid to meet my own reflection. I stumbled into the bedroom. Half undressed, I dropped into bed.

Miss Block capped this experience with her own, confided perhaps in mitigation after she had brought to light, unwittingly, a weakness of mine. She had stopped short in the middle of her lecture; she was without her flagged copy to read extracts: 'Let me see...' Her eye ranged over the English school... I shrank into myself. 'Ah!' – I was looking away, but she wouldn't take the tip. 'Would you be so kind... in my room... behind the... to the left... in front of... on the right... a small red book.'

In utter confusion, I rushed upstairs. Then down again. Of course her room was on the same corridor as mine. It was full of books – open shelves, corner shelves, bookcases. To the right... behind... I pulled out a small red book. It wouldn't go back. Half a dozen spilled out on to the floor, one folding a delicate page. I jammed them all back. The perfect order and tranquility in the room mocked me. I was pulling out red books at random. I could be here all day. No way out. I had to go back.

Miss Block apologized: '... perhaps I left it in the bedroom...'

That evening she crossed me in the corridor: 'By the way,' she called, to my retreating back, 'that book was *exactly* where...' I had to explain that any unexpected practical task, however simple, demoralized me, making me irrational, helpless.

'How extraordinary!' she said. 'I would never have guessed... But irrational, inexplicable things do happen. It happened to me once...' As an undergraduate at Holloway, reading in bed after a concentrated day, she looked up, to see herself standing by the door, sharp and clear, her cameo brooch at her neck. 'Shut your eyes,' she said to herself, 'you are imagining. Count ten, and there will be no one there.' She opened her eyes, and there she was, standing, waiting. She turned out the light and tried to sleep, and forget the silent figure.

Lydia, liberated at last by the £100 Granny had left her in her will, had taken a secretarial course, and was now a typist in London – at £2 a week!

Bee, at her own request, left school at sixteen, inspired by youthful altruism to save Daddy money – he was always complaining of expenses. This was just when she was at the peak of enjoying school with plenty of friends, games, and when the bogy of lessons no longer seemed to matter. She pressed it home with youthful ardour, Father would never have deprived her if he had understood her motive. After a miserable hiatus of two empty years at home with absolutely nothing to do, she was taking a diploma in domestic science at Reading University, Father's college plan making a nonsense of her earlier sacrifice.

At Reading, Bee with her jolly sunny nature, comely looks and fresh complexion, was grabbed, like Audrey, by a purposeful practical girl with plenty of go, as her perfect foil and companion. She dragged Bee along to dances, social fixtures, etc. Bee, shy and inexperienced, happy to play second fiddle.

It was at a point-to-point that Bee and her friends came right up close to every flapper's dream in the twenties – the Prince of Wales. He rode up 'looking wonderful, in white breeches and a scarlet polo jumper. He had a marvellous complexion and bright blue eyes.' Bee's friend raised her camera. He was half backing but he swung his horse round and smiling waited for the take. Then he made for the jump. As the horse rose, he pitched over its head and landed on his shoulder. He was knocked out.

An ambulance drew up. A nurse rushed out, and a young man arrived on the scene. Blood was pouring from the royal nose. The nurse asked if anyone had a handkerchief. Bee, the only one with a clean one, gave hers.

The Prince was coming round: 'What's this? What's happened?'
Somebody said he'd fallen off.

'I what? What the bloody hell!'

'No, Sir,' the young man said. 'The horse shied, and knocked you off. We're getting you a stretcher, Sir.'

'I bloody well won't go on a stretcher!'

But he did. Bee was very shocked at all the foul language.

In her diploma exam Bee had a section on economics – 'I never knew what this was all about,' she said. In the social science paper there was an essay on 'Marriage as a Career'. Bee, with visions of holy marriage, babies and love, simply wrote: 'I think it is disgusting to talk like that.'

So she left without her diploma. But she had learnt cake-making and got a job 'all found' at fifteen shillings a week in a ladies' home-made teashop. The impecunious widow, her daughters and Bee slaved away in the kitchen and shop. Bee with the strength and jollity of youth finding it all great fun.

My chief interest in vacation, apart from the thrill of the theatre, was prowling round second-hand bookshops. They drew me. I sifted and sampled, looking for gold. I was influenced now by the academic ivory-tower mythology that venerated, made sacred cows of certain old, now esoteric tomes, as the hallmarks of taste and discrimination. In particular Burton's *Anatomy of Melancholy*. (Compton Mackenzie cherishes it in its halo when he writes about Oxford days in *Sinister Street*. Malcolm Muggeridge confesses in his autobiography that in early days he lugged it about the world, unread, as a kind of cultural 'totem'.) I remember my satisfaction when I acquired my bulky second-hand copy. I still feel some regret that, when the bombs were falling and my mother insisted that I clear out my papers and books from the old black trunk in the attic, I reluctantly jettisoned the dismembering volume. If it were still on my shelves it would no doubt be diffusing its quaint faded emanation of cultural pot-pourri. An essence deriving from Miss Block's observations, because I never discovered anything in it myself – I doubt whether I ever read more than half a dozen pages.

Back at college, the St Trinian episode was over – I had only been roped into the cast. Now I had to escape from the red brick into my own inner world of introspection. To divorce myself from the conforming routine

125

that would inevitably lead into the adult prison – in the school or at the desk. I retreated, biding my time, into a congenial climate, that had evolved, I suppose, from childhood's nourishment in enchantment and magic. This was a still green adult world of sensibility, with a secret intense delight in nature as a vivid solitary experience. I was to discover and enjoy Sylvia Townsend Warner's *Lolly Willowes,* and the escape into fantasy of David Garnett's *Lady into Fox,* and to recognize in Rose Macaulay's *Orphan Island* and *Crewe Train* the struggle of youth against the conforming adult world, betrayed at last through ardour into a final acceptance in marriage of the approved duties and demands of the social pattern – something that could never happen to me.

I probably read a review of Henri Frederic Amiel's *Journal Intime* in the *London Mercury.* In the post-war vogue for extreme sensibility and for escapist literature, Amiel was, I suppose, a find. I still feel a faint echo of the pleasure I had in the two small volumes in smoky purple boards streaked with lilac.

I get a clue why it was congenial to me at this time, from the prefatory biography. His friend reveals him as a solitary – retreating, burying his talents, and with all his accomplishments achieving nothing but trivia. Incapable of approaching a subject direct, obliged first to skirt all round it exploring its ramifications, placing, categorizing, and finally ending with no more than an inventory of what could be said about it.

When the biographer had written urgently begging him to fulfil his promise, to write, to take up the position his friends believed he should hold, he had replied – after a delay of three months – that it was in his nature to be afraid of what gave him pleasure, to postpone what attracted him in favour of what was a penance. Though sociable, refreshed by contact and conversation and plunged into impotence when solitary, he was, he said, destined to spend his life in stifling isolation, inuring himself to solitude.

These failings only endeared him to me. And the fact that in the end, with the publication of his *Journal,* all his weaknesses were discounted and rated now as the attributes of a rare spirit, I found most satisfying. His reflections, all in a vacuum with no impact of the outside world, conveyed to me in my immaturity a way of escape, of living in the mind, of ignoring the practical realities that made me helpless and inadequate, and of opting out of the conformist society where I saw no congenial place for myself. (Opening the journal today, I can hardly believe I ever did more than flirt with trying to read his introverted self-communing, and interminable contemplation of the infinite.)

126

As I grew up in Brazil I was aware that outside the familiar family perimeter lurked danger, beauty, adventure, and I always had at the back of my mind the expectation, the promise of a vivid future. But in England, everything outside was predictable and rigidly prescribed, all laid down by never-to-be-deflected rules – a conforming enclosing process that would slowly kill you. The forlorn hope to discover a chink, a way of escape, to break out in time – into the risk, the danger of being young and alive.

From my sheltered standpoint, and in my father's shadow, the bastions of established order and hierarchy seemed immutable, unassailable. I had no inkling of the immense dislocations of war, of the profound shock-waves of the Russian Revolution, the time bombs, the depth charges ready to detonate in the social and economic structure and in the intellectual and emotional climate – to change everything.

Today, when we live perpetually aware, caught in the constant current of universally shared instant experience, instant news, it is difficult to recapture the empty excluded calm, the isolation of a home-county suburb thirteen miles outside London. A segregated society with strict social barriers; leisured class–working class, middle class knowing their place, sticking to it socially, and migrating from it geographically only as prescribed and with their own kind, and the working class by necessity almost static. Each on their own side keeping the rules, knowing little, caring little about each other – no means of communication. The quiet air, the quiet road – an errand-boy whistling by on his bicycle, the jingle of the tradesman's trap delivering at the back door. The static silent wireless – head-phones still in use, and the cabinet set not carrying outside the closed door. I remember the first time I clamped on the ear-phones, I thought I was going to intercept messages flying through the ether – what I did receive was an instructive talk read on one high clear note. The nine o'clock news gave us, in a smooth editorial flow, official hand-outs delivered with complacent authority in impeccable English. Opposition, minority views, briefly dismissed, the militant actions of 'agitators' omitted as unsuitable non-events.

In the cinema, *Pathé News* invariably showed a royal incident (cutting the tape, or the stately progress down the rigid ranks), a racing event (horses or cars), a local or crafts feature, and, in the political field, an avuncular statesman or churchman bumbling platitudes to a respectful audience or a cheering crowd.

Father's *Times* was his perquisite, Mother had her *Daily Mail,* the kitchen the *Sunday Pictorial.* I never looked at any of them. I turned over the pages of our weekly *Illustrated London News,* and I read the jokes in *Punch.*

In the four years I was at college, I never saw a newspaper, never heard a political subject discussed. I identified politics with the prosy close print of *The Times.* In my last year we were given a small common room, supplied with a few dull periodicals. It was generally cold and empty – like a waiting-room.

In my time, I can only remember three lectures from outside. I think it was in my first year that two young Russian students appeared one evening in the lecture theatre. Dark, attractive, speaking in halting English, one took up the story from the other. After he had told us about their hardships, they both smiled. In the winter, she said, desperate for fuel they had had to burn some of the woodwork in their college to survive. They were very serious about their work, their need to study, to fit themselves to help their country. They were short of textbooks; they had to share in groups, take turns to read. They were smiling again. In their youthful confidence there was no end to their optimism. I felt warmly engaged, drawn into their struggle. I wanted to help. But these two strong young students asked us for nothing – all they seemed to want was our goodwill. (I remembered my father fulminating, working himself up into a state about Russian expropriation without compensation, spittle collecting around his mouth.)

The second lecturer was a slight, dark young man who read a paper – written with studied elegance – in some literary subject. He obviously hated the solid feminine ranks that encompassed him. I remember the venom in his phrase: 'the monstrous ribaldry of women'. His passionate aversion rather endeared him to me.

The last lecturer, Lena Ashwell, as she still preferred to be called (she was the wife of a leading surgeon and physician, Sir Harry Simson, who attended the royal births), had made her name on the stage at the beginning of the century. In the 1914 war she organized concert parties near the front for the troops in France. After the war she sponsored repertory companies, named after her, performing in and around London and based in a little theatre in Bayswater.

I was invited to sit next to her at the high table at dinner, because I played a part in the college dramatic society. In her fifties now, well preserved, she seemed to me a hard, worldly woman. We disliked each other at sight. I didn't find it easy to talk to her. But I did discover that there was a system of pupils in her companies. For a premium – £50 I believe – would-be actors of both sexes could come on probation. After three months, if they showed any aptitude, they would be accepted. At the end of a year, likely pupils could hope to join the company as paid members.

As she talked, the way ahead opened up. It was instantly clear to me. *This* was to be my escape! Out of the dead academic world, out of the suburban desert, away from my father – into the theatre, into life!

I tackled her straightaway. She saw no difficulty in enrolling me as a pupil. At the same time, her cold eyes were discouraging. Privately, she dismissed me as 'not the type'. But I was indifferent to her judgement, she was only the vehicle for my release. I had made up my mind.

Now that I was in my last year, I knew how to get by. I no longer worked through the night. If I spent the evening with Richardson chasing Clarissa, I skimped the work I had in hand. I was procrastinating, standing still in the present, resolutely refusing to face up to Doomesday Week that crawled my fate a little nearer every day.

Miss Block's colleague in the English school stopped me on the stairs. She was a comfortable young-middle-aged woman.

'A word of advice! If you get down to some *really* hard work, it may make all the difference . . . [she is going to to warn me that I risk getting a third!] . . . between failing or picking up a third.'

I thanked her, and walked away very thoughtfully. Her warning kept me awake. Now there was no reprieve. I had to face up to it.

As usual, it had to be the hard way. All the interesting modern literature that we were only now approaching chronologically, had to be jettisoned. Too late for Browning – almost a stranger – why had he written so much! I had been put off by all those fulsome Victorian admiration societies. Now, sadly, he had to be scrapped. And for everything after him, I would have to rely on my own superficial acquaintance. I must concentrate on the centuries where I had already blasted the rock in early conscientious days.

But the main problem was philology. I concentrated on this, and I worked out a chart covering the essential minimum that must be memorized to get by. When I had finished it, it was the only really good job I did at college: a tight overall inclusive synthesis, the essential framework that contained, related everything. I knew that this potted short-cut would be invaluable to generations of English students. Just before finals, I put it carefully away in one of the tiny drawers – and never saw it again.

129

Three weeks or so before finals, we were liberated. No more lectures! Free at last to go our own way. Now, for the first time, I could delve at will in the library. I strayed and stayed in the eighteenth century – Gay's Virgilian *Eclogues,* Shaftesbury's philosophy – enjoying myself. (Miss Block told me after finals that my best paper covered the eighteenth century.)

For the first time too, London University admitted we existed. We had never had facilities to attend lectures or functions, but now it was open to us to take finals at University College, instead of in our own lecture theatre. I was the only one who chose London. I stayed in a flat in Battersea with my school-friend Celia and her young medical-student husband – soon to qualify as a doctor. Each morning, the fresh perspective of the Thames – a coal barge moving deep, seagulls, cranes – broadening, widening my horizon.

And now, at last, in the stimulating air of London, going up the wide steps for the final adventure!

In the jostle of the cloakroom afterwards, a bunch of girls were comparing notes. 'Wasn't it the *limit*!' Their lecturer, who set the paper, had taken them through one or two almost identical questions!

At night I couldn't relax. My brain was still sparkling, it wouldn't fade out. After four sleepless nights, I went to a chemist for a powder – I suppose Celia's husband advised me. But that didn't work either.

In the last paper, with twenty minutes to go, my eyes gave out. I couldn't see to write any more.

Back at Holloway, a glorious orgy of tearing up. Freeing myself from the grey thrall of four lost years.

Goodbye to Miss Block in her contained haven. She gave me a testimonial – assuming that I would be carrying the torch. I would be 'an enlivening colleague' and 'likely to command the attention of those I taught... my outstanding dramatic ability would be an advantage to me in the teaching of English... my work had an unusual quality of succintness and point.'

Goodbye to the kind lecturer, Miss Willcock, who had warned me about failing. 'You must write,' she said. 'It doesn't matter what, film scripts – anything. But write.'

I was amazed. What could I write *about?* I didn't know anything. Sitting all by myself, scratching my head? Film scripts? Insuperable technical difficulties. I dismissed the whole idea as impossible.

Pat, a college friend, and I went for a fortnight on the river in a camping punt, in the direction of Maidenhead. She knew how to pump a primus and how to moor up safely above a weir. Lovely to be no more than a body, waking in the green sappy dawn, tying up at twilight, arms stiff with the pole, glad to stretch out on the cushion, and to roll up in a blanket and go to sleep with the birds. Church bells over the meadow. A curious water rat propping his snout over the edge of the boat.

The village shop for apples, a loaf and eggs.

And now, for the last time, past Magna Carta Island, and back to the college boathouse.

I picked up my faithful battered bicycle, abused, crashed (as I braked suddenly down Egham Hill), overburdened, never oiled. I tied my old suitcases on, and bits and pieces on the handlebars. Arrived at the station, it chose the right moment to fold up. Disentangling my things, I abandoned it where it lay.

Moving away in the train – lovely, lovely, to say goodbye! Goodbye for ever to the Higher Life! Goodbye to 'the toil':

> Of dropping buckets into empty wells,
> And growing old in drawing nothing up!

– 5 –

Discovering on the Stage

MA Campbell's heels came tapping upstairs with the hot water. Betty and I were instantly awake, sitting up in her double front-room, in twin beds – waiting.

A dainty tray for each of us – small fried egg, two buttered halves, a one-cup pot of tea (bed and breakfast 12/6 a week). She was a nervy little spinster, still girlish, with earrings and black frizzy hair. No 'Ma' about her. The jocular address was typical of Lena Ashwell hearty patronage.

Now she was pulling, or rather adjusting the curtains, just so, for the neighbours – Westbourne Grove – only the correct span of daylight with clumps of curtain either side. She nestled a towel round the hot water. And as she turned round – every morning it was the same – her surprise! She couldn't believe it. Betty and I had gobbled it all up, every scrap. Two bare trays ready to take down.

Neither of us had had anything to eat since tea-time yesterday. I had popped into the ABC for a roll and butter (1½d) and a pot of tea (4½d). The waitress wouldn't expect a tip – not for a sixpenny tea.

At dinner time I was making up carefully in the big cold dressing-room at the Borough Hall, Greenwich: thick spiky eyelashes and peachy cheeks for my walk on and off in cap and apron. Betty was playing at the Masonic Hall, Camberwell. We were both too absorbed and involved to think about food. In any case we couldn't afford it.

When we unlocked the dark door at Westbourne Grove, the silent street empty, only a distant taxi – we were both starving. Sometimes kind little Ma Campbell left us a thermos, a bonus of hot coffee, or even, once, thick tomato soup! It never occurred to either of us that we could buy a loaf and a lump of cheese. Where could we keep it? You didn't store food in the bedroom. Food was kept in the larder, eaten in the dining-room – except, of course, breakfast in bed – or ordered in a restaurant. As for a nourishing pennyworth of chips! If you found yourself in the kind of street with a fried fish shop fouling the air, you crossed over to the other side and held your breath. As for actually going into the rough place and expecting to come out with anything remotely edible – the idea was quite fantastic.

Betty was sporting and sweet-natured; leggy and fair she was a natural for the *ingénue* parts of sexless English girlhood, and she had just the right 'Keep your distance' in her voice to make her instantly acceptable to the Lena Ashwells.

Only two doors down the road, and we were in the tiny Century Theatre. Three productions were in rehearsal. Irene Hentschel was in the foyer, ebullient, laughing, ready to start on a light comedy. Kynaston Reeves (Philip Reeves as he appeared on the programme) was joining her cast. He came in with his two rangy mongrels and carrying a little antique leather book, said to be Greek verse – or was it bawdy *Decameron?* The dogs collapsed under chairs. Just as well not to get too close; urban animals, they were apt to emit sharp stinks.

A big solid Boadicea stalked in, red-gold hair, cowboy-style hat rakishly on one side – everybody hailed her. Our leading lady, Esmé Church. A bit of a hag she seemed to me (Bee who only saw her over the footlights – beautiful as she acted – thought she was in her late twenties. I assumed she was in her forties! She was in fact thirty-three.) She tramped through the auditorium, careless of her appearance, to rehearse on the stage. Freddie Leister greeted her, forty-ish, attractive (elderly to me), a smooth considerate producer.

I found my company in the basement hall. It was *The Tempest.* Disappointing! I wanted to plunge into the contemporary – something modern and alive today. I had had enough of the literary past. Too recently dissected in the lecture theatre, inducing sadly a feeling of nausea.

Beatrice Wilson, the producer – dark and interesting – was abstracted, half her cast not yet assembled. No Ferdinand, not enough wrecked nobility. We sat down for a rather ragged first reading.

No Godfrey Kenton for Ariel ...

'You read it,' she said to me.

Ariel! Incredible! But almost at once as a reflex I rejected it. Miscast! I could hear it in my head, clear and strange, but my voice could never convey it. I was only supposed to *read* it, give the cues, not to *be* it. All the cold repressive winters, the chastening of good form that had flattened my native exuberance, pushed me to retreat, opt out, not to make a fool of myself, or to show off. Cowardly, I filled the gap unobtrusively, like a typist reading it back.

This was the key time when pupils were being assessed. Beatrice Wilson, imaginative and sympathetic, was probably the most congenial of the Lena Ashwell producers – Leslie Banks was to join us later on – and my idiotic negative approach may well have led on to the stereotype casting that was to be my lot in the company. But I remained obtusely unaware and cheerful.

It was at the dress-rehearsal that the young – probably nineteen-year-old – Laurence Olivier appeared! I had never seen him act, but already he carried unmistakably the air of young theatrical royalty, a vital physical presence, striking good looks and a confident assurance. Maybe he had heard from Beatrice Wilson – whom he tells us in his autobiography he liked and admired – that she was producing *The Tempest* and that the island was still undermanned, and so, between engagements, he was ready for a fill-in and a walk on. A year earlier he had done a season with the Lena Ashwells, whom in retrospect he dismissed contemptuously as the 'Lavatory Players', ready to set the scene in any old makeshift hall. Or perhaps it was Basil Radford, who was playing the usurping Duke, who had told him about it. At any rate, there he was, at this last rehearsal. He fraternized only with the men. The lanky young Ferdinand, embarrassed at having to wear white satin doublet and hose, was assured by Olivier that no, he didn't look like the principal boy in pantomime, his legs were too thin!

We opened at the Century Theatre. The thunder sheet which had been pealing and banging away for the shipwreck, was silent now. I sidled cautiously round it, to discover on the other side, Olivier standing in the wings. The ideal blunt masculine profile, almost boyish, the fire and the finesse, latent, in reserve. Miranda was on the stage, her long dark hair framing her face, a serene classic oval of Hebraic innocence. But she moved and spoke in her own prosaic world, wooden, never on the enchanted island, turning it all into painted canvas and green cloth. The ancient Corney Grain, who had been originally with Ben Greet, had a noble profile as Prospero, but sadly he was too advanced in years to hold the long part. He fumbled and paused, and only just retrieved it. Only the spirits and the comedy were alive: a fawn-like Ariel, Caliban letting out all the stops, Trinculo very professional. I was still the literary graduate, critical, detached. And now Basil Radford was subtly, wickedly, indulging his bent for comedy – playing up to Olivier grinning in the wings – picking at the Elizabethan prose with tweezers, inflecting the lines ironically, half-surprised, hesistant, as though it was all Greek to him. I had a fellow feeling with the two of them, and I tried to catch Olivier's eye. But instantly I was made aware that he was alone. (Shades of the heroes in uniform who had ignored me.) Theatrically he was already destined for the Olympian heights, and I, as a pupil in my first show, was less than the dust. I was in a rather tatty faded green tunic, pulled crumpled out of a wardrobe trunk, waiting to trip on for the masque with the other nymphs and the odd reaper, to trace a sketchy roundel, Ceres and Iris our maypoles. Put theatrically in my place, I remained a commoner, observing him fitfully in his glass coach.

But now the ancient Prospero was in trouble. He was pulling a pause ... beyond the limit ... At last, a tired old horse, he made for the stable: 'Our revels all are ended ... '

Before they had even begun! He had jumped it – cut our scene! We hastily shed sickles, garlands, scythes, snatched up rugs to cover our bare arms and legs, ready to plunge in on all-fours in the black-out 'in the shape of hounds'. This was too much for Olivier, he doubled up, convulsed – like a schoolboy.

In the train on Monday, our first night on circuit, there was Ferdinand and Basil Radford – but no Olivier. I assumed that he had had enough. Betty's version was different. His ribald attitude had been noted, and the Lena Ashwells had not extended the engagement beyond the week!

Pupils were absorbed straightaway into the company, learning as we went along, walking on as maids – or a butler – only one male, a graduate, who wanted to produce, not act, and was hugging his secret first play that hinted discreetly at the sweets and perils of homosexuality at the Varsity. The other four were girls. I was the eldest.

We made ourselves useful packing the clothes in the big baskets, helping with the props, doctoring burnt sugar into whisky and coffee, holding the prompt copy. And quite often we were tried out in bit parts. Casting going on every three weeks for another three plays.

Beatrice Wilson after my dead Ariel, probably reported back to Esmé Church and the other producers: 'Hopeless. No feeling at all. Nothing there.'

I was too dumb to be aware, walking on as a silent maid, with a carefully laid on beauty bloom and purple eyelashes. The delight of flesh as canvas, and the new inviting tools! The sensuous thick smell of greasepaint, and the melting wax of purple sticks dripping into a blackened spoon over a candle stump.

135

Olive Walter, warm and plump, had initiated me in the dressing room. I watched her kneading, working her broad malleable face into what she wanted, using No 5, No 9, carmine, etc. She had started on the stage as a child – the original Tyl-Tyl in Maeterlinck's *Blue Bird* in London, and in the war, like Esmé, she had interrupted her career playing three years in France to entertain the troops.

Esmé Church set her own style as leading lady. She strode into the dressing room – all the women shared one small room – her fresh complexion London-pale free of powder and make-up, and in her heavy masculine leather coat and sensible shoes. She carried in with her a strong sense of purpose, an aura of endeavour, but her mouth was set, her eyes disillusioned now. She was handsome in a solid Anglo-Saxon way, but getting too heavy, a little brawny. High-minded, Spartan, straightforward, she was the dominant influence in the company. Her bracing asexual outlook set the tone. Men, if not the weaker sex, were patently fallible and helpless, their foibles mirth-provoking. Women's role to set an example, to keep them up to scratch, be tolerant and helpful and jolly them along.

It was Esmé who was the main attraction for our public. She had a big strong stage personality, imagination and power. She could eat up the meaty parts easily – Shakespeare, Shavian heroines, Nan in Masefield's tragedy, a natural for St Joan – tender, tough, homely, beautiful, soaring into poetry, immense vitality in comedy. As a young actress, she could have made a big name for herself – perhaps another Sybil Thorndike – if she had not too generously devoted her youth and talents – for twelve key years – exclusively to Lena Ashwell.

It started in the war, when she was twenty-three. After RADA, and a debut at St James's Theatre, zealous 'to do her bit', she volunteered to join Lena Ashwell's venture of concert parties for the front in France, and theatrical companies near the base camps. Artists either gave their services or if they had commitments at home, received a small salary; they were of course billeted and fed from the funds collected. They played without scenery or lights, in barns, huts, hangars, fields, anywhere, in discomfort and danger from air raids.

Lena Ashwell tells the story in her autobiography, *Myself a Player* (published in 1936). She just gives Esmé Church a mention by name (in brackets) as one of the artists 'working in the Base Camps in France with the Repertory Companies'. The whole enterprise, generously supported by actors, singers, musicians, writers, etc., carried on successfully and won great acclaim for the main organizer, Lena Ashwell. She

136

basks in the applause. She records verbatim in her autobiography the tribute read by a sergeant shaking with nerves who mounted the platform to deliver it, after her own recitation to the troops:

> Madam, In the name and on behalf of the NCOs and men of the 3rd Army ... at this Rest Camp ... we beg to express ... deep appreciation ... recollections of dear old Blighty ... helped us to realize again that we are fighting for the Empire, Home and Beauty ... go back with firmer will ... hearten and lighten the lot of His Majesty's troops. You have been and are the fairy-godmother of us all, and we are proud and grateful to be able to look you in the face today, and to say from full hearts Madam we thank you ... respectfully request you ... to accept a small souvenir ... utterly inadequate ... deep gratitude of over 1500 soldiers of the King ... the boys of 15 Divisions of the 3rd Army.

Each member of the company was presented with a souvenir spoon.

After the War, Lena Ashwell received the newly created Order of the British Empire, and 'all the artists who had been to France contributed to give me an emerald and diamond pendant, presented to me on the night when Ciro's closed.'

The Ministry of Reconstruction commented in its blue book on Adult Education: 'that the work done under Miss Ashwell's organization was not only recreational but educational in a high degree ... indicating what might be done introducing good drama and music to the home population in normal times'.

Lena Ashwell saw her peacetime venture in more glowing terms: 'Thousands of people ... could be made happier if our work continued in time of peace as a relief from ugly and sordid conditions in town life, for the education of the soul, the taming of the passions, the awakening of broader interests ... for the stimulating of all that is highest, best and most adventurous in the human spirit.'

Esmé Church, after the adventure and the comradeship in France, joined Lena Ashwell's company in England to put her heart into another good cause. Maybe she was also a little under the Lena Ashwell spell.

The company opened at the baths in Bethnal Green, with what was left over from the money subscribed for the concert parties. After a struggle, they were beginning to make their way, when the premises, significantly, were taken over for conversion into a cinema. They moved to Stepney. Major Attlee was the mayor and the chairman of the Labour mayors. He arranged to let them have the use of the baths and town halls in certain Greater London boroughs at nominal rents and to send out their advertisements with the rates demands. Other boroughs followed suit. Later the Bijou Theatre in Bayswater was taken over and rechristened the Century. The Lena Ashwell company found its feet with the new down-to-earth mission of putting on good plays in poor neighbourhoods with cheap seats (6d the lowest price) with civic co-operation. The company wanted to run on co-operative lines, and Lena Ashwell agreed to this. But there is a revealing sentence in her autobiography on the finances which suggests that her altruism had perhaps in practice a sharpish edge. She writes: 'When I tried to work on a co-operative basis, I found that the financial committee would vote for funds to be paid out which had not been earned.'

The Lena Ashwell Players finally folded up in 1929, and she pays a valedictory tribute in her autobiography to the leading personalities: 'Beatrice Wilson with her great knowledge of poetic drama created productions of beauty and distinction out of raw human material and the rags and tatters of our inadequate wardrobe. Irene Hentschel acted many parts charmingly but was more interested in feeling her way as a producer.' And last of all comes her acknowledgement to her leading lady of ten years' standing who attracted and held her public: 'Esmé Church worked from the first days in Bethnal Green to almost the end of the enterprise with unfailing energy, self-sacrifice and courage.' Lena Ashwell, the retired star – with her 'beautiful old Georgian house in Grosvenor Street' – the 'fairy-godmother' who took everything Esmé had to offer and never waved a wand for her, reveals herself, in the final assessment, incapable of conceding anything at all to Esmé as an *artist,* and ends up giving her no more than a character reference!

When Esmé left the Lena Ashwell Players she went to the Old Vic to play Rosalind, Lady Macbeth, the Queen in Hamlet, etc.

By the time Betty and I joined the company, the sense of mission had, with changing times, worn pretty thin. I never supposed that with our repertoire of Ian Hay, A.A. Milne, older evergreen popular successes, a few mediocre new plays that had failed to see daylight elsewhere, a sprinkling of Noël Coward, the occasional Shakespeare, Galsworthy, Drinkwater, we were trying to do more than attract the public and stay solvent. It was true that in the three-week run of each production, with one week at the Century and a fortnight on circuit, the one-night stands did include the poor neighbourhoods of Deptford, Camberwell, Ilford,

Battersea, but also the comfortable suburbs of Sutton, Watford, Winchmore Hill and Staines. It was evident that Esmé Church was disillusioned now. She was of course aware of the company's precarious future – it was in fact to wind up two seasons later. We pupils, ignorant of politics and finances behind the scenes, had no idea of this.

Lena Ashwell made occasional brief appearances in the theatre. Once she gave the pupils the privilege of star 'tuition'. She set us the task of tackling the big scene in *Mrs Dane's Defence* where she made her name as the fascinating Felicia Dane confronted with the guilt of her seduction in girlhood.

We were fluttering nervously in the wings mumbling the words, trying to work ourselves up from stone cold into the abject depths of a broken woman begging for mercy: 'I was only a child ... '

Composed and elegant in the stalls, she called us out by name, to put us through the ordeal as though we were on audition. Every now and then she sang out, flaying our stumbling attempts. Mary's treble rose shrill, piping into falsetto, and now Betty was struggling, desperately earnest ...

'Go away child,' her voice cut in. 'Break your heart ... and come back ... try again.'

I don't think she called me out. I was the mouse that escaped the cat's claws. As she sat there, the odd remark came into my head. It was the wardrobe mistress who had let it drop – her dresser once I suppose. We were sorting through 'the rags and tatters' for a period grey bodice and skirt. I had pulled out a yellowing confection. 'Lena Ashwell's wedding dress,' she said solemnly, fixing me with her wall eye. 'She was sick all over it on her wedding morning. It was a job to get it clean in time.'

And now Lena Ashwell was coming up on to the stage, to show us, after our pathetic failures, how it *should* be done. I can see her getting down on her knees, and bowing her head. (Of course! A broken 'guilty' woman would never stare straight up into the face of her masculine accuser.) She clasped her hands before the empty chair. But as to the star performance itself, it has left in my memory no impression at all.

Later in the season, she came round to our dressing-room. This time she noticed me: '*Much* better,' graciously. 'Gooood ... '

I was beginning to smile.

'... I could hear *every word* you said.'

After she had received her usual rather formal accolade, she vanished.

Esmé was fastening on long fair plaits as the young wife, hungry for

139

love and tied to an old man in the Nordic gloom of *The Witch*. She trussed up her solid bust into the taut span of a corded corselet; careless of her sex, she stuffed one side up and the other down. Olive remonstrated, and laughing she sorted herself out.

Kynaston Reeves, his pointed scholarly profile under a clubbed wig and pouched velvet hat, was ill-assorted, improbable as her young paramour. He made elevated love to her with restrained nobility, putting out a cautious hand to encircle her waist and avoid the overbulge.

I was hovering in the background as a runic beldame, adding to the hard grey local colour. This was my very first chance in a speaking part of any length, and I was determined to put into it everything I could, to make the old woman convincing. A long make-up with blanched cheeks and heavy runnels.

When we were at the Century, kind Beatrice Wilson intercepted me in the wings: 'I misjudged you,' she said on a friendly impulse, 'I didn't think you had it in you.'

In the play I had to quaver a few lines of pious hymn, and Coatsie had drilled me carefully over her piano to try to get me to keep in tune and not change key every few notes. Kate Coates and Honor Bright were vintage members of the company, vestal virgins of Esmé's intimate entourage. Coatsie in charge of the music – piano and violin – she herself composed, I believe. And Honor Bright, with a haughty nose, prominent eyes and no chin – an Osbert Lancaster caricature – the most improbably ugly woman one could expect to find on the stage. Very fittingly, I remember, she was cast as Caesar's wife.

When Esmé was in genial mood, there was a hearty jolly atmosphere, a ping-pong of banter, that assumed a general consensus of no-nonsense sporty loyal feeling. The cheerful badinage was extended benevolently every now and then to take in the pupils. If you felt at home and could match up on this plane, you were admitted into the jovial sorority. But if you were a little withdrawn with a reserve of unvoiced opinions, you could still qualify, outside the circle of Christian name buddies, as a bit of a character, with a jocular adaptation of your surname. Uplift or jollity it was all rather heavy going for me, but I tried to fit in as best I could. I came to be known as Cruttie.

Olive Walter, a little too low-brow and earthy to be always quite at home in Esmé's Spartan climate, was her good-natured foil, her familiar and cosy cushion. When Esmé was gloomy, she would jolly her with little jokes and a ready belly-laugh, and flatter her with cosy compliments, ignoring her snubs when her praise had been a shade too fulsome.

The permanent company attracted actors who were prepared to go along in this 'healthy' moral climate. In those days deviations were always private, but here even heterosexual excursions were tactfully kept very much out of the picture. It was a pleasant friendly company, no back-biting, no intrigue, no crawling. The men nearly all war veterans, one big kindly bear of a man, a former shell-shock case, was apt to dissolve in helpless giggles. The juveniles of course were too young to have been in the army – Alan Webb, Godfrey Kenton, Patrick Gover, John Ruddock. With its convenient little London theatre in Bayswater the company was useful to actors making the grade in the West end. Walter Fitzgerald and Cecil Trouncer were both in the company in my time.

Now that I had shown that I could cope with a character part, I was given another. I worked hard to make the cockney convincing, using teeth and breath. Then I was a neutral aunt. Now I was in a Maeterlinck play, one of the ghastly sisters – Fates, Eumenides, spectral chorus, or whatever. We stood frozen in the background with raised claw-like hands uttering in turn and together cataleptic oracular nothings: 'They are not watching ... ' I practised the dead voice *ad nauseam,* trying to get it drained, empty of feeling. (After a series of grey parts I was dying now to feather my eyelashes and part brilliant lips in a carmine smile.)

'Don't make your hands so decorative,' Leslie Banks had reproved me at rehearsal. I was, I suppose, half-consciously trying to assert, before a sympathetic masculine eye, my baulked feminity.

But when I did get my chance to play a juvenile, perversely, stupidly, I didn't take it. It was because the old part I was first cast in was so impressively long. A lavender lady who pottered in and out of the action with her silver-haired twin. This twin was to be played by a seasoned actress well in with Esmé and the nobs. Being paired with her, I felt, would give me a big lift. But just before rehearsals, somebody else was lined up to take my long part, and I was to play the tiny juvenile. Now I was feeling aggrieved, and hankering for the old part. Leslie Banks was the producer. He joined us, the unimportant ones, for lunch at Ma Campbell's, instead of eating somewhere more sophisticated with the other producers. He was always charming, approachable, an artist with no side at all.

Two or three times a week, out of loyalty and to economize with a big cheap meal, Betty and I steeled ourselves to tackle her shilling 'workman's lunch'. Heavy meat, swamped and sweaty in thick stale-fat gravy, with veges plonked on all together on the plate, steaming on her red check table slips.

'You *want* to keep the old lady?'

Leslie Banks's tone of voice and his look gave me a twinge of doubt, a warning that I might not have ignored had I not been immediately distracted. Ma Campbell was clearing our plates, and two nuns passed by the half-net frontage. She darted a terrified glance, dropped the plates and vanished behind her bead curtain. We waited and waited – but there was no pudding. At last I discovered her, dark eyes and earrings peering up behind her settee. She had taken cover.

'They've come to take me back, because I ran away ... They'll do *anything* ... '

She would reveal no more. Warily, at last, she got up, served us with our fluted cake shape with pink sauce.

Leslie Banks gave me back my long old lady's part. (Very likely it was he, out of kindly consideration, who had been instrumental in at last casting me in a juvenile role! I was too inexperienced to make the assessment.) Now I had cooked my goose. From then on it was powdered hair, white wigs, wrinkles, falsetto treble, never under forty, often over sixty.

Occasionally on circuit a town hall offered the leading ladies a separate dressing-room, and we young ones escaped the restraints to be free and light-hearted on our own. Oriel Ross joined the company as Myra in *Hay Fever* (I, of course, played the 'Tea for Two' maid, and Betty, Sorel). She wound her lovely Nefertiti head up in a turban, and, flouting Lena Ashwell decorum, stripped down into something diminutive, to make up topless.

On Saturday night at Watford, as the last lines were being spoken by the Bliss ménage in their riverside cottage, the whole fabric began to quake and sag. Jock was going round undoing all the knots making ready to strike the set, in anticipation of his weekend take-off in the lorry, with all of it aboard.

I dozed in the train going home from Victoria, and walked half-asleep through the dark suburban streets in the midnight silence dangling my light suitcase.

I never understood why it was that my father made no difficulty about my going on the stage. He had been paying up for my college fees after my scholarship folded up and might well have expected me now to take on a reasonable job on the strength of my degree. (Miss Block had sent me a postcard to say I had a good safe place in the second class, nearer the top than the bottom. I hadn't bothered to attend the ceremony to have my degree conferred, nor had I asked my father for the two guineas, or whatever, to join Convocation and get my new gown.) I expect it was the Lena Ashwell prestige that decided him, the flavour of good works attached to her companies, their intense respectability. The Board of Education in their *Teaching of English* had praised her for 'popularizing good plays', and hoped that her work would be extended with the co-operation of more local authorities. I remember no row or fuss about the payment of the £50 premium. But even that was not the end. He was giving me I believe it was £1 a week for food and lodging – never quite enough – and going to keep that up for the better part of a year.

The mortifying searing encounters with my father were all clashes of temperament – that I had the audacity, ventured to criticize, call in question, etc. I can remember no difficulties about money, or anything else. But Bee recalls a row about a new dress.

Lydia and I were going off to a dance, and came in to say goodbye to Mother. I was in my new green frock, low-waisted, three layers of overlapping petals touching my knees, swaying when I walked. My father stared disgusted over his glasses.

'Ottilia!' threatening. 'Are you going to allow that child to go out in that frock?'

Bee says that I was thrilled with the dress, which I bought in Wardour Street, and that I certainly had a short petticoat on. Apparently I was furious. A terrible row. Mother resolved it with a thread of green silk, crouching down and sewing together the lowest picot-edged petals, closing the gap.

The stage as a career was I suppose trendy at the time (Noël Coward's 'Don't Put your Daughter on the Stage, Mrs Worthington'), but that would hardly influence my father. I believe there was a brief economic revival, things were looking up – this may have helped. Father had his car now, and went on golfing holidays with his cronies. Whatever decided him, he did generously give me my chance to freedom – to find my feet, and in the end to discover 'real life'. The home atmosphere no longer oppressed me. I looked forward every weekend to coming back to my mother. But now it was my choice, not my fate – it made all the difference.

On Monday morning, it was back to London for rehearsal. I was running for the train and practising a martial voice for a messenger in *Julius Caesar* (to appear in cardboard breastplate and knees smeared with No. 9): 'Prepare you Generals ...!' Two men at a distant corner turned

143

round and hesitated ... Did I need help? I dropped into a slow walk and stared hard into the privet hedge.

One of the company's financial arbiters was probably the manager, Harold Gibson. He was an impressive James Mason type, in his forties, with a monocle on a broad black ribbon. He was a bit of a mystery, inviting speculation. Was he stage-struck (he occasionally played parts – Esmé's old husband in *The Witch,* and in *Tilly of Bloomsbury,* the once gentlemanly now alcoholic father come down in the world), or did he fancy himself as an impresario? Was he backing the company as a business venture, or did he subscribe to the Lena Ashwell culture myth, and aspire to be a patron of the arts? He had a Sunday-school side that put him in Esmé Church territory (it was he who later on arranged the company's tea-time visit to the Archbishop of York), and a worldly side that made him a little suspect, sometimes earning her unspoken disapproval. Like James Mason in his theatrical roles, he had a rather ambiguous personality. Was he going to play the mixed-up not-quite hero? Or was he to be the half-baddie with a soft centre? (Lena Ashwell does not refer to him in her autobiography.)

He was at the stage when he was thinking of settling down, ending on friendly terms a liaison with a society woman, who turned up at functions, toothy and emaciated but still chic. Now it was youth that attracted him. He approved of Betty and was avuncular and mildly flirtatious with her. He and I eyed each other with a little suspicion sugared over with friendliness. I teased Betty about him. Too old, and bogus, I warned her.

But then Mary came along as a pupil. A big baby doll, with the broad open china face, the round blue eyes, starry eyelashes and exactly the same mouth as my doll Lucy in Petropolis. But her thin cupid's bow with its scallop of underlip could widen and spread generously into a disarming grin. Her long straight fair hair was just like Lucy's that I used to comb and plait. She had been disciplined in childhood like a boy, and made to scrub white the decks of her father's yacht in the frosty dawn. Now she was making up for it, aware of the appeal of her high-pitched treble and the inviting stare of her blue eyes, yet she was still implacably hedged behind conventions and inhibitions as unyielding as the sleeping beauty's entanglements. When I teased her about Gibbie, she pleaded that he was, all the same, 'raaather sweet!'

We were going into the provinces for the summer repertory. This year it was a fortnight in Leeds and six weeks at York. Betty was dropped as a redundant juvenile in favour of Mary, although she had had a longer

144

experience in the Lena Ashwell's and was certainly the better actress. I was included, scoring this time with my useful character parts.

I loved Leeds, a dark, exciting charged place, a rich mixture of architecture, culture, influences. Something vivid might happen round any corner. A short bus ride outside, and you brushed through trees into green country.

We arrived in the evening. A bus took us near our digs. Humble streets. No traffic. An old woman trundled by on uneven legs. A dog nosed in the gutter. It was getting dark now. 'Let's go back,' Mary was coaxing, 'just for tonight.' She was all for the bright centre and fixing up at some little hotel. I was firm.

We crossed an old bridge over a trickle of dry canal.

No. 9. Its doorstep flush with the pavement. Mrs Gurney welcomed us in with heavy breathing. We sidled past her into the cosy nest of her sitting-room, tightly upholstered, plush, woolly bobbles, potted ferns. Upstairs, a dim back bedroom with a monster wardrobe. The huge double-bed absorbed us under the glazed plummy eiderdown – a new experience for both of us.

At the theatre, later that week, Mary was frowning over a letter. Her young friend – on leave from Portsmouth – wanted to take her out to lunch and tea. Mrs Gurney, Mary decided, could do a nice lunch for the three of us. She wouldn't hear of my leaving them for a tête-à-tête.

He turned out to be the classic young naval officer, fair, blue-eyed, unassuming – just right for the juvenile lead. He stared helplessly at Mary, but brightened up when she suggested a *thé-dansant*. Mary roped in Gibbie and two or three members of the company. We all sat round a big table, and were jolly with theatre jokes in the Lena Ashwell style, and rather superior about the dancing. Mary warmed up for a sweet smile when he had to catch his train.

After Leeds it was York. In the old Theatre Royal the space backstage was enormous. You had to walk right down to get into the wings of the set, to smell the grease paint, the fusty exhalation of wardrobe clothes, and to hear the faint rustle from the front of the house. In the surrounding twilight, the cavernous space, the gloomy height, dwarfed and engulfed you. It dwindled the bright stage rectangle and its patter into insignificance.

The theatre had been built on the ancient foundations of a religious order. The stone shell, with its massive masonry, appeared to have been hewn out of rock. It still preserved its ancient aura. The iron past was waiting to claim it all back, to impose its old silence and flouted piety.

145

The height created the illusion of bated echoes, suspended orisons, muted chants soaring inaudible.

Ancient circular stone stairs gave access to the dressing-rooms, two or three turns to a landing. Most of the cast on the first floor. The stage-manager and some of the men on the second. And we pupils, the small fry, at the very top. Down an elbow-turn into a whitewashed bare room, featureless, high sightless windows. It only came to life with our make-up and mirrors, our stage clothes, and Mary's whiskered pup flattened patient in a corner. The door was immovably propped open with a ten-pound weight. It was in this room that the nun was said to have been immured. If ever the door was shut and the key turned, she was heard to scream, and go on screaming. None of us found it comfortable to be left alone in the room, remote, cut off from sound, the silence grew more and more insistent, oppressive, ready to explode in irrational fear, ridiculous panic.

Every night, at the end of the show, after the stage had lapsed into darkness, Frank, the tall young stage-manager, reached up to flick off the lights all the way down the stone stairs, and as we pupils – always the last with our chores – were making for the stage door, the silent old night-watchman – I never heard him utter a word – would be standing waiting at the foot of the stairs with his glowing lantern. His vigil always started with a heavy tramp up to the very top to make sure that the ten-pound weight was still in place.

Morning rehearsals were brief, our repertoire mostly from shows already played at the Century, only needed brushing up, the principals in their original roles, a few smaller parts to be filled in.

I was so bored now with my eternal character parts that I was getting slack. When I was cast in a play new to me, I tackled my part with the egotism of shallow interest. My slender lines and cues my only concern, I picked up at rehearsal the 'correct' tone and nuance, unaware of the turn of the plot, the concept of the whole, or even sometimes my exact relationship with the character to whom I addressed my last lines. After my exit, the play was a blank, noises off, of no consequence. In *The Whiteheaded Boy,* as Kate, I was a peg in a homely skirt, old blouse, tired make-up, who said this and that – very little – in answer to that and this. I took a lot of trouble to make my lines sound as Irish as possible, but I had no idea what it was all about. It was only in production, with the swing of the dialogue, the rhythm, the feel of the scene, that I began dimly to discover myself and to be aware of the intrinsic quality of the play. I hardly bothered now with wrinkles. As the formidable great-aunt

146

Trafalgar in *Trelawney of the Wells,* in spite of white hair and blanched cheeks, I look much too young in the snap next to Esmé, her solid build negating dangling brown curls and a saucy bonnet as the youthful Rose.

The elegant Green Room, little used by the busy principals, was our haven. Its period prints and cartoons, its aura of sophistication and former glitter, gave us the brief illusion, sitting there at our ease, of being the stars. I was young again, critical and amused, my ancient garb, fancy dress. We passed the time with anyone who wanted a little frivolous relaxation, often John Killner, pocket-size, good-looking, who played comedy and the older juveniles. We had a fellow-feeling of independence from the approved Lena Ashwell fold. We giggled about the expensive present young Douglas, who had a crush on him, had given him for his birthday. Ought he to accept it? 'What am I supposed to do in return?' The day was almost all leisure now. We pottered round benign well-to-do York, sheltered in its silver-grey calm behind ancient gates and walls. A scattering of shoppers and tourists in the narrow old streets. The river meandered politely past tonsured lawns and leisured homes.

I was content to be caught up in Mary's extrovert plans. Her bland eyes, that never browsed in a book, innocent of introspection, could go blank in cheerful determination that we go *her* own sweet way. Once this was achieved, she blossomed, happy in her freedom from family constraints, pleased with Gibby's attentive ways, her small dog's whiskered appeal. She would sigh exuberantly, wind her strong arms round me in a squeezing hug – 'boogling' she called it.

Three cabfulls of Lena Ashwell's set off for tea with the Archbishop. In a country lane we passed a mongrel straining out of a barrel and howling. Mary poked the cabman to stop. She bought the towsled animal for four shillings.

'You're not going to take that dirty dog to tea with the Archbishop?'

'The cabby will look after him.'

It sat slumped on our feet, at the end of a frayed rope.

A demure very plain tea. Small fry at the chaplain's table. Gibby and the principals with the Archbishop. A conducted tour of the 'palace' (in fact a modest mansion). In turn we picked up Wolsey's spoon and fork, complying with the ritual tribute to antiquity and patronage. And now for a stately little procession over the grounds. As we emerged from the walled garden, the sky closed in a deep purple, the lawn lit up vivid as a green lake. His Grace quickened his pace making for shelter. His advance was halted by an eruption from the back of the palace. Skidding over the gravel the happy mongrel burst into our midst dragging behind him the Dickensian cabby, knees bent, grey hair awry. It bounded straight for His Grace, welcoming paws all over the purple apron. Mary rushed in, the ingenuous *ingénue,* to save the situation. She snatched up the dog, cradling it in her arms: 'You naughty boy!' Turning, she dropped it on the path, gave the cabby a friendly push.

Back in our digs, Mary was giving the mongrel a pail-wash. Mrs White was glum. One dog was enough. 'Don't worry, we'll keep him in the bedroom,' Mary assured her.

It was our bath night. We were left alone in the house. In the cosy twilight of their basement-kitchen-living-room, the tub was filled with hot water close to the range. Mary, her fair hair knotted on the top of her head, was overflowing splendidly pink and pendulous when we heard heavy footsteps overhead. They clattered down the tiled hall. Now they were at the top of the basement stairs, leading straight into the kitchen ... Coming down! ... Halted ... Not a sound. Mary and I and the unknown, dumb. He was backing away! Retreating ... noisy down the hall. The front door slammed. Apparently all the keys in the road fitted. The worse for drink, Mrs White guessed, couldn't tell his own front door.

As it was Mary's shopping week we had crab and strawberries and cream for supper. In the morning I felt rotten. Mary dragged me out on the river: 'Much better in the sun!' And the next day, still limp, out again to watch tennis. It was when I was feeling better that a little rash appeared. Now *she* was worried. On the way to the theatre we passed a doctor's plate. Before I could demur, Mary had rung the bell. The elderly man was suspicious: 'From the theatre, you say.' He took my temperature. I must go to bed. He would call in to see me. On his visit he kept well away. I heard him questioning the landlady as he went down the stairs: 'She *says* her face is swollen?' He thought I had scarlet fever.

The next day I was awakened as two burly men were shown into my bedroom. They bundled me up in red flannel, carried me downstairs and into their van. I was driven off to the corporation isolation hospital. On admittance I was plunged into a regulation brown disinfectant bath – my hair too – and put to bed in a large scarlet-fever ward with half a dozen small boys and one tiny very sick girl.

That evening, before the lights were turned on, a gaunt figure in a long cape and with a great hound beside him, appeared in the doorway like something out of *Wuthering Heights.* He shuffled up and peered at me: 'Spots coming out nicely?'

'I haven't *got* scarlet fever.'

He straightened up. His old eyes considered me under shaggy brows. He passed on.

The hospital doctor was away in London at a conference.

The small boys whiled away the long afternoons playing tag. One came flying down and bumped into my bed.

Matron came to see me. I was moved into an empty ward that had been fumigated. I was in total isolation. I couldn't send any letters or have visitors. No way of communicating with the outside world. I could receive things, but take nothing away except the night clothes I came in. A notice, I learned, was posted outside. Three formulas: Satisfactory, Comfortable as can be expected, Deceased.

Every day I was woken at 6 a.m. with a gargle and an aperient. I tilted both into the basin, and slept till breakfast gruel arrived in a tin receptacle with a cup of tea. No human till lunch – generally a lump of boiled fish.

Mary made the long tramride to leave me untidy parcels with buns, sweets, a long scrawl of letter and literature from Woolworths. I feverishly turned it over. Large paperbacks in small type – Edgar Jepson, J. D. Beresford, Warwick Deeping and Anthony Hope. Anthony Hope I found unreadable even in my vacuum.

I declaimed poetry – the empty ward a good auditorium. 'You calling, Miss?' The gardner poked his head in at the window. Now every morning we had a chat. He left lettuce on the window-sill, and slim carrots.

After a fortnight, the doctor back from London came to see me. I had had fish poisoning – the crab. I could go.

I was wobbly after so long in bed. Mary's mother had come to take her home. It was the end of the Lena Ashwell season. She and Mrs White were frightened to let me into the house. They rushed out with a chair. Mary packed my suitcase. I travelled home alone.

My father paid the doctor's bill without demur.

Another family holiday – this time in Normandy. Hotel lunch was in the garden in little summer-houses with thatched roofs. A bucket of shell-fish for hors-d'oeuvre.

I danced with a French boy. He clipped me close, our concave stomachs met and fused blissfully. A Prince of Wales type, country-bred from the North, shy but fiercely independent. We exchanged addresses and corresponded in French for a few months.

149

Betty and I started the new season as paid members of the company! We shared part of a furnished flat in Westbourne Grove. We had our own little sitting-room with a gas ring. I learned from her how to sizzle bacon and egg. From now on this was our staple diet.

The company put on three new plays. One in verse by Alfred Noyes about the greenwood. Esmé played Shadow of a Leaf in green tights. Sir Edmund Gosse, now aged seventy-seven, came to see it. He wrote to Siegfreid Sassoon on 28 December, 1926:

> Nellie and I went last night to the first performance of Noyes' romantic play in verse of Robin Hood in Sherwood Forest. It was enthusiastically received by a crowded audience and is indeed a very pretty thing, but the verse – it is all lyrical – could not be very easily distinguished, though the actors did their best. I shudder to think what the Georgians [the children of Eddie Marsh] would say to such unashamed romance, but none of them were there.*

Betty and I were filling in the background as greenwood followers. Thorold Dickinson was stage manager and he provided folksy provender for us to sit 'eating' cross-legged. I was hungry and swallowed a mouthful of dusty shredded wheat. It stuck in my windpipe and choked me. Whooping and rolling about, I made the merry men more merry.

The hopeful authoress of the second play, *The House with the Twisty Windows*, a big trusting woman, haunted the theatre. On Saturday night when we finished at Winchmore Hill, it was freezing. We travelled back with Jock on the lorry with the props, and carrying a big poster of the show. Down a long icy road we went into a big skid and ended up sideways on top of the hedge. Twisty wheels advertising the *Twisty Windows*. I was in the tilted corner under a pile of two dogs and three men, helpless with laughter. John Killner – who had been in the trenches – called out (rather tactlessly I thought), 'Get out quick before it catches on fire.'

The third new play was a trivial 'modern' comedy very like any other conventional piece of the period. I had to take the curtain up with a cockney monologue as a slatternly comic char. The word went round that the critics were in front. I tripped over my bucket and a dribble of water spilled down to the footlights.

Maybe it was because the play was so weak, and the critics didn't stay very long, but in St John Ervine's brief review in the *Observer* I

*The Life and Letters of Sir Edmund Gosse, Evan Charteris, Heinemann, p.497.

was the only one he picked out for a notice! A good performance if I hadn't under-acted.

The following week I had offers of complimentary sittings at half a dozen photographers. The prints came out looking like something in the style of the studio rather than me. In one I was dark and sultry with heavy eyelashes (nothing more than lick), in the next fair, swan-necked with a carefully marcelled profile, and finally casual, mushroomed on the floor, a collapsed lampshade with curving silk legs. Esmé gave me some sober down-to-earth advice: 'The publicity will only be useful to you if you want to do *character parts*.'

The best production of the Lena Ashwell's that I remember was John Masefield's *Good Friday*. The setting, the cast, the scope were all within our range, and Beatrice Wilson achieved an imaginative production, with moving effects in the crowd scenes. (She roped in an obliging stage-hand to appear stripped and blackened as a Nubian eunuch.) I had only three words to speak: 'Goodnight – and blessings,' and I never got them just right. She sang them out after me in her deep mature voice. It rang in my head – coming out of the night, full of healing. But I could never quite capture it. Young and unachieved, I was trying to echo maturity.

We took the show to Wormwood Scrubs. It was going well, a friendly audience. The big hall had been curtained off down one side. We, the crowd, were waiting behind this to swarm on to the platform in two streams, most of us directly on to the stage and a few of us alongside the front rows and up the steps and on to the front of the platforms. I peeped through the curtains and was surprised to discover the prisoners, sitting close the other side, so strong and good-looking. Our cue! We parted the curtains and out we ran – no steps! I took a flying leap. It caught in the hem of my long gown and sent me sprawling. I did an awkward scramble and heave, arms, legs anyhow, to cheers and laughter.

We took *Trelawney of the Wells* to Haileybury – both my brothers there now.

The summer season this year was at Bath. Betty, Mary and I shared digs in a respectable terrace. Two white-haired old witches toiled up from their basement with heavy old tureens and vegetable dishes for our lunch, eyeing us with veiled disapproval. The crockery so ancient that the chamber pot parted dangerously. 'Too much dancing and prancing,' muttered the one who carried off the jagged halves. In Betty's catering week it was homely stews, steak and kidney, shepherd's pie; in Mary's salmon, chicken (still a luxury), shell-fish. In mine, lettuce, tomatoes, fruit, cheese and ham.

151

On the river in the long afternoons, joined now by Douglas, ready to carry our gramophone and thermos and, better off than we, to supplement our modest buns for tea with iced cakes and strawberries. We slipped through the silent waterway in the green bowl of the valley, past empty meadows. Only the plop of our oars, our voices and the glancing dragonflies. A tangle of wild rose, tall cow parsley, meadow sweet and vetch. We tried to land but the soft clay banks were rotten and slippery. We steered away from the thick floating weed, to bathe in mid-stream. Drying in the sun with the sweet catchy tunes, 'My Blue Heaven', 'Who Stole my Heart Away', 'Why is It I Spend the Day?' ... tickling a little half-asleep sensuous nerve. In the early evening light the slopes were surprisingly flecked with a tribe of snow-white rabbits.

Back into Bath, half-asleep too. The elegant bridge suspended over the dead stream, white arcades of silent houses. The prospect serenely beautiful but the air a little soft and sagging – like the river banks.

The theatre is a blank in my memory except for the lovely Regency interior of the front of the house, all red and gold. Cecil Trouncer was getting engaged to Queenie Russell, and soon afterwards Mary was engaged to Gibbie. They planned after a short spell in London to live in the country.

This was our last season with the Lena Ashwell's – soon to close down. Betty and I had to look for work.

In the autumn, Norah Killner told me she was giving up her juvenile part in *Up in Mabel's Room*; would I like to apply for it?

I waited outside the semi-detached in Brixton. The queue trailed down the lino stairs, through the open front door to the wicket gate in the privet hedge. Casting had been advertised in the *Stage*.

Apparently I was just what the House of Bernard was looking for! Before I had time to explain my lack of experience, Mr Bernard turned a questioning eye to Mrs B – dyed red hair – she nodded and that was it.

I was of course the perfect foil. My enunciation, my gormless aura, the bloom of the higher life and Lena Ashwell rescitude would make the inuendoes, the rude cracks, all the funnier bounced off my bland composure. I was to rehearse for a week at Winchester, go on on Saturday night, and then open the next Monday for a season at Sheerness.

The male juvenile who discovered the compromising cami-nicks under the sofa, in the wrong bedroom, etc., was played very staccato and nasal by a lanky youth. I thought he was terribly good. I enjoyed dancing about in my pink pyjamas and silk negligée bordered with swansdown (clothes found by the actors).

152

A week later, the juvenile vanished. In his place there was a stocky well-filled man with a Marlon Brando stare. His broad face slightly pitted, one cheek slashed by a scar. This was Wilfrid Lawson.

In the wings: 'Are my trousers too tight?'

And at the end of the show, as we linked hands to take the calls – legally paired off at last after all the cami-nicks misunderstandings: 'I suppose this is when we are allowed to go to bed together!' He was knocking the cliché respectability of the vulgar little show, but I misunderstood and walked coldly away.

There were no lavatories backstage. The penny-in-the-slots were outside down a gravel path. The two adjoining communal dressing-rooms were provided with a make-shift bucket with a lid. The partition dividing the dressing rooms didn't reach the ceiling. So every now and then the ladies burst into song, and the men raised a little cheer.

At the back of the stage as you edged your way behind the set, it was bitterly cold. The canvas bellied out. Behind this you could mysteriously hear the sea. How it got there I never discovered. It couldn't be seen from the gravel path. I don't think I ever discovered the sea at Sheerness. Perhaps it was chiefly a utility sea for the docks.

The small terrace house where I had my digs stood flush with the pavement in a cul-de-sac ending in a high wall and a gate that never opened. Although it was unlike anything I had ever lived in before, it felt absolutely congenial, as though I had been born there. Through the kitchen for the outside lavatory, and a friendly word with Mum, plain with glasses. Her son was a wag, he wrote rude doggerel ('Isn't he clever!') and kept up a non-stop leg-pull making out that his mother was a raving beauty. He got her all giggly and confused. He and Dad worked in the docks.

Lawson and his wife moved into my digs. They had the front sitting-room and best bedroom. I was at the back. They were engaged as a joint. I forget the ridiculous cut-price figure that he told me. Mrs Lawson, Girlie to him, was years older than Don (as she called him), still pretty in a gentle rather old-fashioned way, with a very fair lined skin. Don treated her indulgently, rather like the Shah's favourite in the harem. She loved it. In fact she adored him.

When I was helping her wash her long hair ('Don won't let me cut it' – 'What a funny shampoo! The water's bright yellow!') she told me her story about Don. When war broke out he had enlisted, making out he was of age. I think she said he was seventeen. He wanted to fly. Later on he had a plane crash. He lived through it all over again in nightmares, groaning and falling out of bed. She hinted that that was why he had to have his drink.

I had never thought of him as a drinker. He went to the men's morning session at the pub, and came back to a late lunch. But that, as I was discovering, was the usual thing. When I joined them in the afternoon, he never smelt of drink, his speech was never slurred.

He would be lolling in an easy chair in his slippers, arrogant and affable. At one moment he was a friendly tramp with a rolling eye, a cavernous grin and ribald croak, then a jester-clown with a mocking hollow voice, or a disarming simpleton. But most often, the genial potentate, too lazy to exercise his *droit de seigneur*. We never talked *about* anything. Women were a pleasant harem species, and you needn't converse with them *about* anything. His general theme, implicit more than actually spelt out in words, was that as man and actor he was a colossus, he must and would be recognized. London was to be his kingdom, and there he would be offered the crown. This episode in Sheerness was no more than a joke. If it was his pleasure to hood his genius in an incognito interlude that was the good fortune of the House of Bernard. Goosey, as he called me, had to be brought down from her high perch on to the road to reality. For a start, she must recognize his genius and she could do worse than succumb to his male stallion magnetism.

'You seem to think you're a kind of Napoleon or something?'

Shedding a slipper, Don would intrude a lordly foot under Girlie's skirt. However much he tried to outrage and provoke me, Girlie remained placid and indulgent, content to be the audience in our mock combat.

I challenged him: 'You've got an eagle-elephantiasis *complex*...' (that was the popular psychology key word then) – and so it went on.

While I could feel the strength and complexity of his personality, I had to take his acting on trust. In our show, his face, his voice, his general meatiness – however much he soft-pedalled – broke through the rotten fabric, but achieved nothing for him. Towards the end of the season, the blarney, the mellow afternoon assumptions were rudely broken. The House of Bernard were signing up the company for the next fixtures. The Lawsons had been left out, and so had I. The maggoty crawling House of Bernard had taken it upon themselves to drop him, they would see his name in lights in Shaftesbury Avenue, and then the maggots would be crawling at the thought of what they had missed. (Lawson never swore in front of Girlie and me.)

They left before the very end of the season, and his place was taken

154

by a personable young man. His real name was that of a well-known impresario, but he had adopted a stage name, fed up with the lack of family support. He seemed to think that a recital of the charms and delights of his absent fiancée was a good prelude to an attempt to make love to me.

After I had done the round of the theatrical agents, and before I caught the train home to the suburbs, I called in to see the Lawsons in their flat in Garrick Street. This was just after he had got his first break in a season of Shavian plays with the Macdona Players.

The heavy old street door towered as though it was shutting in a warehouse rather than leading to flats. Lawson had to come down to let me in. He was grinning about his encounter with George Bernard Shaw. The story has fogged up a bit in my memory, but the key line was a little ominous. Lawson was rehearsing Dolittle in *Pygmalion*, but he still had to be vetted by Shaw before he could get his contract with the Macdona Players. Teetotal Shaw scrutinized him: 'You look to me already rather mellow, slightly sozzled.' Lawson assured him that he was getting right into the skin of the part, the feel of it. He had conned the old sage. He was in!

Everything in their flat was dark and anonymous. It must have been let furnished. Girlie and Don sat at one end of an enormous dining-room table, they were finishing their tea. Don as usual started off with his masculine bombast, and we were off on our sparring duologue.

I looked at my wrist watch, and sprang up. There was a snap – my bra-strap had burst. Lawson went into a clowny comedy act, half Marx Brothers, half Lancelot Gobbo. What is this phenomenon? He viewed it from different angles. Desperately he tried to draw my attention to the disequilibrium. He stretched out a tentative, helpful hand...I refused to play and be amused. Girlie showed me out into the dark passage. We smiled at each other. I raced down the stairs, and slammed the awful door. I never met him again. But we talked on the phone occasionally in the evenings. Long talks about nothing at all. It was the tone of voice more than anything – going up and down, and dropping, and the pauses – that held me on the line. Then he joined his company and I went on tour, and that was that. After the Macdona Players he began to appear in the West End. Whenever I was in London I would go and see the show. In one play – in Shaftesbury Avenue – he had a brief key scene where he played a ghost. I can still hear the echo of that insubstantial voice as it rose high and thin and pathetic and terrible. All that excitement and vibration evoked in a play so second-rate that I remember nothing else about it. All he needed was a vehicle. I am sorry now that I never sent him a first-night telegram with a few superlatives: 'You were right. You *are* an Emperor...' and signing it Goosey. He would have enjoyed a little whiff of incense.

Before I ever saw Albert Finney on the stage or in film, he materialized, for the first time for me, on television, in an interview. As he filled out on the screen, I got a shock of recognition – Wilfrid Lawson! Much younger than when I knew him, but still unmistakably his blood brother – in bulk, in build, in mannerisms. Slow and powerful, half-asleep and half-challenging. He held his head as though it was heavy. He pursed his lips, or compressed them before speaking, sometimes, teeth bared, he spat the phrase out, or chewed it up and let it out in a mumble. I could see Lawson speaking! The juxtaposition of gentleness, pseudo-softness and strength. In Lawson it was the cat nursing the bully-boy, feral and sensitive. Of course now I have seen Albert Finney in many parts, he has turned into himself and Lawson remains with me as the gnomic figure in the part I last saw him on the stage. This was in the 1962-3 season at the Old Vic, when he played the button-moulder in *Peer Gynt*. (He had of course shipwrecked his career irretrievably long before that.) At the end of the play he was well up stage, a mysterious figure, taking it very slowly. Suddenly his body lurched forward and he almost fell. He recovered himself, assimilated the strange movement into the part – and still he held the stage.

I went on tour in *Dr Jekyll and Mr Hyde*. The actor playing the lead was venturing out with his own tour. He knew me from the Lena Ashwell's, where he had played Svengali in *Trilby*. I was to understudy Mrs Jekyll and take a character part. Wilfred had his own private double life. He was on the best of terms, courtly and attentive to his newly acquired elderly rich wife, who toured with him, and his boyfriend in the cast was in the room upstairs above their double room. But Donald was getting upstage about some No. 3 bookings on the tour – miners tramping in, expecting the customary leg-show and greeting the opening with cat-calls.

One of these small-time bookings was at Ashington in Northumberland. The miners' houses stretched in rows – privies sticking out at the back – all standing on rough earth, and cut off by waste ground. Only the long shopping street was made up and had pavements. You cut across the unmade tract to get to the theatre and join another short interval of street. The dressing rooms were running with damp. Clothes on hangers had to be propped away from the wall.

Attracted by the name, I took a bus to Newbiggin – a young girl clipping my ticket. It was all deserted. A glinting North Sea was breaking on the shore, wind-blown dunes dazzling in the wintry sun, the sand swallowing half-buried chicken-runs. Primary colours bold in the white air, the combs and feathers of bantams, green stakes deep in shining sand. The wind baptizing it all. Not a human in sight.

At the theatre, a long-drawn wail came vibrating up the stone stairs into our dressing-room. Agnes and I exchanged glances. She started off down. I followed. She was North-Country, a sinuous figure, a throaty voice, chinless, ugly-attractive – an instinctive comedienne. Swathed in his silk dressing-gown, Wilfred, tragic, stared at himself in the mirror: 'This is the END! I can't go ON! Donald hates me. He Haaaatzzz me!' He started up, throwing out his arms: 'He doesn't Laaahve me any more.' He went swinging round the small room, beside himself.

'We *all* love you!' She was trotting beside him, turning with him, 'You know we do. We can't help it. You're so wonderful! Be a good boy!'

Wilfred, deaf, hissing, screaming, spittle collecting round his mouth.

A head appeared round the door. She darted up: 'Port – and an egg – *quick*!' I was feebly murmuring a soothing accompaniment to her efforts. A tray at the door. She snatched the drink – made to break the egg, crack it in. It wouldn't give. She bashed it! Hard-boiled! Her head jerked back and she let out a yelp.

Wilfred, shocked, stopped dead, stared at her – the suspended gesture, the glass, the egg, her comedy face – it was too much for the actor in him. In spite of himself he let out a harsh cackle. She let go in a howl of relief. He caught the infection. The two of them were shreiking away uncontrollably.

She hugged and patted him. Curtain up. Only Donald remained sulking in his tent.

The leading lady was young and beautiful – soon to rise to minor stardom – perfect dimples, and a fetching gap between two teeth. She enchanted the visitors to her dressing-room, sitting milk-white in sea-green cami-nicks. As the tour went on they faded and drooped, ending up olive grey. She had a tiny snuffling Pekinese that messed the carriage seats and the carpets in her commercial hotels. She herself preferred to hoist up and do a wee-wee in her dressing-room basin, rather than bother to go down the corridor. Radiant, smiling, she was generous and warm-hearted, all the susceptible men in the company half in love with her.

After staring long and searchingly at me, she told me I *must* pluck my eyebrows. I don't know how I managed through the twenties to preserve my thick brows. They were a constant provocation to women with tweezers and time to spare in the dressing-room. I don't really know why I obstinately defended them. I realized of course that as a startled pencil line was all the vogue, they were much too straight and heavy.

It was after Morecambe that we had a Sunday call to Aberystwyth. We changed at Crewe at midnight, and got on to a slow train through Wales – no corridor. Women in one carriage, men in another. As the dark slowly turned into restive morning, one of us unpacked a long cardboard box. We took quick turns, and finally floated it out of the window, not with complete success. The peke goggling at us, comfortable to do his pools where he sat.

It was too early when we arrived at Aberystwyth to wake landladies. I dozed on a seat in the esplanade. I knocked at last on a front door facing the sea. I dropped asleep in a top bedroom. I had the illusion I was back in childhood on holiday in Seaford.

At the end of the tour, Wilfred fixed up a week at the Q Theatre, Hammersmith. Our leading lady was already booked, so I played Mrs Jekyll. There was still a fleck of spume by his mouth when he slipped back into Harley Street after a Hyde frenzy. I had to shut my eyes as I received his conjugal kiss. I had my own emotional scene at the close, in black velvet and a rope of pearls. All the family were sitting in a row out in front.

Betty invited me up for a week to South Shields, where she was playing the leads in an Alfred Denville stock company. She opened in *The Rosary* and went on into *East Lynne* and *Maria Marten*. I saw her in *The Luck of the Navy*, with a grand court-martial scene, all gold braid. A hush as the wronged maiden made her entrance in a simple white frock. Cross-questioned, she confesses in a quavering voice – that carried to the back of the gallery – 'I am about to become...a mother...' and sinks slowly in a dead faint.

With her usual sporting enterprise, Betty had fixed up riding for us. The horses in the Territorial Army barracks needed exercising. The sergeant tried us out first in the riding school – without saddles we slipped and slithered over the broad backs, then saddles but no reins. After we had landed a few times in the sawdust, he fixed up a morning ride for

158

us on the beach.

Low tide. The breakers dwindled into shallow swathes that spilled and ran on over the glassy sand. We took the horses down to the water's edge, and swung into a canter. The salt and the air, and I felt my horse gather up to plummet into a gallop. We were cutting through a moving carpet of water that ran in shallow spumy circles dizzy in light. Now it was all sweeping back, pulling out under us as we shot forward. It was pulling me too, upsetting my balance...I shut my eyes, let the horse carry me forward, go his own sweet way.

We trotted up the beach, and turned into the thin hard grass leading to cobbles and the traffic. My horse, in front, pulling hard, he hadn't had enough. The sergeant shot ahead and swung round. My horse reared and plunged and I flew into the air. Bang – I was winded. I tried to scramble up but collapsed. His white face stared down as my lungs filled up. Chastened, my horse too, I got back into the saddle.

The agent fixed me up in another tour with a thriller. I doubled as a char and a tart – a melodramatic sequence in Chinatown, lurid local colour for the rubbishy plot as the action moved into Limehouse. In Nottingham I was reading Priestley's *Good Companions*. The city's wide centre, the castle and ancient pub veiled in misty light became romantic. We moved outside into D. H. Lawrence land. The miners stamped into the gallery and upper circle, boots pounding. They spoke the opening lines for me. I couldn't hear my own voice. When it came to Limehouse, the 'Chinaman' playing opposite me hissed: 'Play it *down!*' But the miners were ready to enjoy this. I let it rip.

The tour was doing badly. A gross fat manager turned up, and called us in individually for a 'friendly' chat. The leading man, he confided, was taking a cut in pay. What did I think of that. I agreed that with his big salary it was very handsome indeed. 'Good. I knew I could count on you. I will adjust your pay too.' When I stood firm that my salary was much too small to cut, I found that I was out!

I wanted to get more experience in young parts. To be light and silly, to know how to laugh. I would tighten up when this lay ahead in my part. I had done so much crying, and tough, mostly cockney comedy. I tried the Liverpool Rep. I had an interview with a vague pleasant man on his visit to London. But by the time I had found the obscure rendezvous, he was ready to leave for somewhere else, and his mind was concentrated away from me. In the end I wrote to Dundee. Two plays a

159

week, twice nightly Wednesday and Saturday. Four pounds, I believe. I wondered which photograph to send. I decided the dark sultry one was the most flattering. Too flattering, perhaps. When I arrived at the theatre washed out after the sleepless night journey, he didn't recognize me. However he cheered up. I had a good carrying voice, confidence, and seemingly a fair wardrobe.

With two plays a week there was much more to stuff into the memory. Rehearsals hard and to the point. Effects, business clear cut once and for all. If it was botched, it was *out*. And clothes: my wardrobe couldn't be stretched indefinitely. I hadn't the first idea about dressmaking. The youngish character woman, her solid legs very much on the ground from hard experience, took me to a second-hand shop. She turned over piles of clothing disengaging a fetid whiff. I made an excuse to get outside. I had to improvise with safety-pins and botched tacking. My mother sent me a parcel of frocks discarded by a young friend going abroad to another climate.

My digs were perched high in a grim tenement, with no internal stairs. You scaled the outer walls at the back, up metal stairways giving on to small openwork landings. My front bed-sitting-room overlooked the steep drop of Hawk Hill. At dawn I woke to the rolling thunder of timber waggons rising to a crashing crescendo down the nobbly cobbles. My young-worn landlady was making-do on her husband's tram-conductor's pay. No bathroom. Her bare starchy diet I found so uncongenial that I suggested buying my own food. She had never eaten some of the green vegetables I bought in and didn't know how to prepare them. Potatoes and root crops were her familiar staple. Her salads, a cooked jumble of diced carrots, dried peas and potato stained with beetroot. My catering may have eased things a little financially, but at the cost of more work. Once a week I made my way across an ugly tract fronting the estuary (Broughty Ferry bright and inviting on the other side), past warehouses, over truck-rails, to the municipal baths for a first-class soak – eightpence I believe, including soap and towel – I brought my own. The second and third-class alternatives I never sampled.

At Christmas my kind landlady invited me to share their dinner in the kitchen. We sat at a scrubbed table with a white cloth – I don't remember any decorations. I believe her husband celebrated with a glass of something. Beef. And then the moment for the pudding. It stood solid on the plate, glaucous and pitted with black currants. It cut clean in hard, greyish wedges with dark patches of something crushed. My heart sank, how was I going to get this down. The little boy's eyes glistened.

160

In a gesture of bravado he unbuckled his belt to announce his joyous assault on the crown of the feast.

A local publican treated the company and friends to a coach-outing to Gleneagles – lunch and tea at the famous hotel. An indifferent cold meal was laid out for us at a long table when all but the last delaying residents had finished. A hard stare from one or two as though we should have been accommodated in the servants' hall. The male guests we saw, comfortable in the lounge or diving in the warm indoor swimming-bath, were disgustingly fleshy and pink after the bleached bony Scots of the hard factory streets of Dundee or the grind of Hawk Hill – a different race, glossy and plump, like porkers ready for the market. After tea in the sun-parlour, there was an exodus of our coach party into the writing-room to purloin a sheet or two of headed paper or a bright postcard, as evidence and for future display. Even the moorland country round seemed laid on for trippers and hotel guests.

The actor-manager of the company was a tall debonair, anyone-for-golf type, easy-going, young for his age. His wife and leading-lady, in contrast, tightening, bags already under her eyes. The male juvenile lead – probably her choice – was a big soft vain young man, in love with himself. He liked to show himself off at a central table in the main *café-dansant* and have the local girls compete.

So there was only the 'heavy' man, solid, not bad-looking, a man's man, something of a safe father figure. With the difference that he was the opposite of mine. Blunt instead of acute, a little sentimental, no cynicism, incapable of sarcasm. But the only real point of contact was his masculinity, enhanced by a reserve. No talker. He didn't show his hand.

I first met him, apart from the theatre, when I was buying my portable gramophone. This was outside the shop. I had already chosen my records – mostly Jack Smith and Layton and Johnstone – and now I was hovering, considering, making up my final mind about hire purchase. He suggested that he buy it all back from me when I was tired of it, at the end of the season, to give to his old mother in Essex or somewhere. (At the back of my mind I was wondering how my choice of records would appeal to an old lady.) He carried the lot back for me up to my digs.

'You know he wears a wig?' My landlady a few days later. She evidently thought him too old and unromantic to be coming to tea in my bed-sitting room. (The hair brushed over his forehead *was* a little too thick and brown – but I didn't hold that against him.) And I was deter-

161

mined to play with fire. To find out. Or rather to play with matches, because the potential risks involved never even crossed my mind. In my middle-class suburban world chastity was the conventional rule. (Wartime licence with the boys on leave from the trenches long forgotten.) The hazards of promiscuity, risks and preventatives exclusively a masculine concern.

The way it happened – trivial, unromantic – was I suppose a comment on his way of life. His experience built on snatched encounters, a technique wary of interruption, to accomplish with the minimum fuss. In my room, the door unlocked, the tea things on the table, the landlady's kitchen-living-room a few feet away, no need to undress with caminicks. It was brief, furtive, no more than a poke – to use the ugly denigrating word. Only the stain on my clothes to tell me it had really happened.

That same evening another disillusion. In the play the manager had to kiss me. As usual I turned a cheek, but now he held my face firmly to plant his kiss on a hard mouth. In the last act, when I fainted in the drawing-room, and was picked up, a hand dared to stray. So – my reserved, reliable, almost father-figure was no more than a boastful schoolboy! He had to play the man's man in the dressing-room. What was there to brag about?

While the brief encounters lasted they meant só little, yet paradoxically they taught me so much. The nonsense of the build-up of the supreme importance of taking this step. In fact a nothing compared to the profound disturbance long since, the surrender of the mind and the will to the ravishing pleasures of the imagination and to guilty abasement. The flat reality dissipated once and for all my girlhood dreams of man the conqueror. The fantasy that persisted even after the freemasonry of the stage, where sex was exploited as an act for the show: fetching femininity, tough masculinity, but underneath the rivalry or comradeship of fellow-artists did in fact neutralize, approximate the sexes. Men as bitchy or as cosy as women. But I had grown up in another climate: neutrality, masochism the approved feminine role: 'less than the dust'. Sexuality in women an affront, breasts horrid and vulgar, 'the fastidiousness which compels English boys to keep women at a distance'.* The delusion of man the conqueror had persisted.

But now his urgent whispered question confessed him in the dark, unaware, asking, not making me react, and vulnerable. I didn't answer because I didn't know what 'coming' meant. But I began to understand the

*While I Remember, Stephen Mckenna, 1921, p.75.

162

complexity, the mutual dependence of sensual response, the power of the woman to rape the man's ego, and to deceive. The nullity of half-hearted contact with neither sparking the electric charge. I soon decided that cold intimacy was not a lesson I wanted to learn, a warning how not to mature, not to grow old and tepid, loveless and half-hearted like this kindly dull man. The signals from the other men soon died down, I remained aloof, as 'chaste' as before.

I returned to my Jack Smith records, and I went around a little now with the comfortable homespun character woman. We called on her friends the other side of the estuary. At tea-time: 'Will I cream it?' 'Yes please.' (How original.) But this was only a pretty Scottish euphemism for thin milk.

Our repertoire was not very different from that of the Lena Ashwell's on its lighter side. No Shakespeare of course, and nothing heavier than Pinero's *The Second Mrs Tanqueray*. In *The Faithful Heart* I played the worldly fiancée of the hero (the manager), torn between his loyalty to me and his espousal of a little heart-throb girlie (his wife in pinafore dress, pigtails and flattened in a liberty-bodice). In the either-her-or-me scene, I had to disengage myself, give him up and make my dignified exit: 'No' – a moving gesture of restraint – 'stay exactly where you are.' I got a round of applause – but the sympathy should have stayed with her. A special rehearsal was called. I had to play it harder, colder. I gave it all I had in an arrogant ruling-class voice. But the harder I played it, the more the wee Scots liked it. They understood this kind of woman, they were on my side, against the 'young' interloper. Give it her, the little besom!

On a rare day of spring sunshine, I felt the urgent need to expand a little, to respond to the promise in the air. Discarding the eternal coat, I chose a frock – the only one I had never worn on the Dundee stage – the tart's dress in the thriller tour. It was warm solid-fitting black satin, shiny, slashed with scarlet, tight sleeves spreading at the wrist and flaring skirt. I ventured into a patch of sun at the top of the metal stairs, to test the climate. The boy was coming up; when he spotted me, he gasped, stared and let out a wolf whistle. Hell! I should have to go back and change. I stood irresolute, and then went on down the stairs, to be safely lost, swallowed up anonymously in Dundee's steep dark preoccupied clatter.

The last Saturday night of the season, there was a send-off from our faithful drab audience. Little presents were handed up, a queue formed down the side street to the stage door. Mostly women waiting to kiss

163

their favourite character goodbye. I escaped through the front of the house. I had been handed up one or two tiny presents and some frightful outsize artificial silk cami-nicks. I was laughing about these to the heavy man, who had come to say goodbye.

'They look expensive, to me,' he said rather severely.

Of course – they were from him!

He gave me his address, in case...

'In case?'

'You ever want help.'

'Help?'

'If you're ever in trouble.'

How priceless!

I was loath to part with my gramophone. But he had written to his mother. She was expecting it. I had to let it go. I didn't mind, I had been ready for him to take my maidenhead – leaving me with a rather shabby memory – but I did mind him taking my gramophone, my romantic solace, and all my favourite records.

In August I went on another family holiday to Brittany. When we landed off the Channel boat, Mother had a temperature and her face and arms were red and puffy. The French doctor diagnosed – bugs! She had fallen a victim in the second-, or was it the third-class sleeping saloon? Father, with five children to accommodate, had economized on the tickets – he should of course have booked a cabin for my mother. He himself was going on a golfing holiday. I had slept on deck, flat on a rug, more comfortable than slumped in a deckchair. Our letter of complaint to the passenger line was answered in non-commital terms and carried still pinned to it the internal memo, 'Send usual bug letter.' A comment on the standard of living at the time! The tired old vermin-infested accommodation that spread the pests afield.

After the break it was back to work. With my holiday glow I went the round of the agents. Seaside hair carefully set and undulated with the tongs, in my best fawn three-piece, a silky material flower in the lapel. Nothing doing in Charing Cross Road, only bespoke artists welcomed, for me the inner door closed, the office boy disregarding. I tried my luck in Garrick Street. I was admitted into the inner sanctum, but he was too friendly, I had to make for the door, back away with a still placating smile. Dean Street, more delays and disappointment. I was tempted to give up and relax in the Copper Kettle – a haven run by ladies with their country nieces as waitresses – up old-time steep stairs with cottage posies perched on small ledges, to nibble cress sandwiches and toasted

164

home-made tea-cake. But I resisted, and pressed on to the Stage Guild, the precursor of Equity. Pinned to the notice board, a new repertory, casting now. The actor-manager was affable but unimpressive, a little man talking big: high-class venture, exceptional cast – I had never heard of Ross-on-Wye – every likelihood of expanding into a larger centre, etc., etc. There was a vacancy for a juvenile. For no good reason, and almost against my better judgment, I felt strongly drawn to accept the role. I went home content. No misgivings. Looking forward in confident expectation, quite illogically convinced that this unlikely venture was going to open up the future for me.

From the beginning this little repertory season assumed for me a charm and a character all its own.

It started off just like the cliché opening of the short story in the woman's magazine that in my freelance days I was never to be able to turn out for my bread-and-butter. I arrived at the little country station lugging my heavy suitcase, on a Sunday afternoon in soft September, and stood hesitating. No digs, no addresses. The small market-town un-visited up to now by theatre companies. And just then the 'interesting' stocky dark young man turned up and offered to carry my bag. But, I explained, I didn't know where to go. He had the answer, that is if I didn't mind sharing a sitting-room. It so happened there was a vacancy in *his* digs, and it was quite near the theatre, or rather the hall, as it was in fact. He'd played there in amateur theatricals.

So we set off down the quiet High Street, past the closed shops and silent pubs. I followed him through an unlocked doorway up steep wooden stairs into an old house, and a long room. The sunlight flickered through a tree at the back on to dark furniture, wooden easy chairs, a stretch of bare table. It was like a study, the shelves half-empty, waiting.

The warm West-Country landlady welcomed me, took it all for granted, draped the top half of the table, brought in a big teapot, and settled us down to tea for two.

He was a schoolmaster, but nothing academic about him. A country-man, a local man. I could picture him in leggings on a farm, or in a muddy field in a country sport. He seemed dissatisfied. He was looking to find his way outside, to make the horny old world kind to him. He was stepping out now from the woman's magazine and into a short story by D. H. Lawrence.

But I didn't venture far into that short story. It was the schoolmaster's

165

role to add to the interest of mine, and to put me in just the right place to meet and have daily contact with the man who was to play the leading part in my life for the next fourteen years.

My homely little bedroom tilted over the street so that my bed crawled a little nearer the window every night. It overlooked on the opposite side of the road the bed-sitting room of the stage manager, Ronald Kidd.

It was when we were getting to know each other than Ronald told me his first impression when he met me – that I was so absurdly like his cousin Margery whom he had fallen in love with when he was fifteen. Of course when I started to talk, I was quite different. I liked the way his ears lifted a little when he smiled, his solid round neck, and his big cleft chin. I assumed, of course, that an attractive man of his age would certainly have a settled background. (He was in fact thirty-nine, married, and with a little girl. I was twenty-six.) He had an unselfconscious manner, at ease with himself, and so it seemed the world in general. Although we were both discovering that we had been led up the path and that our 'high-class' rep was only operating in a little all-purpose local hall, he made no attempt, when he introduced himself as the stage-manager, at any status-propping. The word wasn't in his vocabulary. Ronald, I found, had a completely unworldly outlook, and no class consciousness.

It was soon clear to me that he and his wife were living apart. He had his digs in Soho, and she and their child a home in the West Country. Much later on, when I was in his digs in London, and he was moving, I found an attractively designed Wigmore Hall programme billing his wife in a piano recital, to be followed by a *diseuse*. In the same folder there was a photograph of her in evening dress. 'What shall I do with it?' I asked him. 'Throw it away,' he said. It seemed a shame. He told me then that they got married after her father crashed on the stock exchange. He was not her favourite suitor, but she had turned to him. And although Ronald had already begun to doubt their compatibility, now he felt he couldn't let her down. But in his heart, he told me, he knew he was making a mistake. Ronald was warmly attached to his little girl. Her last affectionate scrawl, covered in kisses, was crammed into his wallet, bulging with press cuttings and cards.

Ronald and I rambled together in the enchanting countryside all around. A lingering mellow autumn was keeping the valleys green and the tawny beechwoods still on fire. Ronald with something of the tender romantic sentiment of his Edwardian boyhood days, was still young in

166

heart and ready to fall in love. And I, seeing myself happily reflected in his eyes, ready to respond to his strong, warm nature, the attraction of his experience, and, as I soon discerned, his fundamental integrity and seriousness of purpose. It was only after writing of this time that I began to understand why it was that every year – even when I was becoming an old woman and dreading the approach of winter – as the summer faded and the leaves began to turn, I found my spirits rising, the fountain beginning to spring again, responding to the echo of the unfading autumn of so long ago.

Our rep season came to an abrupt halt just before Christmas. The actor-manager decamped to London, in debt to the company and local suppliers. From now on, without any formal ties to hold us, Ronald and I were to link our lives together. At first we were still separated in between tours, he in Soho, and I at home, although I spent most of my time in London. In the summer we were both engaged together on a sunny tour to the south-coast resorts, and this was virtually our honeymoon.

Ronald came of a medical family, and it was his advice that was to solve for me the problem that was getting more and more of a handicap: the monthly 'curse'. Our family doctor, who used to play tennis with us, and never of course examined me, had been giving me successively stronger pain-killers, and once when I was in a bad way a hypodermic injection. I had learnt on the stage that the sovereign remedy was gin. I would buy a tiny bottle and take the contents with hot water, preferably in bed. I sipped it down, shuddering a little, and by the time the walls were rocking, I was released painlessly in a voluptuous stupor. Ronald persuaded me that a good gynaecologist would be better than gin. A woman, he insisted. 'If you only knew how doctors, among themselves, discuss their women patients.' The gynaecologist I consulted took me into her Wigmore Street nursing-home for a simple curetting operation.

I walked into the operating theatre and was introduced to the young anaesthetist. This was her first operation. She was so nervous, she couldn't find my hand. I had to shake hers. I stretched myself out on the table, and she took over. She knocked me right out with a strangle of chloroform and as suddenly brought me round again gasping. This sequence of choke and revive was repeated more than once – my head thrashing about desperately. At last she dispatched me for good.

When I came to – prematurely I suppose – I felt as if a wild beast was tearing my entrails. I tried to jump out of bed. The nurse restrained me. 'I'll get you a couple of aspirin,' she soothed. 'I expect it's the iodine.' I was moaning, tears pouring down my face. (I have discovered since that I am allergic to iodine.) About ten minutes later, like a tap turned off, the pain vanished. And now I was conscious of my bruised aching jaws.

Next morning, a little old woman crept slowly round the door burdened with a bucket of coal and a wooden box with sticks, shavings and brush. She crawled on her knees, her small bent skull intent on her work, her little claws clearing the cinders, making up the fire. I was half embarrassed to be lying there – restored now – while this great-grandmother crouched at her work.

'Lucky there's a lift!' I interjected. I was on the top floor. 'Oh no!' shocked. 'Too dirty – doctors only.' She turned defensively: 'She's very good to me, is Matron. *She* won't turn me away. I can sit in the kitchen as long as I like.' She went on staring, the past and future written on her old worn face.

The operation did the trick. The pain vanished for ever. My father, the responsible paterfamilias, paid the fees. I always spent what I earned.

In contrast to our seaside tour in the comfortable South, another we shared later on visited the big centres in the hard industrial North. I had a foretaste as we travelled up the backbone of England through the once cruel border country, still uninhabited. The train made its slow ascent through the wide valleys, dwarfed by the barren slopes rising unending either side, not even a glimpse of sheep, only the occasional stream, cutting a white line. A drear no man's land that gave as strong a feeling of the history of the tough island as its ancient castles and cathedrals. In Glasgow I was to discover, away from the prosperous busy centre, in the working-class area where we had our digs, almost another race: children deformed by rickets, adults stunted, shapeless women, young men with bony pallid faces.

With the competition of the film circuits opening up everywhere, touring companies and repertories were closing down. I started to freelance in editorial work, for publishers and the public in general, and I came to live in London, in Ronald's digs in Soho.

Introduced to the London scene, I was coming of age politically. I have written in an earlier book – *Fire Under the Carpet* – much more about our lives together, and especially about the thirties. This was the key time for both of us, the 'low dishonest decade' when the contagion of Fascism was spreading, giving a sense of impending danger. Democratic rights, long taken for granted, were now at risk. Ominously, our own so-called National Government, soon virtually Tory, was appeas-

ing, condoning, even flirting with Fascism. There was high unemploy-
ment, hunger marchers making their way on foot in disciplined ranks to
demonstrate in the capital and put their case to Parliament, treated as a
dangerous element, to be contained by police cordons and baton
charges, and their leaders arrested. It was official policy apparently to
discredit them by associating them with disorder. Ronald's sworn affida-
vit about the use of police *agents-provocateurs* disguised as working-
class men in the 1932 Hunger March whom he saw trying to provoke
aggression and then drawing regulation police truncheons to make
arrests, was one of the issues that was to lead on to the setting up of the
National Council for Civil Liberties – as it was first called – on 22 Febru-
ary 1934. Ronald took on the job of general secretary. I had learned
from experience his uncompromising sense of personal responsibility
that led him, when he was aware of injustice, not just to be content to
deplore, but to get involved, to *do* something about it. And I was ready
now to join forces with him. Since my schooldays I had been looking for
something worthwhile, an incentive for living, and now I was finding it
working for the Council, voluntarily at first, and then as assistant
secretary.

Ronald started to work on the job with enthusiasm and optimism,
without any funds, with no office and no staff, from his own digs,
converting his single room into an office, our modest living quarters
partitioned and curtained off. It was because, in the climate of the
times, the need for a body to defend civil rights was so acute, and the
setting up so timely, that Ronald was able from the first to enrol
influential public figures to sponsor us as vice-presidents – and
contribute a minimum of two guineas apiece. Of course Ronald's
reassuring personality played a key part. His manner and style carried
the conviction of a man with no party-political or personal axe to grind.
Indeed his standpoint – as was that of the Council's first president,
E. M. Forster – was ethical rather than political, although, of course,
Ronald was very politically aware. More important still than the big
names was the voluntary help given us by the legal profession: brilliant
young lawyers ready to draft amendments to parliamentary bills to put
to sympathetic MPs, to give legal advice and to defend cases in court,
with no fees, not even claiming expenses. The work absorbed us both.
After office hours, there was observing to do at outdoor meetings and
demonstrations. Ronald had speaking engagements in the evening, and
often at weekends. It was after one of these, on a Sunday in Hampstead,
that he was knocked down by a car on a pedestrian crossing, and his leg

was broken. He left hospital, with a heavy plaster casing from foot to thigh, to get back to his full load of work as usual. At night he had three flights of stairs to climb to our top-floor flat. The following year he spent time in hospital with an irregular heart condition. In the war years the London blitz took its toll. 1941 was a fatal year for both of us. Ronald's health was failing. He gave up the post of general secretary and took up limited duties as director. I too resigned as assistant secretary. The dislocations of war, the big increase in cost of office materials, had put the Council into serious financial straits. Cuts had to be made in staff, and my mind was now set on being with my mother who was terminally ill with cancer. With her exceptional understanding, and the warmth of her loving nature, she had always respected the independence and integrity of her children. Her care and concern for me included Ronald too, once she had got to know and like him and to treat him as one of the family. It was a daily anguish now to see her strong resilient nature weakened and plagued by pain and still stronger drugs, and to be torn between a longing for her release and the dread of losing her forever. It was at her funeral, when I was standing by my father, that for a split second I saw Ronald as a white-faced stranger, before I recognized him, with a dreadful stab of foreboding.

In the spring he was too ill to go to the Council's annual general meeting. He worked at home, still writing articles for the Council's journal. He corrected the proofs of his pamphlet on the freedom of the press from his bed, the cylinder of oxygen beside him. Till the end he stayed calm, stoical, uncomplaining, harvesting his ebbing strength. E. M. Forster gave a fine tribute to him at his cremation, and included it in his collected pieces, *Two Cheers for Democracy*, published in 1951. Kingsley Martin's broadcast appreciation went out on the Overseas and Empire Service.

In my empty life, I had nothing now to take me on from day to day but fortitude. I suppose the best medicine was having to adapt and work in a completely new environment. I was installed now in the planning division of the Ministry of Works as a temporary assistant principal. I would never have chosen the Civil Service, but in wartime jobs were scarce, and after my mother's death I wanted to fix up something that could take care of Ronald as well, since his health was so vulnerable. The planning division soon broke away to form the key nucleus of the new Ministry of Town and Country Planning, with leading architects and planners co-opted temporarily to prepare the blueprints for post-war Britain, starting with the new towns. But although the personnel was most congenial, I had nothing at all to contribute in that field. When I heard of a vacancy in the Ministry of Information I applied and transferred – as a temporary, I was free to move – into their publications division as a commissioning editor. Now I was in my element, and working with journalists I found it lively and absorbing. But at the end of the war, MOI dwindled into the Central Office of Information. Still doing the same work as before, I was turned into an information officer. All too soon, the Cold War clouded everything, killing incentive, even affecting the slant of our output. The Tory cuts of 1952 did for me what I ought to have done for myself. I was made redundant. I had been ten years in the service and entitled to redundancy pay. I started off doing the sensible thing, chasing, rather half-heartedly, after good lucrative jobs. It was my revulsion when one of these even seemed likely to mature that made me begin to see daylight. The sensible course was never right for me. The competitive office scene held no future for me. I wanted to be on my own. First of all I would have a go at freelance journalism.

– 6 –
So It All Came True

In holiday mood and still luxuriating in my freedom, I made a leisurely start at freelancing. First of all I took the easy, and familiar route – articles for COI. It was fun now to be at the other end, doing the interviewing, collecting the material, never, of course, touching on the Cold War. I did some book-reviewing for small publications, long since deceased, and reportage articles for trade union journals. I wasted time trying to write romantic fiction for women's magazines. The single one accepted earned me the miserly fee of £5. I spent too much time and trouble on all the work I did in relation to the fee. This applied especially to a sketch I read on the BBC Home Service, *Portrait of My Grandmother*. When I started to tune into my dear Vovó in her world of so long ago, I was drawn to browse, with a Portuguese dictionary, on her earliest recollections and her fascinating *History of Brazil*. She quoted the chronicler on the first voyage of discovery. As their ship sailed towards the inviting white sands, the curious friendly Indians, the gentle cannibals, crowded down to greet them. Their hair and skin, he recorded, had the gloss and burnish of birds' feathers and the sheen of the pelt of wild creatures. Not long after, a cousin from Brazil told me of the plight of the descendants of these coastal Indians, long since forced back into the harsh interior, many of them living in destitution, suffering from a chronic infection of the intestine from amoeba in their unhealthy drinking water.

Towards the end of the year it was clear that I would have to bolster up my freelance takings with some other regular form of income. The only one I could think of that would also – as I then believed – give me the spare time I needed, was teaching. Once my bugbear, now, after the major reforms of the Butler Act, something of a challenge. It was the

172

secondary modern school I had in mind. I wrote to the Surrey County Council – my flat was in their area – for advice on how to start. The only way, they told me, was to take two years' teacher training. Out of the question, of course. Instead I crossed the road to have a talk with a progressive headmistress of a good secondary modern girls' school. Not easy, she said. But if I was determined – I didn't of course let on that this was only my financial second string – I could perhaps make it. At present, she went on, her staff were short-handed, some of them away with girls at a summer camp. But I could come and observe lessons in my subjects: English and French.

Next morning I had a very friendly welcome in the staff room, mistaken for a supply teacher. They brushed aside my explanations. A very good little form, for English, my subject. The girls had their poetry books. So that was how I started. In – not at the deep end this time – rather the happy little shallow end, to learn, as I have done all my life, as I went along. Observing was very helpful too, to give me an idea of the contemporary approach.

I was taken on the following term at a mixed school nearby, on a temporary basis to be tested in due course by an inspector. Now I had my own form of twelve-year-olds, with a register to keep in order. This register, and the simple job of collecting and ticking for the dinner money, was turned by a series of meticulous, ridiculous columns into what was, for me, an impossible accountancy problem. All this had to be done at lightning speed in front of the class. I left it all blank. I had the usual quota of cheeky naughty boys, and the silly awkward one who joined in at the end, and always went too far, to land himself as the scapegoat every time. There was a rather beautiful gypsy girl, much older than the others, contemptuous and bored. I made all the mistakes, but I managed in the end to stay put as the boss. I remember one morning after a bad day looking up to the sky for inspiration, and deciding to try to win them with poetry. To start off with, Wordsworth's simple, lovely little lyric celebrating the end of winter with its happy rhymes.

I sang out blithely: 'The cock is crowing . . .'

'OOOEEE, miss!' from the boys, in mock protest, and shocked at me!

'Don't be silly.' I started again . . Now more of them joined in. They were enjoying this. I don't know how many times I bashed it out, before I got on to the second line – which only made it worse: 'The stream is flowing . . .' Now the girls were giggling, and with the third line: 'The small birds twitter' they all joined in. I had to give up. I turned nasty,

173

and we did grammar, instead.

The head had asked me to take on a small group of a dozen boys, who wanted eventually to qualify as draughtsmen, for a lesson in applied geometry. As I hadn't a clue in maths, he gave me a foolproof teachers' guide covering the course, lesson by lesson and stage by stage. I had to get this off by heart, like the script of a play, because I couldn't let these eager children down. I found it rather touching that at such a tender age they should settle down so earnestly to prepare themselves as little wage-earners. It was at this lesson that the inspector turned up – rather unfairly I thought – for my test. I told him that maths was outside my range, and that I was an arts woman, but he put on a very severe face. He didn't expect to start off with excuses and pleas. I had as usual taken trouble to get a very clear and careful figure on the board. The children were on their best behaviour and I trundled out the model lesson, hoping that the approved pattern would last out, and that I wouldn't get any awkward questions. The boys backed me up and stayed silent, heads bent over their graph paper. Before the end, the inspector began to make his way towards the door. 'I think I can leave you now,' he was smiling. 'Oh, just one point,' he turned back. 'I heard you more than once refer to five-tenths. Why not simply, a half?'

You *idiot*, I kicked myself. Of course it was. It had never occurred to me! My brain raced feverishly for an answer. 'Their rulers,' I came out with, 'one side divided into eighths, and the other in tenths. I want them to get used to the tenths.'

'I see,' he said. 'I felt sure there must be a good reason.'

At the end of term get-together, the head in cap and gown was moving among the staff. 'Have you fixed anything up for next term?' he asked me. 'No,' I said hopefully. 'Then I think you ought to get going at once.' This was rather crushing. But just then, as though on cue, there was a knock at the door. A florist's sheaf was handed in. For me! From my form! All the naughty boys had signed the note too! I was surprised and touched, and grateful. After all my shortcomings, they had forgiven, and accepted me. The young are very generous.

I can't remember who it was advised me to get in touch with the head-mistress of a girls' school at the Elephant & Castle in London. She was a strong determined woman, dedicated to helping the deprived girls of this poor neighbourhood, confident that with a good staff she could, through education, open up the future for them. She was prepared to take me on.

Now I was harnessed as it were to somebody else's will. I knew her

174

cause was right, and I could see that she was prepared to help me to serve it to the best of my ability. I had teetered rather aimlessly in freelancing, so I supposed that this was now the best that I could do – something useful. But my heart sank at the prospect of being caught in the hard path of duty, and enclosed in a world of women. I liked and admired my own sex, but not exclusively. I felt I was saying goodbye to part of my own world. I had chosen teaching only as a sideline to help me out. Now it was swallowing me up. My mother, laughing, used to say to me in childhood when there was something unpleasant on the way – medicine or the dentist – 'Courage! mon ami, le Diable est mort!' (quoting, maybe, from *The Three Musketeers*). The devil meant nothing to me, but it was her voice, her spirit, tender and courageous, that fortified me. So now again it was – 'Courage! mon ami . . .'

First day of term. Staff elbowing each other in a friendly jumble in our poky leisure and meal room – an architectural hiccup, stuck halfway above the first floor, up a tight stairway, where our lunch trays had to come up sideways. The coats and sportsgear cupboard projected dangerously over nothing. I was afraid to step right inside in case I crashed through on to the landing horribly below.

In the medley of women, I recognized the inevitable old-time disciplinarian, pinchfaced, chalk-dry; in contrast, the assured science mistress, who initiated the girls in a special, persuasive, hushed-sweet voice on how our bodies worked, male and female. Coming from the Walworth Road, some of them were already learning it the hard way, washing warily at the kitchen sink, and in a few disturbed families it was 'Uncle' doing the job upstairs, if Dad was too persistently away. They were all familiar with the painful birth at home. The big, rather endearing Girl-Guidey sports mistress, who had left her Teddy on the pillow at home, was oiling her bat, ready for the remote suburban playing-field. There was a comfortable, reassuring music mistress, and the assorted young – the dedicated, and those filling-in till life caught up with them.

And now, just in time for assembly, stilettoes snapping up the stairs, a vivid newcomer lit up the scene in her silky-shine scarlet mack. Molly Thomas with her black hair, green eyes and colourless skin had something of a little Elizabeth Taylor face, but mobile, laughing, half-mocking, and a blithe self-confident air of accepting little in the way of rules, making her own as she went along. Mediterranean, I thought, maybe French or Spanish. In the staff room she was exotic. Yet everybody else seemed to take her for granted – the new art mistress.

Molly, I was to find, had no contact with the Mediterranean. She was

175

Welsh, from a mining village in the Garw Valley, over the hills from the Rhondda. At grammar school she had hesitated between English and Art. Art won and she took her degree at Brighton College of Art, taking her turn too in minding the family tobacconist and sweet shop in a sleazy back street in Brighton. Just back from a travelling scholarship in Italy, she was delighted to have landed a job where everyone wanted to be. So now it was the adventure of London!

Molly was twenty-one, I was fifty-two, yet surprisingly, from the start, she cottoned on to me. And it was the impact of her young vital personality that was to enliven and stimulate me, the happy collision of our points of view and our experience, her youthful sanguine – sometimes brash – confidence in her head-on way to achieve, that was to bring colour and interest to what I had dreaded as the hard path of duty, and was in the end even to transform the future for me. Molly had nothing of the usual, the natural egocentricity of the young, her generous creative spirit spilt over and refreshed me too. She and I and another young member of the staff, who was in the same boat, all of us starting on our first firm teaching assignment, made a threesome to go out together after school, to talk and have a little snack supper, sometimes overlooking the river in a restaurant left over from the Festival of Britain.

The head let me settle in easily with a small form of twenty-five rather backward girls. After my big mixed class, I found no difficulty in working with them once we had got used to each other. They were much more responsive and more impressionable than the solid Surrey children from easier backgrounds. But a term or so later I was given a class of thirty-nine thirteen-year-olds, and that did mean I had to be on my mettle and to work hard to arrive at a tolerable state of daily harmony.

Molly went to work with a will in her form. The school photo shows them a rather rag-bob-tail collection of deprived eleven, or was it twelve-year-olds. Molly's youth, her looks, her figure, made her irresistibly the girls' ideal – their film star! (it was still the films then, not yet the universal telly). Admiringly: 'I like your bra, Miss.' Up to now the art lesson had been their opportunity for a good old free-for-all, a general scurry round, with water and paint all over the place. But now Molly held them. They caught fire from her creative drive. She put something exciting on the board, and soon they were all eager to have a go. (I was surprised to discover in my own form how uninhibited these London girls were, how easy it was for them to unlock, and try for themselves, in drama and poetry.) Molly's art classes generated an excitement through the whole school and made an impact outside. When the LCC held an exhibition at County Hall of the output of their London schools, our school was chosen to demonstrate the achievement in art. Molly was invited to take the exhibition stand for a week with ten to fifteen of her girls, in a live art-class display, against a background of their delightful original murals and paintings.

Molly's idea of stimulating interest by entering a nationwide painting competition run by Cadbury, met with an enthusiastic response. Once the girls had attached the stipulated three sweet wrappers, Molly sent in all their efforts, good bad and indifferent – and some were remarkable. The output from our school must have flooded the market. At our end-of-term function, a bulky pile of outsize chocolate boxes were handed out to the joy of the girls. And then it was the *Sunday Pictorial* competition. The winning paintings to be displayed in the prestigious Piccadilly Gallery, and rewarded this time with money prizes. How I wish I had one or two of these stark, colourful and singular paintings on my wall today to attract and remind me.

It was when Molly came to my flat for a Saturday/Sunday weekend, that I discovered that she wasn't nearly as sophisticated as I had at first supposed. On Saturday afternoon when we had finished shopping, we passed a sleazy little café with one or two dead-end types drinking out of plastic containers. Incredibly, Molly wanted to drop in for tea. Then it was the cinema. Sadly, there was absolutely nothing on, a dead-loss all round. But I couldn't deny her twice over. At the big theatre-cinema, dwindling now – the rising-organ turn-off – we sat through a romantic musical with a big Germanic blonde and a plumpish Caruso counterpart. But Molly emerged satisfied, happy. Years later she explained to me the established pleasure-association. Saturday was not Saturday without the treat of tea out, followed by the pics.

A bigger surprise, and this was terms later. We had all been working hard at a big drama festival. Now at the last minute the head asked Molly to design a programme cover. Always ahead of her time, Molly dashed off a zig-zag of bold handwriting – instead of Roman type – with a hint of decoration in one corner. It was informal, and I thought well suited to our school effort. But the head was disgusted. She tossed it back contemptuously. 'Can't you do better than *that*!' Molly withered, turned into a lost little girl. I discovered her, after school, in the empty staff room. She had retreated into the cupboard, her head buried in a big coat. Sobbing, she told me. I rallied her: 'What does *she* know about art? She hasn't a clue. Don't upset yourself. It doesn't matter.'

But most significant of all, when her mother came to London, Molly went dumb, took a back seat to give Mam her due, as the centre of attraction. Even much later on when Molly was married and her mother was staying, Molly pointed out naïvely and with pride at a party how it was her mother who attracted the men all round her. I tried to disabuse her, to tell her that the men were being nice and attentive because they wanted to get into *her* good graces. Earlier on, when Molly and I were teaching, her mother confided in me, as one mature woman to another, how she hoped that Molly would stick to it, and make good to the top of her profession. It was so clear to me that with her looks, her personality, the variety and range of her creative ability, her contemporary flair, Molly would never be contained by the school routine. She was going to have a meteoric career – still unpredictable. I imagined it might well be on the stage. She had an irresistible comedy sense.

I remember at the end of a school week, when a few of the younger ones were still in the staff room finishing off a bag of plums, we got talking about the weekend ahead, the joys of lingering in bed. Molly busy with a ripe plum turned mischievously to Jane, a pretty, very young, good little buttoned-up newlywed, something of a Puritan left-winger. What did *they* do? Breakfast in bed? Innocently, artlessly, she went on probing, while contemplating her plum, delicately nibbling, sipping, licking her fingers. Jane getting pinker, primly struggled to stay detached, not to join in, and get caught in Molly's naughty tender trap. All this was before Albert Finney in the rollicking film *Tom Jones*, used the same device of miming with food in sexy comedy, in his tête-à-tête supper with the fly-by-night as they eyed each other, challenging, across the supper table and exchanged juicy morsels in bawdy courtship.

Another early experience with Molly was the weekend we spent in a country cottage with her hopeful young man. He had glimpsed Molly through the window of a bus as it crawled, and he walked, along Oxford Street. Molly was radiant, glowing with pride after a successful interview to clinch her first job in London. In this electric mood, he caught her eye and smiled, she smiled back. He took a taxi and followed. At Victoria he saw her off on her train. His next move was to invite her to a weekend in the country. Molly agreed if she could bring a friend. I was the duenna. We set off by Green Line, and got off in a leafy lane. There he was, waiting at the crossroads, an elegant, dark, interesting young man. His modest cottage was on a rural hillside overlooking an unspoilt woody valley. The evening meal was strictly vegetarian, little dishes of greenery and radishes and beetroot, but nothing solid and warming, cheesy or eggy. Afterwards, in his cosy sitting room, he pulled down

178

from the shelf volumes of poetry, some of it French. Molly read it to us beautifully. Her Welsh tongue lending itself easily to French. Her mother, as I learned, had French blood in her. Absurdly I felt a little out of it. No one asked *me* to read. The French poetry had taken me back to Brazil and Mademoiselle. I remembered Victor Hugo's: 'Offrant à tout part,/Sa jeune âme à la vie/Et sa bouche aux baisers.' Addressed to a little girl-child, but apt too for Molly – hungry as she was for admiration and love and experience.

He was going next morning to have an early dip in the natural pond screened by trees, and a little way down the valley. Would anyone like to join him? No response. We said goodnight, had our hot baths and then Molly and I in the double bed in his spare room got down to it. 'What did you think of him?' 'Did you like him?' 'What would he be like ...' We went on intimately dissecting him. A muffled cough cut us off dead. The wall behind us was plywood! His head on the pillow on the other side!

Molly was to discover that he was married – hoping for a divorce. She put a full stop to the romance.

Molly confided in snatches the highlights of her after-school Cinderella escape into West End night-life, and back in the small hours into the shared basement flat in Earl's Court Road. She had splashed right into the centre. It had all started after she had been joined by another Brighton girl – the one who had everything: the comfortable family home in the desirable quarter, the successful father with contacts in wealthy London circles. Molly was included in her invitation to a Christmas party in a grand art-deco house in a fashionable square in Knightsbridge – used later on as a setting for Mick Jagger's film, *Performance*. The blue-eyed, fair-haired eldest son of the family, a little younger than Molly, was instantly taken with her. Now he was her escort to the with-it night clubs and parties. She was invited on Sunday to teas at home with the family. He was still at the youthful stage and put her on a pedestal. A little stupid, Molly thought him. And when he did, at a favourable moment, attempt a close-up – I was amused to find that as Molly told it me, she winced, screwed up her face in distaste, Chapel and 'mortal sin' still reinforcing her own virginal reaction. And this after earlier tender passages with a boy in Brighton. 'Did *you* like it?' she pressed me. Or maybe it was even '*Do* you like it?' Surprisingly Molly put me on a level footing, as a contemporary, still in the picture, still engaged in the tender struggle.

But it was not the young man who held her interest for long. It was the sixty-four-year-old father she wanted to talk about. Shall we call him Cuthbert, Bertie for short. He had invited her to supper – melon and smoked salmon – in his own, out-of-this-world gorgeous flat, quite apart from the family home. Music floated through it, television in every room, an intercom talking system. He had fallen in love with her. She was his princess. He wanted to help her in her career, to introduce her to a television producer, have her paint his settings for film. He had in mind a yachting cruise in the Mediterranean and she could invite her friends. He wanted to teach her to play backgammon. 'Backgammon!' That put the lid on it. 'Whatever for?' Molly insisted that I must visit this extraordinary, interesting man, and see for myself. He would be delighted to meet a friend of hers.

So at last I did. Molly was thawing me. Maybe I was getting a little silly too! Bertie's flat was in what was advertised as a luxury block, with its own underground car park, squash court, swimming bath, restaurant and shopping centre. After I rang his bell ... I had to call out to assure him that I was I, before the door unlocked and the heavy curtain parted to admit me. I stepped into an Aladdin's cave of Eastern delight. Concealed neon lighting and a glittering candelabra lit up the purple, dull scarlet and old gold of tapestries, soft curtains, fine rugs, heavy silks that covered, draped, walls and ceiling. The centrepiece there was a circular gilt-framed goddess in old-master oils. The ample sofa-bed was covered in a rich purple and gold thread altar cloth, deviously acquired, so he told me. A thick carpet and expensive Eastern rugs. A door to one side ajar led into – was it a conservatory? I could see green creepers and pots of flowers – in fact it was the bathroom, with gold taps and a television. Cornucopias of fruit for decoration instead of flowers. Bunches of purple grapes, outsize peaches and ripe melons, exuding a sickly-sweet, softly fermenting aroma in the cloying central overheat. The window in an alcove recess was swathed over, not a glimpse of sky or daylight. We were cocooned away from the outside world.

Bertie himself was bleached, bald and hairless. A hard-boiled pink-and-white solid-built urban ... what should I call him? Picturing him theatrically, I could visualize him as a showman, and in that pseudo, contrived setting, that was almost how he was casting himself. He could have taken the stage in a topper and with a gold-top cane and done an elderly, agile, quick-foot routine as the band struck up, to the accompaniment of his own smooth, non-stop patter. Much later on I discovered him in my 1949 *Who's Who*. He described himself as a scientist, inventor and politician (Tory of course). He had a long career entry, and among the credits: honorary rank of colonel, and the French decoration of Chevalier de la Légion d'Honneur.

He was, in fact, engaged now in that soft-voiced patter. But not a word about Molly, his princess; he was selling himself to me. First of all as a cultured man-of-the-world, and then putting it over that he and his flat were the cynosure to attract a wide circle of questing women, the married – and their daughters, the young and ambitious as he had the know-how and the experience and the contacts. There was a little judicious name-dropping from the theatrical and social world. All of this conveying an association with aphrodisiac delights. He burbled on. Finally, we had something to eat, ready prepared in his kitchen, off left. While he was out, I noticed a big silver-framed portrait of a handsome woman – his wife – prominently displayed to disabuse a bemused visitor that Bertie might have any serious intent.

'Molly,' I told her next day at school, 'the man's mad.' She would be nutty to waste any more time with him. Her dream flat was a tarted-up bedsitter, airless and with the fruit going rotten. His influence, his contacts, like his yachting days, all in the past. His know-how, his advice to her, decadent, as useless as his rotting fruit.

And yet, it was through Bertie – although Molly was the deciding factor – that I was to meet my future husband.

John Scaffardi like me had a Latin grandfather, an Irish grandmother, and a strong loving rather beautiful mother. So now for an outline of *his* story. It was when Eugenio Giovanni Scaffardi, in his home in Northern Italy, learnt that he was to be sent to Milan to be educated as a priest, that he decided to run away. He emigrated to England. First to Birmingham, where, supported by funds from his family, he learnt the craft of cabinet-making, and then to London. He met and married an Irish girl, Helen Dole. Money from Italy dried up when it was clear that he did not intend to go back, and that he had broken away from the Roman Catholic Church. His son, also Eugenio Giovanni, was John's father, and like his father a cabinet-maker. Dark-haired and good looking, he married Elizabeth Champney, ten years younger and the daughter of a hansom-cab driver. I met John's mother only in her frail seventies. A rather beautiful, strong-minded old lady, with large sad eyes, but still ready to enjoy a good bit of gossip and a laugh. As a lovely child she was noticed by an artist, invited to pose in his studio, given a golden guinea, and sent home by cab. He found her so patient and good at sitting still that the visits continued till his picture was completed. The family recall the artist, a little vaguely, as Maynard Brown. Could this, I wonder, be

181

Madox Brown, then elderly and established, and she a tender seven or eight? Elizabeth had thirteen children, five of them, in those harsh years, dying in infancy. One of them in her arms in a tram on the way to the doctor. John was the eighth child and so he was christened Henry. And Henry, of course is always turned into Harry – my favourite name for a man, taking me back to my silly young, falling-in-love days – if only there had been someone to fall in love with – 'I'm just wild about Haaareee, and Harry's just wild about me!'

But sadly I got to know him as John, his office name – given him for a reason I no longer remember. When John was a little boy he was run over by a cycle. He told no one, but later on, when his back ached intolerably, his mother took him to the doctor, who told him it would get better. But it didn't. It was only when the spine began to show signs of curvature that he received treatment, and was sent to a hospital in Surrey to be kept strictly lying on his back. Finally, when he was discharged, he had to wear a bone harness that fitted over his head and was strapped across his back. John was followed on his way to his special school by jeering urchins. He discarded the harness. No hospital aftercare in those days, the curvature returned. The family had fallen on hard times. His father, getting older and lazier, preferred to make up a book of bets in the market, without a licence of course, to following his craft. He was picked up and fined, he fell into debt. John, leaving school at fourteen, went to work to help keep his mother. His first job was working on a lathe, without any protective shield; the burning sparks blistered his chest, he would come home exhausted, and his mother would give him supper in bed. For a short while in the thirties John joined the Communist Party, as did a number of the brighter boys he knew. With his generous nature he undertook too heavy a load of voluntary work: selling the *Daily Worker*, distributing leaflets, chalking up notices, etc. He told me about an incident at a meeting in a side street in the East End – typical of many I came across when I was working for the National Council for Civil Liberties. The young cockney speaker on his makeshift flimsy platform, seeing a clump of policemen approaching, called out 'Stand firm, Comrades, we are in our rights here.' Two burly coppers picked him up, platform and all, and pitched him over the paling, and then broke up the meeting, batons at the ready. John took refuge in a doorway to shelter his vulnerable back.

He was working now in the rag trade with a French silk firm. He taught himself French, going to evening classes, and he was good at maths and could readily turn French decimal measurements and money into their English equivalents. Molly remembers too, when she was running her boutique, his expertise in advising her on the texture and colour of materials. It was now that John won about £800 on the pools. He gave presents to all his family and relatives, bought some new clothes and went for a weekend to Paris – the Folies Bergère, the Louvre, Versailles, the lot. A charming young French girl, related to one of the French sponsors, had come to London for a working visit in the firm. In the summer, at holiday time, finding herself short of funds, she asked John if he could lend her £100 to fly to the Riviera. Smiling, she added, to see her lover. John parted with his last £100 from the pools – 'and she didn't even kiss me,' he told me ruefully. 'Lucky for you,' I said when I heard the sequel. She had died on holiday, of galloping consumption. (I had the same feeling of incredulity and shock when I was on the stage and learned that the pretty young juvenile, so full of life, whom I had just been touring with, had died suddenly of the same disease.) The French girl had told her lover to be sure to contact John Scaffardi, when he returned to London, presumably to repay her loan. And her lover was Bertie!

I would much rather that it had been Molly, with her intuitive perception, who had the idea that John and I should meet – but she hadn't even seen him then. It was Bertie's sympathetic hunch. He felt indebted to John, not only the unpaid £100 but for the trouble he was taking, helping out, and straightening up faulty technology in the flat. On his first visit John had found Bertie engaged in do-it-yourself. He had spotted that some of the points were heavily, even dangerously overloaded. He put new ones in for him, and that started him off generally lending a hand. He was quite a regular visitor now, and Bertie was getting attached to him. He wanted to teach him to swim in the baths at the flat building, and he also wanted to do him a good turn by introducing him to me. He put it to Molly. She tells me today that he gave her no idea of any social gap, speaking of John Scaffardi as a friend, he told her of his sensitivity, his sense of humour, and Molly felt that as we both had warm Latin blood, we should get on well together.

Bertie phoned me to say that a friend of his would very much like to get acquainted with me – as a cultured person – or some such nonsense. He went on to tell me something about John – quite misleading. All I can remember was that he dressed well – I think he was trying to build him up. I asked Bertie to invite him to tea with me on Saturday. Teatime came and went, and no sign of him. I rang Bertie to ask, rather crudely, 'What about this type who was supposed to show up for tea?' I was assured that he was on his way. He had been helping in the flat. Bertie didn't tell me that at last John had to be pushed out. He was getting cold feet.

I had conjured up a picture in my mind of a tall, lanky, indeterminate Oxbridge type. Instead, when I opened the door, there was a tough little man, no taller than I, half defiant, but all the same engaging, with a Bob Hoskins appeal. I had an old perm that was growing out, and I hadn't bothered to dress up. We were both of us amused and surprised at each other. 'What did *you* expect?' I asked him. Bertie had told him that I was young and charming. He was smiling, tactfully not in disbelief. I told him my age. (Molly was right, but it wasn't only the warmth of his Latin blood, but the tact and finesse that went with it. The source that prompted him to write his first letter to me in French, 'pour te fair plaisir'.) As we talked the contrast in our lifestyles, which he uncovered so frankly, only added to the interest – and the attraction – we felt for one another. From the start we were happy together, and the more we got to know each other, the more we found we had in common. He was a darling, big-hearted, generous and unselfish. And such good company. He was just as interested in people, their quirks and mannerisms as I was, and a delightfully amusing mimic. How I wish I had on tape his perfect imitation of the confidential chatter of seagulls – so different from their long plaintive cries – that he first heard on our honeymoon in Devon, and that I got him to repeat to me time and again.

John was much more charitable about Bertie. He thought him a harmless old eccentric, and even in his funny way inclined to be benevolent. But he hadn't repaid the loan! John would have overlooked this, but I felt that on principle it was wrong. He was letting his dead girl down. I believe that it was after we were married, when I wrote to him thanking him for the silver-box wedding present, that I reminded him, of his oversight as I put it. It came by return.

I can't remember exactly when it was that the question of marriage came up. I thought about it and hesitated for so long, that at last John lost patience. 'Forget it,' he said, 'don't worry about it any more. We will just stay as we are.' That decided me. I wanted to grab him, and hold him tight. So at last I decided to join the married women's trade union. We were married at Finsbury Register Office and afterwards went to a party at his family home in Myddelton Square. His brother, Jim, organized everything beautifully – including white carnations! Lydia, and Bee and her husband came – Charlie and his wife were away on holiday – and of course, Molly. John's mother looked lovely in a

184

black dress, with a lacy white pinny, and John's favourite niece, Rita, with her red-gold hair. We danced to the gramophone, and afterwards we had supper at Bertorelli's. Then John and I were motored back to our flat in the old car we had just bought for our honeymoon. It was an ancient, almost vintage Hillman Minx, with solid bodywork and leather seats. Jim drove us down to Devon, as John was still a learner. We were staying at Mrs Ada Gammon's cottage, at the top of the cliffs at Morthoe. John made it daily, coaxing the old car that tended to jump out of second gear up the one-in-five gradient with an abrupt right turn at the critical top.

And so it turned out – through an unlikely link-up of separate happenings – that what my music mistress had read in my hand in 1918, when I was sixteen – that I would get married in my fifties – did in fact come true at last in 1956! Of course I had forgotten all about this trivial, disregarded incident, until I began to turn my thoughts back to the past and to write about it.

A year later, at the end of the summer holiday, after our last term at school together, Molly was married. Before she met Michael, she liked to get my angle on the current front-runner, something to bounce off, before she made up her own mind. But now she told me, I don't care what anybody thinks or says, I know what I want. Yet she tells me today that at the last moment she had serious doubts. Her mother bought her an ultra slender white wedding dress from a model at Harrods incredibly reduced, because it was the one worn on display by the mannequin. Now Molly had to tailor herself to fit her dress. The wedding photo shows her hollow-eyed and wispy. But everything was perfect to delight Mam and the Aunties. A church wedding, the small dark Welsh on one side, and the big blond Anglo-Saxons on the other. Bertie in a top hat, accompanied by his elegant wife. The order of the service noting music composed by the bridegroom. And after the service an impressive reception in Mr and Mrs Bertie's handsome house. The approved send-off with good wishes and confetti. As the car sped away trailing its honeymoon funnies, Mam clasped her hands, and looking up to heaven, declaimed dramatically her heartfelt plea, 'Pray God for their happiness!'

John and I started our close-together life in tune. No disagreement on fundamentals, the rights and wrongs, and happily we were so in sympathy that most often our instinctive likes and dislikes coincided. He was tolerant of my weak points, and I found *his* rather endearing. We didn't irritate each other in our own little ways and habits. He was now getting integrated with and appreciated by my family, with Charlie and his wife and my very dear niece, Christine, who lived near by, and with Bee and her husband and Lydia in happy visits to their home in Eastbourne, attractive today, in contrast to its forbidding face in our schooldays.

I wanted now to branch out in a completely new line, to pick up the domestic skills that most women acquire in their youth and that maybe turn into a boring chore, but to me in my ignorant fifties still presenting an interesting novelty. First, cooking. I bought an attractive illustrated tome, to tell me everything, and started off. It was very satisfying, and much easier than I thought, if you cut out all the frills. Then dressmaking. It was the variety and range of John's patterns that stimulated me. It was more fun and much cheaper to make my own – at first – simple things in *my* choice of colours and material, rather than to make do with the current range on offer. I went back to school in evening classes to understand patterns and how to cut out, while John on another floor learnt car maintenance. John taught me to drive. An impossible task I had warned him. He said that was nonsense, and proved it, making me stick to the wheel on holidays in twisting country lanes, with the surprise of a hay-wagon round the corner. In the end I passed my test first time. We had happy breaks on our holidays discovering the natural delights of rural Wales. In Pembrokeshire, behind the farmhouse where we were staying, a Merlin green field with mysterious smooth, round white stones rising all over out of the ground, like giant mushrooms, while armies of foxgloves tilted crazily outside an impenetrable witches' thicket. On a village green in the Gower Peninsula, a family party of animals: ducks, geese, a huge sow, and, in a group, stallion, mare and young foal; and on a wide stretch of beach, a distant ring of oxen, seated at first – the smallest in the centre – and then as the tide turned, narrowing the stretches of sand, they made their leisurely way back, away from the sea breezes. In Snowdonia, a blue lake enclosed in black and gold in the sunlight.

I was teaching now only on supply, in response to a call from the Surrey County Council Education Department, getting an interesting impression of a variety of schools, but with no long-term commitments. It was when a café opened on the street level, below the flats, and attracted an intrusively noisy hooligan element, that our flat, once so comfortable and congenial, became intolerable. One spring morning I got into the car and drove off. I discovered a For Sale notice outside a house that attracted us both. It had been called Hill-Top Cottage, when houses had names, and was built on what had been farmland with old fruit trees lining the road as well as decorative double cherry.

Now, in the morning, I woke to the dawn chorus, and at dusk the thrush sang like a nightingale in the walnut tree. John with his practical know-how took on the house, making it draught-proof. When we moved in, a breeze blew under the front door to connect up with the flow round the French-window and the draught down the chimney, to raise the carpet a little in windy weather. He turned the cottagey dark brown paint into white, and had the floors – edged with the approved dark varnish of the thirties – scraped clean to reveal pleasant-smelling pine boards. I took on the garden, a never-ending labour of love. Half of it wild, the original woodland, and looking after itself, grass and trees and naturalized bulbs, and wild flowers in season. First snowdrops, then wild violets, and wood anemones, followed by daffodils and narcissus, and, in May, bluebells and honesty.

The happy everyday pattern was livened up by the theatre and the cinema in London. I would leave the car in free parking on a grassy patch off the Outer Circle by Regents Park, and take a quick bus back – buses running by all the time, no waiting in those days – to meet John in his office in Upper Regent Street. (He was in the very same big block, not far from the BBC, where I used to work, just before the war, with the National Council for Civil Liberties, the rent very generously cut down for us.) A little supper, and then the show, very often with Molly and Michael.

It was Molly who brought us in to see the sparkling comedy turns in *Beyond the Fringe* which I think of as the champagne send-up to introduce the new tempo of the sixties. Satiric sketches, written and acted by the young Jonathan Miller and Alan Bennett, and with two other coming stars, Peter Cook and Dudley Moore to make up the cast. Together with Molly and Michael we went to show after show at the Royal Court in its sixties' heyday – that did in fact start in the late fifties with John Osborne's *Look Back in Anger*.

I am not going to attempt to write about Molly in the light of a career woman as she made her own swinging way in the sixties and after, setting the pace and making the headlines, because John and I came into her life always on the personal, the family side, with her little girls as they grew up, and her mother, and Michael, and then Patrick. For me, she was always at heart the Molly of our schoolteaching days, although, of course, I had seen even then the potential for the adventurous career

187

that was to follow.

At first she was painting all the time – one of her pictures chosen by the Contemporary Art Society for the Tate. I have four of her strong, individual paintings to make my sitting-room interesting and attractive, and a sensitive pencil sketch of John's mother which she made when she was staying for a short while before her marriage in their home in John's former room. Painting was the easiest to combine with starting a family – two lovely little girls, Sarah, my godchild, and then Sophie. John and I used to visit them in their cosy little home, one of three small Dickensian houses – modernized inside – Mary Holland in the second, and David Jones in the third. All of them hidden behind a high wall, down a narrow blind-alley, beside a leafy churchyard. Sarah and Sophie as toddlers, played with their toy wheelbarrows in their enclosed front-garden, unaware of Notting Hill going its sometimes stormy way outside. And then Molly and Michael arrived in Chelsea, in Old Church Street, and now their house could accommodate thronging parties. It was when Molly was in her fashion and television stage that she pulled me into her programme on BBC 2, *One Woman's Week*, for a little chat about old times together. I shed my gardening clothes, scrubbed the earth out of my nails, put a wig on over my untidy hair, and arrived at Molly's house to find her sitting-room draped everywhere with a profusion of vivid materials. Sophie, as I could hear through the hatch, was doing her bit to open the programme, ordering over the telephone, in her unselfconscious little girl's voice, groceries for her mother. Then it was our turn. Molly came in to find two unoccupied chairs – I had no idea what we were going to talk about – but she soon steered it into an easy path for us both. The film showed John too, as one of her close friends. And now, thanks to Molly and the BBC, I have a big blow-up of him in front of me, to keep me company as I sit at my typewriter.

From fashion editor at *Nova*, then *Harpers & Queen*, she went on to the *Sunday Times*. I remember, at the end of this fashion and journalism episode, when she left, to write novels, her goodbye meeting with the staff at the *Sunday Times*. Molly sitting on a table, swinging her legs, to be joined by Harold Evans, with a friendly arm round her and at the end a hug and kiss with good wishes for the future. Molly's yellow vintage Rolls Royce, waiting outside. This was a present from Hector, a long-time admirer, who hoped that she would be free one day to marry him, give him a male heir, rejuvenate him, and bring to life again his family estate, Pampisford in Cambridgeshire. A tall order – which happily Molly never took on. Hector (Eton and the Guards, and now – so he

said – a socialist) had an interesting profile. A nose that could prosaic-
ally be called a boxer's – maybe a casualty of Eton's Wall Game or,
more romantically, Norman, identical with the profile on the Bayeux
Tapestry of the warrior, whose nose under the helmet, ran straight
down in the same line as the forehead.

Molly had an open invitation to come for weekends to Pampisford
with parties of her friends, and John and I enjoyed some happy, topsy-
turvy times there with her, a mixture of *Alice in Wonderland* and L. P.
Hartley. A never-ending drive through neglected woodlands opened up
at last to a prospect of lawns, and then the gravel approach, the only
part of the grounds kept reasonably tidy. The mansion itself with yesterday's pattern of living, hollow now, an empty shell. Hector alone. No
resident staff. But all our bedrooms made ready for us and inviting with
their outlook over lawns and big ornamental trees. But the nearest one,
blackened and ghastly, lightning-struck, still left standing, an ominous
ghost. Hector, affable and benign in the background, waited for Molly
to take him in charge, to drive out with him to stock up with provisions.
'No need to buy potatoes,' he objected. 'Plenty in the vegetable garden.' We had already wandered into that wilderness, the greenhouses
cultivating monster weeds, sheds stacked with sacks of flabby sprouting
potatoes. 'We'll leave them for *you*, when we've gone,' Molly said
sweetly. One moment we were the make-do staff, improvising meals in
the kitchen, and the next, the guests sipping vintage claret, and taking
afternoon tea in the elegant period drawing-room. Before one visit,
Hector told me he had engaged two Brazilian peasants, man and wife,
to attend to the house. In fact they were a sophisticated couple from Rio
de Janeiro, driven away by soaring inflation and the high cost of living,
and hoping one day to start a little café-restaurant in London. She was
amazed to find they were the only staff. The gentleman, she told me
rather plaintively, expected her husband to light fires in all the bedrooms. 'And look what he has given me!' A great black-metal of a
Widow Twankey sewing-machine, and a pile of torn fine-linen sheets to
mend. She was having a go with her own up-to-date machine. I advised
her to fold them all up, showing no tears, and put them back where they
came from. And both of them, to leave this dead-end and get back to
their friends in London as soon as they could.

My Indian summer of happiness ended on the last day of 1971. John
had not been well. The doctor diagnosed angina. He needed a complete
rest. The heart specialist gave us a more optimistic verdict. On the way
there John had let me drive, but now he took the wheel to go back

189

home. The forecast was that quite soon he might be able to resume work part-time. I privately made up my mind that he would do no such thing. No work of any kind until he was quite himself again, and wanted to start. Barely a week later, at night, he had a massive heart attack. The next morning he was in hospital. At midnight, his hand still warm in mine, they told me he was dead.

Today, as I look back at that time, when I had to unlink myself and to face living my own hard life alone, and when, overnight, I turned into the old woman that I had never understood I was while John kept me young, I realize how lucky it was that I had something to fall back on. I had always wanted, hoped, that one day I would write – not, as I had attempted, in freelance journalism, but at my leisure, to satisfy myself. And so, after I had achieved some equilibrium, I started, in my seventies, to do it the easiest way. To tell my own story where the plot and the characters were all familiar and I only had to make it come alive.

It was when I had finished the hard slog of writing about civil liberty in the thirties, that I had the heart-warming experience of being pulled right into the centre again, when the NCCL, celebrating its fiftieth anniversary, invited me to be the representative spokeswoman for those early days. First with the press in the send-off in the crypt of St Martin-in-the-Fields, where we met in 1934 to launch the Council, and then at the lunch at County Hall, to have a happy meeting with colleagues of former days and of today. On one side of me at the table, Lord Elwyn Jones, the Lord Chancellor from 1974 to 1979, whom I knew in the thirties as an eloquent, brilliant young barrister, very ready to lend us a hand, and on the other side, our generous and long-lasting vice president, Naomi Mitchison.

I had, of course, all through the intervening years kept in touch with the NCCL, occasionally in the fifties speaking at meetings, or proposing a motion at an AGM. I brought Molly in as a new member to our Twenty-First Birthday Celebration in 1955 and, later, I even persuaded Hector to join, but not – as I tried – to make out a banker's order. Today the NCCL has to work as hard as we did in the thirties. And sometimes for the same old causes: against the misuse of the Official Secrets Acts, the abuse of police powers, and in defence of the disadvantaged. In particular today, their concern is to get a legal redress against the disconcerting encroachments on the individual right of privacy, threatened by the widespread collection and use of personal information, political vetting

190

in employment, wrongful disclosure of police information, and the use of monitoring devices. And all of this heightened with the introduction of centralized computers. And for women, their right at work to equality of treatment, payment and opportunity.

As it turned out, it was the key time in the thirties when I worked with Ronald Kidd for civil liberties, that was the first part of my autobiography to be published, in 1986. Happily, this coincided with a repeat of a programme on television when I was interviewed on Channel Four by Mavis Nicholson, in a series concerned with older women still active: the politician, Barbara Castle, the actress, Irene Handl, the film critic, Dilys Powell, and myself, the surviving former assistant secretary of the Council from its birth.

Now that I am well into my eighties, I am finding, in the savage, destructive, and philistine climate of today, that I have the same feeling of revulsion, the same acute sense of disquiet that I used to have in 'the low dishonest decade' of the thirties, under the shadow of Fascism. In a completely different political context, our own increasingly authoritarian government centralizes more and more power in the executive, while diminishing the scope and funds of elected local government, and of the trade unions, and economizes severely in its financial support for education, the universities, research and the health and social services, while relieving the tax burden on the rich. Most significant of all, it identifies its interest as the government in power with the national interest, claiming as its right the support of the established Church, and the media, fostering a nationwide climate of assent as the duty of loyal patriotic citizens, so that independent critical spirits, investigative journalists, critical moralists, are classed as subversives. Fascism with its false values, its disregard of accepted standards of justice and humanity, is universally condemned now that history has recorded its resultant horrors and disasters. Yet, paradoxically, its mainspring in action, its two cardinal vices, ruthlessness and aggression, have been adopted today, laundered and acceptable, even promoted as essential qualities to be rigorously applied in competition and exploitation, to achieve the goal, the Jerusalem of a prosperous economy. This attitude of mind sets an antisocial, amoral standard of behaviour, with the resultant social dislocation that we see today all around us and that is filling the prisons to overflowing.

It was when a green leaflet dropped through my letterbox that I had the exciting experience, in reading it, of recognizing a new way, a hope for the future! 'Everything that I had always believed in, put into the

191

aims of a political party.' Not my words, but those of an intelligent, attractive young woman in her twenties, with a modern upbringing and education and an idyllic childhood in Sweden. I had asked her what was her first reaction to the Green Party. Her prompt reply expressed exactly what my tired old brain was fumbling to formulate. This identical reaction, in spite of the generation gap and the contrast in our early formative environment and upbringing, underlines the universal appeal of the movement.

The Green Party, tied to no sectional interest, has an international outlook embracing all classes, races, religions and political parties – left, right and centre – since it deals with the ultimate interest of all of us: healthy peaceful survival in harmony with the natural world and its creatures on the planet on which all of us are dependent. To achieve this means a revolutionary change in outlook and politics. In the first place, a halt to the headlong consuming and squandering of natural resources, to the pollution of land, sea and air, the abuse and degradation of animal life, and the destruction of green life. An end to the policy that puts profit before people, and that believes that still greater production and consumption, more and more growth, is the answer to all our problems. I am not going to attempt to outline the Green Party programme, but only to mention one or two aspects that convinced me. First of all, the uncompromising honesty of declaring for unilateral nuclear disarmament, no nuclear bases, withdrawal from NATO and the international arms race; in civilian life, a low-energy economy based on renewable sources; considerably added help for the Third World. This cold, bald itemizing gives no idea of the glow I felt, the recognition that here at last was a move away from down-grading materialism, to a sane, healthy alternative with an altruistic confidence in the potential of humankind, and also with the effective imperative lever for the reluctant, that the alternative – in the long run – was the endangering of our own species.

Today I am still in the same home that John and I shared together, but the house, which in his charge was so well looked after, is now sadly neglected. The garden, my province, not only half of it wild but most of it allowed to go its own way. The beautiful walnut tree was uprooted in the storm – to deprive the squirrels as well as me. The birds, discouraged by tree-felling and the traffic, no longer sing in chorus at dawn. And now urbanized sparrows are trying to muscle-in and with their harsh metallic reiteration to drown out and take over from the song birds. But the garden is still green. In the spring, the bulbs come out, and the hardy survivors still flower in the summer. The blackbird, the

192

father of the chapel of birds in his garden, like a good trade-unionist, reproves me harshly when I take repressive measures against the sparrows. But soon he relents and repeats again and again, and always at dusk, his reassuring, engaging little tune.

I heard on the radio the other day – I missed the context, some informal gathering, I assumed – that the Prime Minister answered the question that started my story, and that I put to my governess when I was a child: 'What is society?' There is no such thing, she tells us, only individuals and families. So today we are all at sea, all on our own and vulnerable. No more communities, no cohesion, no centre to hold. I only hope I live long enough to see all this utterly disproved.